Courtrooms and Classrooms

Courtrooms and Classrooms

A Legal History of College Access, 1860–1960

Scott M. Gelber

JOHNS HOPKINS UNIVERSITY PRESS BALTIMORE

Printed in the United States of America on acid-free paper
9 8 7 6 5 4 3 2 1

Johns Hopkins University Press
2715 North Charles Street
Baltimore, Maryland 21218-4363
www.press.jhu.edu

Library of Congress Cataloging-in-Publication Data

Gelber, Scott M., author.
Courtrooms and classrooms : a legal history of college access, 1860–1960 / Scott M. Gelber.
pages cm
Includes bibliographical references and index.
ISBN 978-1-4214-1884-1 (hardcover : alk. paper) — ISBN 978-1-4214-1885-8 (electronic) — ISBN 1-4214-1884-3 (hardcover : alk. paper) — ISBN 1-4214-1885-1 (electronic) 1. Educational law and legislation—United States—History. 2. Universities and colleges—United States—Admission. 3. Actions and defenses—United States—History. I. Title.
KF4119.G45 2016
344.73'079—dc23 2015014322

A catalog record for this book is available from the British Library.

Special discounts are available for bulk purchases of this book. For more information, please contact Special Sales at 410-516-6936 or specialsales@press.jhu.edu.

Johns Hopkins University Press uses environmentally friendly book materials, including recycled text paper that is composed of at least 30 percent post-consumer waste, whenever possible.

Contents

Acknowledgments

I am grateful to Julie Reuben, as always, for focusing and clarifying my scholarship. Michael Olivas and Gregory Britton have also supported this project with good humor and timely advice. I am indebted to the National Academy of Education and the Spencer Foundation for postdoctoral funding and, especially, for enlisting William Reese, Pat Graham, and Michael Olivas to serve as mentors. John Thelin and Adam Nelson wrote letters on my behalf and provided helpful feedback.

I have been blessed by the encouragement of my colleagues at Wheaton College in Massachusetts: Mary Lee Griffin, Vicki Bartolini, and Linda Eisenmann. Robert O'Neil, Robert Hendrickson, Chris Schmidt, Neal Hutchens, Harold Wechsler, Ethan Hutt, Chris Loss, Philip Lee, Jack Schneider, and Benjamin Justice generously commented on portions of the manuscript. Andrea Walton, Christine Ogren, and Hilary Moss gave valuable feedback as discussants at conference sessions. The staffs of state archives, law libraries, and university special collections across the country worked to fulfill my requests for research assistance.

Much of chapter 6 was published in an earlier form in "Child Support Litigation and the 'Necessity' of American Higher Education, 1926–71," *American Journal of Legal History* 54 (January 2014): 39–72, and parts of chapters 2 and 4 appeared in "Expulsion Litigation and the Limits of *In Loco Parentis*, 1860–1960," *Teachers College Record* 116 (December 2014): 1–16.

The ultimate message of gratitude goes out to Emily, Sam, Sid, and the rest of my family . . . thank you!

Courtrooms and Classrooms

Introduction

In 2003, when Justice Sandra Day O'Connor expressed conditional support for race-conscious admissions in *Grutter v. Bollinger*, she noted that the United States Supreme Court had always exhibited "a degree of deference" toward colleges and universities. A decade later, an affirmative action opinion penned by Justice Anthony Kennedy was less solicitous but still acknowledged the court's traditional respect for institutions of higher education.[1] Portrayed by these twenty-first-century rulings as a timeless custom, an informal doctrine of "academic deference" seemed to discourage courts from questioning the actions of faculty or administrators except when confronted with evidence of blatant discrimination, malfeasance, or arbitrariness. Not only were institutions of higher education granted the same immunities as other charitable or governmental entities, but colleges and their faculties also seemed entitled to a special brand of legal autonomy. Rooted in the customs of medieval Europe and absorbed into American law by the antebellum Supreme Court case of *Dartmouth College v. Woodward*, this independence was predicated on the understanding that overzealous or misguided judicial oversight could suffocate the intellectual and moral vigor of higher education.[2]

The remarks of Justices O'Connor and Kennedy notwithstanding, the increasing prevalence of higher education suits and the tenor of some recent opinions seemingly constitute a significant departure from the level of deference displayed by earlier courts. Before the 1960s, American judges appeared to exhibit nearly absolute respect for academia. Two principles seemed to undermine most lawsuits filed on behalf of students, in particular: the theory that higher education was a privilege rather than a right, and the presumption that colleges acted in loco parentis to serve the minors under their supervision.[3] Scholars and administrators routinely contrast the intense legal exposure of the contemporary campus with this earlier era when students rarely sued and academic deference seemed extremely robust. For example, the general counsel for the University of California once remarked that the university used to be "a citadel where administrators governed students virtually unfettered by legal constraints." At the end of the 1960s, the nation's most accomplished scholar of higher education law concluded that the student-university relationship had been practically "inert" before that dramatic decade. A prominent higher education law textbook continues to characterize nineteenth-century higher education as "a Victorian gentlemen's club whose sacred precincts were not to be profaned by the involvement of outside agents." The scarcity and apparent unanimity of earlier higher education decisions have seemed dull, almost prehistoric, in contrast to the contentiousness of the post-1960 terrain.[4]

This historical backdrop can give the impression that the current legal landscape constitutes a radical departure from an older and more respectful relationship between students and colleges, and between colleges and the courts. Indeed, the frequency of student-initiated litigation has increased markedly since the 1960s. Of all college student suits reported prior to 2010, more than 90 percent were litigated after 1969.[5] The landmark federal case of *Dixon v. Alabama State Board of Education*, which established a new constitutional basis for student rights in 1961, is commonly cited as the beginning of the end of wholesale judicial deference toward higher education.[6] According to the conventional narrative, the *Dixon* ruling, a wave of campus protests, and new federal statutes combined to erode the moral as well as legal foundations of traditional student-college relations.

However, the gravitational pull of the 1960s has caused scholars to overestimate the extent to which earlier courts deferred to college faculty and administrators. Rulings dating back to the nineteenth century actually exhibited a range of perspectives, with some judges espousing academic deference and others expressing a predisposition in favor of student rights. Although judges almost always sided with college authorities in cases related to faculty employment, property disputes, and personal injury, they were less deferential when adjudicating suits that petitioned for *college access*.[7] Courts regularly intervened on behalf of students who challenged admission, expulsion, or tuition policies. According to state and federal reporters, students won slightly more than half of these suits between 1860 (the decade of the first reported college access case) and 1910.[8] Nineteenth-century courts sometimes limited institutional control over entrance requirements, reinstated expelled students, or held public universities accountable to statutes that required tuition-free higher education.

Courts did not begin to defer more consistently to institutions in admission, expulsion, and tuition cases until the early twentieth century. Students won just a third of reported college access suits from 1910 to 1960 (the eve of *Dixon*), and all but three of those victories occurred in cases litigated by the National Association for the Advancement of Colored People.[9] Aside from desegregation suits, courts no longer intervened on behalf of students during this fifty-year span—an era in which universities enjoyed elevated status and increased respect for their administrative as well as intellectual expertise. Reluctant to second-guess faculty or administrators, midcentury courts expressed their enthusiasm for higher education when adjudicating disputes within the private realm of child support law but refrained from promoting access in cases that challenged university policies. Nevertheless, students prevailed in more than a third of reported admission, expulsion, and tuition suits between 1860 and 1960.[10] I believe that the NAACP's legal campaign contested the principle of academic deference and should be included in this analysis. But even if desegregation suits are omitted, students still won a quarter of college access suits during the hundred years before *Dixon*.[11]

Interpreting these cases in conjunction with the institutional history of higher education, this book argues that academic deference was a fluid principle that dominated college access suits for a rather short period of time. Legal oversight of college access was relatively robust during the nineteenth century, less intense during the early twentieth century, and reinvigorated (to some extent) during the modern civil rights movement. American courts scrutinized college access policies with varying degrees of intensity that correlated with broader perceptions of higher education and administrative expertise. These patterns highlight the inconstancy of judicial deference and demonstrate that the twenty-first-century case for academic autonomy rests uneasily on a history of contention rather than on doctrinal bedrock.

Secondarily, this book uses legal sources to chronicle the evolution of modern attitudes toward higher education. Between 1860 and 1960, the trajectories of college access litigation reflected the embrace of selectivity and institutional differentiation, the decline of de jure segregation, the rise of contractual understandings of enrollment, and the triumph of vocationalism. Each of these developments prompted legal debates over whether college access should be considered akin to a privilege or a right.

To be sure, this distinction was largely rhetorical—there was no firm basis for defining higher education as an absolute or natural right. Yet judicial decisions regarding access to state colleges and universities evolved alongside conventional notions about whether public higher education resembled a rarefied endeavor or a basic government service. Similarly, decisions regarding access to private institutions reflected the extent to which Americans viewed enrollment as either a reverential or contractual relationship between students and schools.

This book focuses primarily on tracing how these attitudes evolved in concert with debates over academic deference—it does not systematically assess the impact of judicial decisions. Nevertheless, I periodically offer tentative observations about the reciprocal relationships between higher education law, policy, and access. As predicted by a robust scholarly literature, courtroom victories did not necessarily prompt significant institutional change.[12] Whereas some cases exerted almost self-evident influence on college access, litigation exerted more modest or oblique pressures in many other instances. Yet although it is often difficult to identify smoking guns, the timelines of judicial intervention and higher education policy exhibit striking similarities—courts and colleges both tended to foster access until the 1910s, at which point they tolerated or endorsed restrictions to access until the emergence of the civil rights movement decades later.

Legal History and the History of Higher Education

This book examines all admission, expulsion, and tuition cases that were reported between 1860 and 1960.[13] When coupled with evidence from other sources (including university archives, institutional histories, trial briefs, and testimony) these opinions reveal not only jurisprudential trends but also the corresponding and dissenting views of students, parents, faculty, administrators, and state leaders. Since students sued all sorts of institutions, these sources also have the merit of documenting challenges to collegiate authority that occurred beyond the prominent colleges and universities that have been most frequently examined by historians of higher education. And to the extent that American courts have been sensitive to political pressures, the outcomes of these cases reflect broader public perspectives about higher education.[14]

Still, one must exercise caution when drawing conclusions about academic deference from a tally of cases "won" or "lost" by students. Reported cases sometimes hinged on technical errors made by attorneys or lower courts rather than substantive analysis of higher education.[15] Some rulings were more purposeful or more influential than others, and it should be noted in particular that students lost both of the nondesegregation college access cases that reached the Supreme Court between 1860 and 1960.[16] Reported cases also document unusual situations in which suits went to trial and culminated in published decisions during an era when litigation was relatively uncommon. The extreme circumstances that precipitated these suits may well have skewed their results in favor of students. One should also note that most reported cases were appellate rulings, which represent an imperfect sample of higher education litigation because some types of suits (such as those challenging segregation) were more likely than others to produce appeals.[17]

It is especially important to recognize that judges evaluated access suits in light of relevant statutes and precedents, rather than simply according to their own beliefs about the nature of college. Admissions, expulsion, and tuition cases encompassed a complex interplay of local circumstances and transcendent legal principles that sometimes had little to do with perceptions of higher education. In particular, courts often looked to the tenets of contract law when adjudicating suits against private colleges and consulted legislative or constitutional language when adjudicating suits against public colleges.[18] Desegregation cases revolved around interpretation of the equal protection clause of the Fourteenth Amendment. Expulsion cases, among others, emphasized debates about due process. Family law principles shaped the level of support granted to the college-bound children of divorced parents. Each of these legal frameworks had an independent history that could exert as much influence as judicial sentiments about college access per se.[19]

Despite these limitations, reported cases provide robust, national, and longitudinal evidence of judicial and (to a lesser extent) popular attitudes about higher education. Although some decisions pivoted on technicalities or clear-cut readings of black-letter law, others required judges to answer substantive and debatable questions about college access.[20] Furthermore, courts often supplemented their rationale for particular decisions with dicta that editorialized for or against judicial oversight of admissions requirements, discipline codes, tuition policies, and related matters. Because this book focuses on charting the course of academic deference, I examine this commentary as much as the overall count of wins and losses or the internal justifications for particular rulings. This approach sometimes causes me to deviate from the disciplinary conventions of legal scholarship by comparing and contrasting the rhetoric employed in cases with dissimilar contexts. For example, disputes about judicial deference emerged in cases that debated the level of scrutiny that courts should apply when reviewing constitutional challenges to university policies, as well as in cases that debated the amount of discretion granted to universities on statutory grounds.

Yet this promiscuous approach is consistent with the academy's early legal status—a status defined as much by sentiment and tradition as by constitutional provision, statute, or well-defined body of case law. Nineteenth-century courts regarded colleges as "neither fish nor fowl" and often resolved higher education suits by resorting to ad hoc mixtures of principles borrowed from cases concerning governments, corporations, charities, and families.[21] As a number of scholars have observed, judicial deference to higher education was a "loose" doctrine that lacked a uniform set of precedents. It resembled a predisposition more than a formal rule. Early courts rarely cited academic deference, pure and simple, as the main justification for a ruling.[22] So although this book mentions the primary grounds for most decisions, its central argument about the instability of judicial deference often emphasizes supplementary dicta drawn from different legal circumstances.

Historical context also explains why this book does not consistently differentiate between suits that challenged institutional policies (such as disciplinary procedures) and suits that challenged faculty expertise (such as disputes over grading or graduation standards). Although courts have deferred more readily to specialized academic authority since the 1960s, there was no stark difference between "academic deference" and "institutional deference" during the nineteenth and early twentieth centuries.[23] College faculty assumed a wide range of duties in the nineteenth century, including direct responsibility for admissions and campus discipline. Typically, a college's president was its lone senior administrator until the first decades of the twentieth century. Moreover, faculty regarded the character development of their students as essential to their vocation; research and scholarly expertise were generally not prioritized until after the turn of the century.[24] As a result, many nineteenth- and early-twentieth-century college access cases do not fall neatly into either a purely academic or purely institutional category. Therefore, this book uses "academic deference" in its broadest sense in order to avoid anachronistic distinctions.

Judicial Oversight of College Access, 1860–1910

As detailed in the chapters that follow, early judicial scrutiny of higher education often stemmed from the perception that nineteenth-century colleges and universities were not especially distinct from open-access elementary schools (also known as "common schools"). The statutes, students, and curricula of higher and lower schools often resembled each other. Leaders of all sorts of institutions emphasized their service to the state while campaigning to recruit larger classes. Colleges typically enrolled underprepared students on campuses that could be difficult to distinguish from normal schools, preparatory academies, or even fledgling high schools. At public universities, in particular, enrollment could appear to be a bureaucratic procedure rather than a discretionary or quasi-judicial endeavor. This observation prompted some courts to prevent governing boards from enacting policies that limited access without express legislative approval. Meanwhile, private colleges could not always persuade courts that they pursued a higher purpose that entitled them to greater autonomy than other corporate entities. Some courts viewed these institutions as ordinary businesses or associations that were expected to abide by contractual understandings and adhere to general principles of due process.

After all, nineteenth-century American higher education consisted of a patchwork of marginal institutions—a far cry from the influential network that would eventually play a central role in state and national affairs. Enrollment grew sluggishly in relation to the expansion of the college-age population, as colleges competed with commercial training programs, correspondence courses, and apprenticeships. Most colleges struggled for respect (and often for survival) while fighting to establish that they provided public benefits worthy of tax-exempt status and legislative appropriations. While small private institutions attracted little formal oversight from the state, their autonomy was limited by denominational control, tuition dependence, and the influence of local leaders. Due to one or more of these factors, almost every campus involved in litigation during the nineteenth century verged on financial or administrative crisis.[25]

The broader political and legal contexts of the nineteenth century also attracted judicial scrutiny to institutions of higher education. Politically, populist impulses promoted suspicion toward elite academic expertise.[26] Anti-elitist rhetoric routinely surfaced within admission, expulsion, and tuition rulings that restrained collegiate authority. Within local courtrooms, Christian sensibilities and a variety of allied reform movements also encouraged nineteenth-century judges to favor underdog plaintiffs.[27] Just as courts sometimes interpreted contractual agreements and corporate charters in order to promote the public interest, judges also used these tools to influence college access policies. While judges often deferred to college authorities and sometimes even cited a broad commitment to laissez-faire ideology, a significant proportion of rulings reflected the assumption that colleges should honor their traditionally porous access policies.[28] The fundamental rationale for the regime of common law—the belief that local judges were well suited to interpret local conventions—encouraged courts to interpret student access cases in the context of this customary relationship between colleges and their communities.[29]

These customs were sometimes codified in ways that opened the door to judicial oversight. Although it is common to assume that the laws governing nineteenth-century higher education were meager, haphazard, or even "insignificant," early legislation and constitutional provisions related to higher education only appear inconsequential when compared to the current state of campus affairs.[30] In particular, nineteenth-century statutes or constitutions sometimes required public universities to remain "open to all persons in the state."[31] When interpreted aggressively by the courts, this language could support challenges to institutional authority on behalf of college access. At a time when the fundamental legal contours of public higher education were still emerging, these laws invited judges to evaluate the competing claims of students and collegiate authorities.

These statutes help to explain why early judicial intervention occurred most consistently in cases filed against state universities, state colleges, and state normal schools.[32] Students persuaded courts to intercede in the affairs of public institutions in three-quarters of the college access cases reported before 1910.[33] Whereas the boundary between public and private institutions had been hazy prior to the Civil War, the mission of the public university crystallized in the late nineteenth century alongside the overall expansion of the American state.[34] Although judges occasionally ruled against private colleges, public institutions were much more likely to be subjected to statutes that provided grounds for litigation. These laws typically instructed public universities to avoid religious sectarianism and to enroll students from all regions of their respective states.[35]

In stark contrast to these limits on administrative discretion vis-à-vis students during the nineteenth century, faculty members were typically hired on a year-to-year basis with no guarantee of ongoing employment. Furthermore, some statutes explicitly empowered trustees or presidents to dismiss professors at will—a phenomenon that has contributed to the perception that nineteenth-century colleges enjoyed virtually absolute legal authority. The establishing act of the Kansas State Agricultural College, for example, authorized its governing board to remove professors "whenever the interest of the college shall require."[36] Even in cases that did not involve statutes, courts almost always sided with colleges when professors sought reinstatement. Although this pattern is cited as a prime example of academic deference, these cases also reflect the lack of due process rights among all workers in the nineteenth century.[37] Furthermore, faculty termination suits demonstrate that courts exhibited little reverence for those who performed the actual academic labor of higher education. As routinely noted by scholars of academic freedom, these cases often resulted in rulings that favored institutional rather than professorial academic freedom.[38] When judges allowed governing boards to fire faculty for almost any reason, they bypassed the claims of professors in favor of the lawyers, businesspeople, and clergy who served as trustees.[39] Understood in this fashion, the legal authority that nineteenth-century governing boards wielded over faculty did not flow from any great reservoir of principled deference toward academia.

The Rise of Academic Deference, 1910–60

During the early twentieth century, the expansion of higher education in America and the evolution of the nation's legal culture combined to reduce the judiciary's willingness to entertain student-initiated suits. The intensification of academic deference coincided with the rising profile of American universities, which benefited from the prestige of increasingly professionalized faculty, larger enrollments, and closer ties to the state. Universities began to regard faculty publications and the proportion of faculty with doctorates as sources of internal pride and external status. The formation of the American Association of University Professors in 1915 signaled a growing, though still inconsistent, level of faculty authority. Fueled by an expanding pool of high school graduates, rising wealth, and the increasing economic value of a college diploma, student enrollment grew by 60 percent in the first decade of the century and doubled during the 1920s. While much of this growth occurred at large universities, even small liberal arts colleges became more confident as they distinguished themselves from high schools and became the standard route into postgraduate professional training. For the first time, clear distinctions could be detected between secondary and higher education across the country. State governments expressed their confidence in public colleges and universities by raising appropriations—albeit to levels that rarely satisfied institutional appetites. Legislatures also passed new statutes that expanded the discretionary powers of academic officials or legalized previously ambiguous practices, especially in the areas of admission and tuition.[40]

Meanwhile, developments within American jurisprudence encouraged courts to defer to faculty or administrators when students pursued college access suits. Twentieth-century courts reacted to the increasing power of corporations and the state by emphasizing individual rights—a focus that encouraged vigilant enforcement of particular constitutional provisions but eroded the earlier rationale for promoting college access in the name of custom or general language about the public good and the education of "all" students.[41] Starting in the 1930s, for example, students could only expect to win admission suits if they established that institutions had violated the Fourteenth Amendment.

Increasing respect for administrative expertise throughout the legal system also prompted judges to allow greater leeway when universities interpreted the vague statutes and charters that governed college access. In response to the growing scale, heterogeneity, and inequality of American society, Progressive legislators and governors sought to regulate corporate excesses by empowering officials who staffed public utility commissions, industrial accident boards, and the like. The administrators of these agencies were regarded as better qualified than judges or legislators to resolve most disputes within these domains.[42] As law schools solidified their position as the lone gateway to the bar, judges exhibited more faith in university-trained experts. Felix Frankfurter and other legal scholars encouraged the courts to treat these administrators with "intellectual hospitality" by respecting the deliberative nature of their decisions and limiting judicial oversight to cases involving extreme procedural errors or clear violations of legislative mandates. By the 1930s, an array of public agencies enjoyed substantial authority over rule making, fact-finding, adjudication, and enforcement. Courts sided with administrators in most disputes over the interpretation of their enabling statutes and sometimes hesitated to intervene even if officials violated internal agency guidelines.[43]

This extension of administrative authority discouraged courts from overruling the decisions of faculty and university officials who governed campuses that were growing steadily in size and complexity.[44] One of the central justifications for administrative authority applied with special force to academic policies: the recognition that specialized matters sometimes required expertise that lay beyond the grasp of judges. This rationale had long persuaded courts to defer to the decisions of professional licensing boards, such as bar associations or state medical authorities.[45] Progressive reformers were especially inclined to respect academic authority because they viewed institutions of higher education as natural allies that could counterbalance private corporate interests. Indeed, university-trained civil servants filled the ranks of state and federal administrative agencies, while college professors sometimes joined in common cause with elected officials to develop social-scientific responses to civic problems.[46]

Of course, professors, college presidents, and trustees were not archetypal administrative agents—especially when they worked within private schools. Even faculty and officials at state universities had a relatively diffuse legislative mandate, a relatively ambiguous legal status, and only a tangential connection with the classic domains of administrative regulation (such as utilities or public health).[47] Courts also defined state universities in various ways, depending in part on differences in their founding statutes and constitutional status. Some universities were regarded as relatively independent corporations, whereas others were treated as ordinary public agencies.[48] Even those universities that were established by state constitutions still depended to a significant extent on judicial interpretation, legislative appropriations, alumni support, accreditors, and public opinion.[49]

Nevertheless, colleges engaged in quasi-judicial administrative processes when they reviewed the fitness of applicants, conducted expulsion proceedings, and determined eligibility for scholarships. When faculty and college officials undertook these tasks, they possessed increasing authority as a result of their association with this new model of administrative power and this new breed of specialized public official.[50] It hardly seems coincidental that judicial deference toward academia peaked between 1910 and 1940, a period that corresponds with the heyday of popular confidence in administrative expertise.[51]

Organization of the Book

With few higher education precedents to draw upon, early college access opinions routinely cited cases that addressed elementary and secondary schools. As I demonstrate in chapter 1, the "common" nature of these schools influenced college access law before the development of sharper lines between elementary, secondary, and higher education. This ambiguity helps to the explain the lack of academic deference during the nineteenth century, when collegiate obligations were sometimes derived from rulings related to schools that were required to educate virtually any interested student.

Focusing on admission cases, chapter 2 illustrates how this early debate over college access evolved into the semiformal doctrine of academic deference. Whereas nineteenth-century rulings sometimes emphasized the traditional accessibility of public schools and limited the discretion of college officials, twentieth-century cases permitted state flagship universities to institute admissions restrictions as long as these policies were not explicitly prohibited by statute. In the process, these decisions defined higher education as closer to a privilege than a right. Chapter 3 reveals how these admissions cases reemerged as part of the NAACP's campaign against segregated state universities. Although suits against racial discrimination were somewhat distinct from other challenges to university authority, they invoked earlier rulings that had verged on establishing a right to enrollment for qualified applicants.

Whereas admissions litigation tends to attract the preponderance of attention during the twenty-first century, expulsion generated the greatest number of college access cases between 1860 and 1960. Chapter 4 begins by documenting how some nineteenth-century courts responded to these suits by interpreting state statutes (regarding public institutions) and contractual obligations (regarding private institutions) as meaningful protections for students. The second half of the chapter chronicles the failure of all reported expulsion suits from 1910 to 1960, while arguing that this apparent triumph of academic deference masks the extent to which students remained entitled to a modicum of due process even before *Dixon v. Alabama*.

The book's last two chapters focus on litigation related to financial access. In chapter 5, I analyze suits challenging public universities that charged "fees" in states where legislators had prohibited "tuition." These cases, along with two unusual suits that questioned the purpose of merit-based scholarships, indicate that the gradual development of deference toward tuition policies was encouraged by the perception that public higher education primarily benefited individual graduates and only secondarily aided the state as a whole. Whereas the rest of the book focuses on suits filed by students against institutions, in chapter 6 I examine child support suits that asked parents to contribute toward college tuition. During the middle of the twentieth century, when judicial deference to colleges and universities was most pronounced, divorce courts began to require parents to defray the costs of higher education. The different trajectory of child support cases, as opposed to suits against institutions, highlights how the obligation to promote college access has been shifting from the public to the private sphere.

The book concludes with an overview of college access law during and after the transformations of the 1960s. The quantity of litigation increased substantially in these decades as students and courts became more sensitive to possible abuses of university power. Colleges and universities became, once again, vulnerable to student lawsuits (though courts have continued to rule in favor of institutions and faculty more often than not). This shift reflected a number of factors, including a broad rebirth of Fourteenth Amendment protections, a growing list of higher education statutes, the increased economic importance of the college degree, and challenges to the authority of universities in the wake of student protests.

Courts have often recorded and sometimes influenced the history of American college access—a dual role that has been obscured by presumptions about the historical supremacy of academic deference. Although judges have always hesitated to question academic authorities, they have communicated shifting standards for determining the sort of arbitrary, unreasonable, or discriminatory actions that could justify external oversight. In light of the transformation of American higher education between *Dartmouth* and *Dixon*, it would have been extraordinary if a single doctrine of judicial deference had consistently settled most disputes. It is less remarkable to discover that the jurisprudence of college access fluctuated over the course of a century and a half of dramatic institutional change.

During the nineteenth century, before the emergence of a distinctly higher form of education, American courts regularly intervened on behalf of students in admissions, expulsion, and tuition cases, especially those involving public universities. In hindsight, some of these rulings may appear to be extreme or unusual interpretations of common law or state statutes. Indeed, many early cases were overturned, circumvented, or ignored during the twentieth century. Yet other early rulings that favored students resurfaced in landmark twentieth-century decisions that championed college access. The invocations of nineteenth-century rulings in cases such as *Dixon* indicate that the expansion of student rights in the 1960s was not a sudden unprecedented shift but a resurgence of one side of a long-standing debate. In total, the doctrine of academic deference dominated college access law for less than three decades—from the 1910s through the mid-1930s. Certainly, academic deference remains a powerful (and largely salutary) impulse, especially when students question grades or pose other direct challenges to faculty expertise. Yet it requires only mild exaggeration to conclude that judicial deference to higher education reigned supreme during a brief and singular era after colleges and universities differentiated themselves from secondary schools but prior to the civil rights movement.

Furthermore, these turn-of-the-century cases deepen our understanding of the public expectations that, for better or worse, confronted American institutions of higher education during a pivotal stage of their development. With each passing year, the postwar golden age of the American university seems more like an exception than a rule in terms of public funding as well as overall state-academy relations. Careful study of the pressures at work during the earlier and more fragile era of American higher education is warranted in order to comprehend, and perhaps even appreciate, the challenges of today.

Understandably, faculty and administrators tend to question whether these sorts of external demands can play a constructive role in debates about higher education.[52] Yet the history of college access litigation should temper our instinct to call simply for deference when faced with potential restrictions on either institutional or professorial authority. Academic deference is a mutable and historically contingent concept that has rarely freed faculty or administrators from the obligation to articulate how our legal autonomy serves the public interest. Indeed, some scholars have observed that the doctrine has been imperiled by the recent "privatization" of higher education and the growing perception that colleges are merely run-of-the-mill businesses.[53] The legal history of college access suggests that faculty and administrators who wish to contest this characterization should accentuate the substantive, rather than customary, justifications for our privileges.

1

Common Schools

In 1882, the Supreme Court of Indiana ordered Purdue University to stop requiring applicants to promise that they would not join fraternities or secret societies. The ruling, titled *State ex rel. Stallard v. White*, concluded that Purdue could not reject fraternity members because the university was legally analogous to the public elementary schools that were required to educate virtually all students. This element of *Stallard*, a decision that is discussed at greater length in the next chapter, highlights one of the drivers behind judicial oversight of nineteenth-century higher education. *Stallard* reasoned that Purdue's trustees were obligated to honor the same commitment to accessibility that guided the rest of Indiana's public school system. After all, many of the students who attended the fledgling universities of that era received remedial training that overlapped with the curriculum of local elementary schools (known as "common schools" in nineteenth-century parlance). The opinion explained that Purdue was comparable to other public schools that served the "common interest." In the process of making this claim, *Stallard* cited seventeen cases involving students from these lower schools and only two cases involving college students.[1] The judges who presided over the case had little choice but to invoke common school precedents—only one other college admissions ruling had been published at the time. Yet the manner in which *Stallard* referred to common schools also suggests that Indiana's high court viewed access to lower and higher education through a similar lens.

Using *Stallard* as a focal point, I argue that common school precedents invited nineteenth-century courts to monitor college access policies, particularly at public institutions of higher education. After presenting an overview of nineteenth-century education law, this chapter traces the competing interpretations of lower school admissions, suspension/expulsion, tuition, and segregation rulings that initially weakened judicial deference toward institutions of higher education. Even though courts often deferred to the decisions of teachers and administrators, a number of nineteenth-century common school cases emphasized student rights and championed access to public education. Then, as the boundaries between higher and lower education solidified during the twentieth century, most college access opinions no longer cited this older prostudent strand of common school decisions. Lower school case law began to support district authorities more consistently, and those college access opinions that continued to cite lower school precedents did so almost exclusively for the purpose of bolstering administrative power. The final section of the chapter focuses on the lower school racial equity cases that constituted the exceptions to this trend by remaining integral to decisions that stripped universities of their authority to exclude black students.

Of course, the mere presence of lower school case citations does not prove that they provided the primary basis for a higher education ruling. Yet the extent to which these cases appeared within college access litigation during the nineteenth century indicates that students, colleges, and the courts routinely blurred the distinction between access to higher and lower education. This pattern suggests that institutions of higher education were not originally entitled to a unique brand of legal authority over access policies, despite their comparatively elite status and despite the fact that they enrolled older students who attended on a voluntary basis. In all likelihood, the murkiness of this distinction helps to explain why nineteenth-century courts exhibited a relatively fragile commitment to academic deference when they adjudicated the college admissions, expulsion, and tuition cases that are chronicled in the chapters that follow.

Public School Law

Nineteenth-century education statutes were relatively limited in scope; legislatures rarely provided specific guidance about the substance or procedure of school discipline. Because of this statutory vacuum, litigation sometimes played a particularly important role in defining the authority of teachers and school boards, since districts were often unaware of (or indifferent to) the existence of state laws unless they were confronted with a suit.[2] Yet a number of factors combined to suppress the frequency of education lawsuits during the nineteenth century. First, districts were able to settle the majority of conflicts by meeting with disgruntled parents and residents. New York State even established a separate dispute resolution system (presided over by the state superintendent of education) in order to prevent school cases from burdening the courts.[3] Lacking access to modern-day legal services or advocacy groups, most potential plaintiffs were also dissuaded by the expense of hiring counselors.[4] Rather than cope with the costs, delays, and arcane rites of litigation, parents were more likely to ignore unpopular regulations, elect new school boards, or appeal directly to legislators. As a result, most nineteenth-century education suits addressed school finances or district politics rather than questions related to access or curriculum that concerned individual students.[5]

Still, the proportion of student-centered suits gradually increased over the course of the nineteenth century. These cases accounted for 8 percent of school litigation between 1887 and 1896, compared with just 2 percent between 1810 and 1846. The total volume of education cases also expanded relative to population growth—a trend that was largely driven by the bureaucratization and professionalization of American schooling.[6]

Although courts tended to interpret sparse legislative or constitutional language as a source of broad discretionary power for teachers and school officials, parental or student "victories" were not uncommon during the nineteenth century.[7] Indeed, the conventions of common law and the republican theory of governance endowed parents with a great deal of authority over their children—especially prior to the spread of compulsory education statutes.[8] Presumed to understand the best interests of their families, parents could challenge school discipline procedures and, on rare occasions, even demand the arrest of assertive teachers. Judges sometimes reasoned that parents voluntarily transferred their authority to schools and could revoke this consent if teachers did not fulfill their expectations. Even during the 1880s and 1890s, after many states enacted compulsory attendance laws, courts still did not always interpret these statutes as a wholesale reassignment of power from parents to schools. Parents became obligated to educate children, but they often retained the right to determine the form and substance of schooling. For example, courts authorized parents to send their children to the schools of their choice and even supported parents who wished to opt out of curricular elements.[9] Indeed, judges sometimes regarded state efforts to boost enrollment as evidence of a legal obligation to accommodate students and parents in all but the most extreme cases. Fueled by dedication to republicanism, Protestant Christianity, and industrial development, most states promoted comprehensive public schooling by the end of the Civil War. The most obvious evidence of state support for educational access took the form of constitutional or statutory language enabling towns to build schools and collect school taxes. States also established school bureaucracies and funded teacher training.[10]

Unlike institutions of higher education, which were governed by high-status trustees and never expected to educate every young person, common schools were dedicated to universal enrollment and governed by local leaders who rarely commanded special deference from parents or neighbors. Particularly within rural districts, key decisions about school policy (including curriculum and staffing) were often made in town meetings rather than central offices. County and state superintendents had little formal authority, and teachers received little in the way of training, compensation, or job security. Schools were casual institutions with short sessions and erratic attendance.[11] When disputes made their way into court, judges sometimes invalidated teacher actions or district regulations that excluded students. These prostudent decisions were consistent with the tendency of Gilded Age courts to prioritize individual freedoms over state regulations.[12] To be sure, judges occasionally upheld district policies and penned opinions instructing lower courts to defer to educators.[13] Yet other common school rulings provided ammunition for the students and attorneys who petitioned for judicial oversight of college access.

Exclusion in the Nineteenth Century

Since common schools were expected to educate virtually every young person, nineteenth-century courts rarely distinguished between students who were denied initial enrollment and students who were suspended or expelled during the school year.[14] Instead of separate categories of "admission" and "expulsion" cases, a wide-ranging and inconsistent corpus of jurisprudence addressed both kinds of exclusion. As noted above, state education statutes rarely included details about the sorts of behavior that could justify exclusion. Most legislatures simply authorized school boards to suspend or dismiss students who repeatedly violated local regulations or committed acts of "gross immorality." Despite frequent remarks about the broad powers of teachers and administrators, nineteenth-century courts responded unevenly when asked to interpret these statutes. Courts disagreed over several basic questions, including whether schools could exclude students for skipping class, misbehaving outside of school, or refusing to study particular subjects.[15]

When cited in *higher* education cases, these disagreements invited courts to evaluate whether colleges, too, might have exceeded their legal authority when rejecting applicants or expelling students. In the nineteenth century, these comparisons occurred organically because the academic distinctions between higher and lower schools were relatively minor. A lack of robust secondary schooling meant that most private colleges would have risked insolvency if they rejected students on the basis of scholarly qualification. Public colleges, meanwhile, were expected to educate almost anyone who possessed rudimentary academic preparation.[16] In order to accommodate these students, many of whom were younger than eighteen, colleges and universities provided a great deal of remedial instruction.[17] Therefore, judicial opinions that limited the powers of schoolteachers or district officials could be perceived as readily applicable to the realm of higher education.[18]

Rough quantitative analysis of the relationship between lower and higher education exclusion rulings indicates that the appearance of common school citations correlates with the likelihood of a court ruling in favor of a college student. As noted above, the simple appearance of a common school citation does not prove that the precedent had a significant impact, especially because courts sometimes mentioned these citations in order to dismiss their reasoning or relevance. Nevertheless, it is striking that courts cited common school cases in 70 percent (7/10) of college admission or expulsion rulings that favored students between 1860 and 1910, compared to just 27 percent (3/11) of rulings that favored teachers or institutions.[19] Regardless of whether common school cases influenced the outcomes of these decisions or merely provided additional heft for opinion writers, courts that sided with college students were more likely to invoke comparisons between lower and higher education.

State ex rel. Stallard v. White, the Purdue fraternity case discussed at the beginning of this chapter, provides the clearest example of how debates over common school exclusion manifested in decisions that intervened on behalf of college students. Written in an era when most colleges were struggling to distinguish themselves from other sorts of educational institutions, the briefs submitted by both parties emphasized lower school rulings.[20] Ultimately, the Supreme Court of Indiana relied on these common school cases when it ruled that state universities had broad authority over the behavior of students once they enrolled but almost no authority to reject initial applicants.

Although it ultimately sided with the rejected fraternity member, *Stallard* acknowledged several common school cases that favored officials who excluded disobedient students. After all, obedience was a core objective of nineteenth-century educators, both on principle and out of necessity (a single teacher was often responsible for large classes with students of varying ages).[21] *Stallard* recognized this traditional emphasis by citing an opinion penned by Lemuel Shaw, an influential chief justice of the Massachusetts Supreme Judicial Court. Justice Shaw, who had previously served on the Boston School Committee, believed that courts should defer to teachers and district officials in most instances (including, as we shall see, cases in which school boards required racial segregation).[22] Justice Shaw first articulated this belief in *Spear v. Cumming*, a ruling that prevented the parents of an expelled student from seeking damages from a teacher. Issued in 1839, the ruling was based on procedural grounds (Justice Shaw reasoned that the power to expel was vested in the school committee rather than the teacher), but it also delivered a broader endorsement of judicial deference toward teachers and school officials. *Spear* instructed lower courts to avoid second-guessing educators and concluded that the job of protecting parental rights belonged to legislators rather than judges. In the absence of specific statutes to the contrary, Justice Shaw concluded, schools were authorized to develop and enforce their own expulsion policies.[23]

Stallard conceded that several other rulings echoed this conclusion. Three decades after *Spear*, another Massachusetts decision favored a school committee that expelled a student for "whispering, laughing, acts of playfulness and rudeness to other pupils." In what would become a standard rationale for academic deference, the opinion explained that school officials should be presumed to act in good faith and were better informed than judges about the proper threshold for exclusion.[24] Similarly, the Supreme Court of Wisconsin upheld an expulsion in 1878 while praising "the ability and good judgment" of district officials.[25] *Stallard* also cited *Dritt v. Snodgrass*, a Missouri decision that expressed concern about whether holding school board members personally liable in expulsion suits would deter "responsible and suitable men" from seeking those offices. In that case, a school committee enforced a rule prohibiting attendance at parties, even though the student had his father's express permission. Ultimately, *Dritt* concluded that suits for damages should be dismissed as long as judges could discern any rational basis whatsoever for a school policy.[26]

This section of the *Stallard* opinion also acknowledged decisions that allowed districts to expel students who raised religious objections to school policies during the 1850s and 1860s. These suits challenged officials in districts that had responded to the arrival of Catholic immigrants by infusing their curriculum with Protestant emphases. Confident that their faith epitomized the nation's democratic ethos (one textbook stated that Protestantism was the "best in the world" for forming republican citizens), many district leaders believed that public schools should promote an ostensibly nondenominational form of Christianity.[27] Teacher-led prayer and use of a Protestant Bible as a text for literary instruction were not uncommon practices, locally authorized at first and then occasionally mandated by state legislatures. When Catholics and other religious minorities challenged these policies in court, they rarely received sympathetic hearings. Between 1854 and 1924, judges sided with school districts in three-quarters of suits that challenged the use of the King James Bible.[28]

Stallard could have noted several other prodistrict decisions that Purdue's attorneys included in their briefs.[29] For example, one judge dissented from the majority opinion in *Stallard* while highlighting another of Justice Shaw's opinions. In *Sherman v. Inhabitants of Charlestown*, Justice Shaw stated that it would be "strange" if schools could not protect students from "the noxious influence" of immoral classmates. He stressed the qualifications of school board members "chosen by their fellow-citizens for their supposed capacity, impartiality and fitness," and rejected the claim of a student who asserted that she possessed an "absolute and indefeasible" right to attend her local public school.[30] Purdue's brief also cited an Iowa ruling from 1871 that sided with a district that suspended a student for truancy. The boy's father argued that compulsory attendance policies violated parental authority over children's "up-risings and their down sittings, their out-goings and their in-comings."[31] In its successful response, the district asserted that school officials possessed a "quasi judicial" authority that could not be questioned except in cases of malicious intent.[32] Despite the challenges posed by truancy, one judge dissented on the grounds that the state required districts to educate "all the youths of the state" regardless of their attendance patterns or conduct.[33] As indicated by several other decisions cited by Purdue's attorneys, that dissent communicated a minority perspective.[34]

However, despite all of these rulings that favored teachers and administrators, common school case law was not monolithic. Other nineteenth-century precedents provided fodder for students and parents who wished to challenge college admissions policies or disciplinary practices. The attorneys who represented the rejected fraternity member responded to Purdue's argument by citing a rival body of exclusion rulings that emphasized the right to attend public schools.[35] These lawyers were even able to counter Purdue's brief by invoking another opinion by Justice Shaw in which the influential jurist distinguished between the power to expel disobedient students and the power to exclude students categorically. In *Nourse v. Meriam*, Justice Shaw concluded that a town could not honor the terms of a vindictive bequest that contributed funds to a public school on the condition that its directors promise to exclude the descendants of nine particular families. Shaw called the ban "repugnant" to the nature of the institution and contrary to the state's education policies.[36]

Attorneys for the Purdue applicant also cited *Morrow v. Wood*, a Wisconsin Supreme Court decision from 1874 that condemned a teacher who pulled a student's hair after he refused to study geography.[37] In court, the boy's father explained that he instructed his son to skip geography in order to concentrate on math and basic literacy.[38] The father's attorney argued that teachers had the right to chose subjects and determine who qualified for promotion to higher grades, but they lacked the authority to punish students who did not study. The lawyer reminded the court that most schoolteachers were "mere boys and girls" who could not possibly stand in place of parents.[39] The court noted that the legislature stated that geography "shall" be taught in common schools without stipulating that the subject "must" be taught. The court also editorialized that the father's reasoning was not "unreasonable or inconsistent with the welfare and best interest of his offspring."[40]

Instead of relying on *Morrow*, the *Stallard* opinion emphasized two Illinois Supreme Court rulings from the 1870s that also ruled in favor of parents whose children were suspended or beaten after they refused to study certain subjects. According to *Stallard*, these decisions recognized a "right of admission" that, while not absolute, invited a substantial degree of judicial oversight.[41] In particular, suspension and expulsion suits that stemmed from curricular disputes received inconsistent treatment from nineteenth-century courts. These cases occupied a legal gray area because they sometimes involved students who were excluded despite the fact that they had not been disruptive or engaged in deviant behavior. It was debatable whether education statutes authorized school boards to punish children who merely sat quietly in their seats. While early treatises on the student-teacher relationship may seem to suggest that parents transferred their authority to officials during the school day, British precedents actually stated that schoolroom discipline needed to be directly related to educational ends. Especially before the passage of compulsory education statutes, this stipulation prompted judges to question whether districts could punish students whose parents told them to study some subjects but not others.[42]

For example, one of the curricular rulings cited in *Stallard* awarded damages to a student who was expelled because her guardian believed that it was "foolish" for girls to study bookkeeping. The guardian also stated that the student's deceased father was a war hero, a status that entitled his ward to a free education in any district in Illinois. Charged with the management of more than two hundred students in a school that employed only four teachers, Principal Henry Rulison worried that exempting students from any part of the curriculum would jeopardize classroom order. The student, Frances Post, claimed that she had "as much right and authority" as the principal and continued to attend the school until she was forcibly removed.[43] Although state law empowered school boards to expel students "for disobedient, refractory or incorrigibly bad conduct," the Supreme Court of Illinois emphasized that the "paramount object" of school legislation was for free public education to be made available to all children. In *Rulison v. Post*, the court held that any policy that tended "to hinder or deprive the child of this right can not be sustained." Only the most "incorrigible" students forfeited that right, the court concluded, and only after educators had exhausted all other "reasonable means" of correcting their behavior. The court determined that Frances's behavior did not justify expulsion, especially because the legislature never directed school districts to require the study of bookkeeping.[44]

The *Chicago Daily Tribune* heartily agreed with *Rulison* and welcomed the prospect of additional judicial oversight of common schools. The paper noted that parents elsewhere in the state had complained about districts that required courses beyond the branches enumerated by the legislature (reading, writing, spelling, arithmetic, geography, and history). According to the *Tribune*, teachers and administrators were not authorized to expel students who wished to focus on the basics. The column also criticized the disciplinary tactics of Chicago school officials and claimed that "the child in Chicago, no matter how obedient and tractable, who can get through a year's schooling without being suspended or expelled two or three times, is fortunate." The paper invited more judicial intervention because "school boards, as a general thing, magnify their office, and forget that the schools are not their private property."[45]

Two years later, in another opinion that would be cited by *Stallard*, the Illinois Supreme Court sided again with a father who wished to excuse his child from a particular subject. In *Trustees v. Van Allen*, the court ordered a high school to admit a student even though his father had forbidden him from studying grammar.[46] The father believed that his son was too frail to undertake a full course load and decided that grammar was the least important element of the common school curriculum. Having already sued a business partner in order to enforce a contract, the father was primed to turn to the courts when the school rejected his son.[47] As in *Rulison*, the court determined that the state's public school law intended, first and foremost, to increase access to education. Even a high school could not operate "for the benefit of some to the exclusion of others" because all children residing in the town had "equal rights of admission" as long as they had enough preliminary instruction to profit from higher training in some subjects. In contrast with school regulations related to attendance, discipline, and grading, which the court deemed to operate for the benefit of all students, the high school's exclusion of semiprepared students only served the interest of the "favored few" who could still qualify for admission. Furthermore, the state had always recognized the right of parents to govern their children's education. The court undercut the traditional rationale for academic deference by stating that familial affection and intimacy rendered parents better equipped than school officials to make decisions for their children.[48] Although denying grammar instruction to one's offspring would constitute neglect in the twenty-first century, this nineteenth-century father may have been proven correct years later when his son became a doctor.[49] Regardless, both *Rulison* and *Van Allen* supported parental authority over the curriculum, while determining that common school statutes limited the ability of officials to restrict access.

The prominence of these lower school cases in *Stallard* proved to be somewhat unusual, but hardly exceptional. During the remainder of the nineteenth century, college admission and expulsion rulings that favored students also invoked common school rulings that circumscribed institutional authority. For example, a Missouri appellate court cited *Dritt*, *Morrow*, and *Van Allen* when it reinstated an expelled college student in 1887. *Dritt* was directly applicable to this case, which also concerned a student who attended a party after the end of the school day. *Morrow* and *Van Allen*, meanwhile, suggested more generally that courts should intervene if teachers or school boards overstepped the limits of their authority.[50] Also decided in 1887, the Pennsylvania case of *Commonwealth ex rel. Hill v. McCauley* cited *Rulison* and *Van Allen* when rebutting a private college's attempt to argue that courts did not have jurisdiction over the relationship between teachers and pupils.[51]

The *Hill* opinion (which is discussed in greater detail in chapter 4) also asserted that an Indiana expulsion suit that was ruled in favor of a school district in the previous year did not apply to the case at hand.[52] Similar to the *Rulison* and *Van Allen* suits, the Indiana case of *State ex rel. Andrews v. Webber* concerned a student who was expelled for following his father's instructions to avoid a subject (music in this instance). A Civil War officer and prominent banker, Abram Andrews felt entitled to control the content of his son's education.[53] Claiming that local school leaders were just being "cranky," Andrews's lawyer declared that fathers made better judges than school officials when it came to the welfare of children.[54] The district responded by arguing that expulsion was subject to the discretion of school boards "composed of gentlemen who would not be inclined to do anything that would be unreasonable." The board also emphasized that district officials should be granted full power over the curriculum because many foreign-born parents were "incapable of determining one study or book from another" and were often "less wise than the children."[55] Although the court ultimately sided with the district, in large part because the father never explained why he objected to the study of music, *Andrews* suggested that state courts could determine whether a school regulation was "a valid and reasonable exercise of the discretionary power conferred by law."[56] *Hill* concluded that this reasonableness requirement, along with *Rulison* and *Van Allen*, demonstrated that courts were entitled to oversee the substance and procedure of school discipline at higher as well as lower institutions of learning.[57]

Given their liminal status between lower and higher education, it is not surprising that normal schools (the predecessors of teachers colleges) also invited comparisons to common schools in suits filed by excluded students. In 1898, for example, the Nebraska Supreme Court pointed to two lower school decisions while ordering a state normal school to reinstate a student. In the first case, *Perkins v. West Des Moines*, the Iowa Supreme Court objected to the expulsion of a student who unintentionally broke a school window and refused to pay for a replacement.[58] The student's attorney followed the well-worn path of arguing that the state's constitution and legislature not only promoted mass enrollment but also stipulated that students could only be excluded for extreme immorality or persistent transgression.[59] The court agreed that it would be "very harsh and obviously unjust" to suspend or expel a student on account of an accident.[60] The Nebraska ruling also mentioned another decision that reinstated a common school student whose father forbade her from studying grammar. That ruling maintained that parents possessed a level of authority "paramount to that of the trustees or teacher" and should be presumed to understand their children and seek their best interests.[61] Similarly, an Ohio court cited two common school cases from the 1870s while ordering the reenrollment of a normal school student in 1899.[62]

Exclusion in the Twentieth Century

Whereas common school decisions laid the groundwork for *Stallard* and like-minded higher education cases during the nineteenth century, this foundation eroded at the turn of the twentieth century when courts began to rule more regularly in favor of school districts. As Progressive reformers consolidated and standardized district practices, judges exhibited greater deference toward the newly professionalized administrators who came to dominate school governance. This trend intensified during the 1920s and 1930s, when courts increasingly regarded schooling as a state interest as opposed to a predominantly personal or parental matter.[63] By the 1940s, American courts tended to define education as a "highly technical" arena with complex disputes that required oversight by specialized experts rather than parents or judges.[64]

After decades of lax enforcement, officials also began to enforce compulsory attendance laws, and courts agreed that these limitations on parental authority were acceptable applications of the state's police power (a constraint on individual liberty for the sake of public health, safety, and well-being).[65] Furthermore, as one-room schoolhouses gave way to larger, graded schools, teachers and administrators were able to make stronger claims on behalf of their academic authority. When classrooms became organized according to age and experience, courts became more willing to abide by policies and truancy regulations that kept students on track within their respective grades.[66] District leaders emphasized these arguments in court as soon as graded schools began to proliferate. One brief convinced a judge that graded schools would be impossible to administer "if parents [were] allowed to supersede the school board."[67] In 1913, a Massachusetts court exhibited this new level of deference by allowing a district to expel high school students if they failed more than two subjects. In contrast with *Van Allen*, which compelled a high school to enroll a partially qualified student, the opinion reasoned that graded schools required teachers to evaluate whether particular students could profit from advanced instruction. "It is obvious that efficiency of instruction depends in no small degree upon this feature of our school system," the court stated. The determination of a student's fitness to proceed to higher grades was "an educational question" that could only be answered by teachers and administrators.[68]

Although two high-profile United States Supreme Court decisions bolstered parental authority to some extent during the 1920s, they did not fundamentally alter the emerging legal dominance of administrators, in part because the cases did not involve direct conflicts between students and public schools. *Meyer v. Nebraska* invalidated a legislature's ban on German instruction, while *Pierce v. Society of Sisters* rejected an Oregon law that would have had the effect of eliminating parochial schools in the state.[69] Yet when lawyers for expelled college students tried to invoke these precedents during a suit against the University of California, the court responded that they were irrelevant to an expulsion case.[70] *Meyer* and *Pierce* amounted to fairly modest reactions to the Progressive Era surge of state authority over education. Neither decision shook the confidence of a high school principal who maintained that courts granted "extraordinary authority" to administrators during the 1930s.[71] Even the Supreme Court's celebrated decision in favor of students who refused to salute the flag during World War II did not unleash an appreciable wave of subsequent prostudent rulings.[72]

Regardless, college access rulings cited lower school cases with decreasing frequency during the first few decades of the twentieth century, the peak era of academic deference.[73] In particular, precedents that reinstated elementary or secondary school students all but vanished from reported higher education rulings—a trend that reflects the extent to which lower school case law coalesced in favor of administrative authority during the Progressive Era. Courts no longer considered the prostudent common school rulings of the nineteenth century to be relevant guideposts for college access cases. If judges cited these decisions at all, it was only in order to reject their reasoning or distinguish them from the cases at hand. These patterns are consistent with the theory that prostudent lower school rulings influenced (or at least mirrored) the less deferential nature of higher education law during the nineteenth century.

The United States Supreme Court case of *Waugh v. University of Mississippi*, discussed more fully in the next chapter, heralded the beginning of this indifference toward prostudent lower school cases. Issued in 1915, *Waugh* disregarded all of the common school rulings that attorneys invoked on behalf of a student who unsuccessfully challenged a fraternity ban similar to the one that had been invalidated by *Stallard*.[74] In the initial state court phase of this case, the student's counselor presented an extensive catalog of common school decisions, including a ruling in which the Supreme Court of Mississippi ordered the reinstatement of a student who refused to study at home during the evening. Noting that the boy's father chose to take him to nighttime religious services, the court proclaimed that schools could only regulate "matters which would per se have a direct and pernicious effect on the moral tone of the school."[75] Yet in *Waugh*, that same court explained that this lower school decision was irrelevant to a university case because students had a legal right to attend common schools but not institutions of higher education. Ultimately, the nation's highest court reinforced this interpretation.[76]

In the wake of *Waugh*, college expulsion opinions only cited lower school decisions if those rulings deferred to the authority of teachers or district officials. A Michigan ruling from the 1920s, for example, upheld the expulsion of a student from the Michigan State Normal College while invoking thirteen cases that supported the disciplinary actions of local schools.[77] In the 1930s, a judge rejected a suit by a former University of Texas student while citing opinions that deferred to lower school policies regarding fraternities, vaccinations, and cosmetics.[78] In the 1940s and 1950s, decisions that emphasized the discretion of teachers and school boards appeared in half (5/10) of college expulsion rulings, including a Massachusetts opinion that granted college professors and administrators "at least" the same control over their students as their elementary school counterparts.[79] Throughout the first half of the twentieth century, courts tended to defer to institutional authorities in both sectors when adjudicating student exclusion suits.

Tuition

Relative to their significance within exclusion rulings, common school cases played a small role in college tuition litigation. Nevertheless, lower school lawsuits also initially undermined collegiate authority before ultimately bolstering institutional control over tuition and fees during the early twentieth century.

Although tuition-free education emerged as a defining feature of the common school, the achievement of this goal was not preordained. Despite the ambitions of many national leaders, a coherent system of free public schools did not develop during the immediate aftermath of the American Revolution. Federal land grants provided some resources for state systems, albeit in a haphazard manner that proved unable to support mass education. In many locations, children attended a patchwork of institutions, often with no clear distinctions between the public and private sphere. Until the middle of the nineteenth century it was not uncommon for private schools to receive state funds or for public schools to charge tuition or require in-kind contributions. Some school districts operated free of charge until state funds were depleted and then required tuition for the remainder of the term. Nevertheless, educators united behind the ideal of the free common school during the antebellum era, especially in the Northeast and Midwest. After the end of the Civil War, the United States Congress required all states to promote free public schools.[80]

This mandate encouraged courts to overturn almost every attempt to charge tuition (though exceptions were sometimes allowed for nonresident students or students who exceeded the legislated age range for common schools).[81] In 1885, for example, the Supreme Court of Wisconsin reinstated a student who was expelled for refusing to collect firewood when returning from recess. Not only did the court determine that this regulation fell outside the proper sphere of school board authority, but it also expressed astonishment that "any intelligent teacher or intelligent board of education should suffer such a case as this to reach the courts."[82] Indeed, since the tuition-free status of the common school went almost without saying, these unusual cases were rarely cited in higher education rulings. Neither of the major college tuition opinions of the nineteenth century (see chapter 5) cited a common school case. Instead, the courts that adjudicated those cases consulted state constitutions and statutes to determine whether public universities were subject to the same constraints as common schools.[83]

Nonetheless, two suits that successfully challenged the scholarship policies of public universities around the turn of the century (see chapter 5) referred to common school tuition cases. These scholarship suits claimed that states could not allocate tax revenue to subsidize the education of a small fraction of college students. Opponents of a county scholarship in Missouri defeated the policy in court, having based part of their argument on a common school case that outlawed favoritism toward the children of veterans.[84] In a similar suit that invalidated scholarships to the University of Kentucky, a judge likened the university's preferential treatment of recipients to a district funding policy that discriminated against African American schools.[85]

Yet similar to the trajectory of exclusion cases, lower school tuition precedents began to promote the authority of institutions of higher education in the early twentieth century. In particular, the Supreme Court of Oklahoma permitted a state university to institute new fees in the 1930s while citing *Bryant v. Whisenant*, an Alabama case that allowed school districts to charge students for firewood and water. *Bryant* reinforced the university's contention that "fees" for incidentals or activities did not violate statutes that prohibited or limited "tuition."[86] The Supreme Court of Montana also invoked *Bryant*, along with a case concerning the tax-exempt status of a Georgia private school, in another decision that upheld state university fees during the 1930s.[87] Aside from the two unusual scholarship cases, common school rulings tended to augment collegiate authority over tuition policies in the early twentieth century.

Segregation

Compared with exclusion and tuition cases, the historical interplay between lower and higher education segregation rulings has been much more thoroughly documented by legal scholars. Although de jure segregation gradually faded in northern states after the Civil War, many schools remained racially distinct because of residential discrimination, whereas other districts simply ignored integration statutes. Some black parents responded by petitioning courts to enforce legislative bans on segregation, while others demanded implementation of state laws that purported to guarantee "separate but equal" education.[88] These cases yielded a conflicting set of lower school rulings that provided grist for both sides of college access suits.

Nineteenth-century courts tended to uphold the constitutionality of segregation, but advocates for racial equity occasionally persuaded courts to rule that school officials lacked the authority to discriminate against African American students. Black parents won desegregation suits in states that outlawed the practice and persuaded a number of courts in other states to prohibit towns from funneling disproportionate tax revenue to white schools. In those northern and western states that permitted segregation, judges sometimes ruled against districts that excluded black students or diverted them to small inferior schools. Some of these court orders required integration, while others allowed towns to provide private tutors for black children or form more substantial segregated schools in combination with neighboring districts. Nineteenth-century courts also delivered inconsistent responses to suits that challenged unequal facilities, leaving scholars to debate whether judges exhibited a streak of racial liberalism or merely ruled in favor of black parents only when statutes left them with virtually no other choice.[89]

Regardless, some courts deployed common school citations to reinforce rulings that deferred to segregated state universities, while others used these cases to bolster rulings that invalidated discriminatory policies. Among all higher education desegregation cases reported before 1960, half (3/6) of prosegregation opinions, and just over half (11/21) of prointegration opinions cited at least one common school case.[90] This practice dates back to the 1930s, when a relatively obscure Ohio Supreme Court opinion cited six common school cases (out of a total of seven citations) when it ruled against a black student who was excluded from a dormitory affiliated with the state university's home economics department.[91] Lawyers for the National Association for the Advancement of Colored People (NAACP) also regularly cited common school cases. In 1935, Thurgood Marshall and Charles Hamilton Houston included over a dozen lower school rulings in their brief for *Pearson v. Murray*, a desegregation suit (discussed at greater length in chapter 3) that targeted the University of Maryland. Ultimately, the Maryland Court of Appeals cited most of these lower school cases when it handed the NAACP its first higher education victory and ordered the university's law school to admit a black applicant.[92]

In 1938, the United States Supreme Court cited two common school segregation cases (*Cumming v. Richmond* and *Gong Lum v. Rice*) in the landmark ruling that ordered the state of Missouri to provide in-state legal education for black students (see chapter 3).[93] *Cumming* and *Gong Lum* were the lower school segregation cases that appeared most frequently in higher education rulings—not only because they were issued by the Supreme Court, but also because each ruling contained statements that endorsed segregation as well as statements that could limit the extent of discrimination.[94] Even though *Cumming* allowed a Georgia district to operate a high school that only enrolled white students, it also instructed lower courts to intervene if segregated districts evinced any "hostility" toward black students.[95] Similarly, *Gong Lum* upheld a Mississippi Supreme Court decision that assigned a Chinese American student to a "colored" school but also affirmed that all children had "the right to attend and enjoy the privileges of a common school education."[96]

Given their prominence and ambiguity, it is not surprising that lower school cases such as *Cumming* and *Gong Lum* appeared in university desegregation rulings. Somewhat less predictably, these rulings were also cited in cases concerning the admission or expulsion of white college students. And yet it was not uncommon for analogies to racial oppression to appear in higher education suits filed by white petitioners.[97] Lawyers for white college students sometimes cited cases that ordered elementary or secondary school officials to provide access to equal, albeit often separate, education to black students. In response, university attorneys presented prosegregation rulings that highlighted administrative authority over admissions policies.

In *Foltz v. Hoge*, an 1879 case examined in the next chapter, two white women who sued for admission to a California law school cited a common school case that guaranteed equal educational access for black students.

They asserted that statutes and constitutional provisions pertaining to educational access (at all levels) should be interpreted in favor of students unless state law expressly stipulated otherwise.[98] In response, the law school cited the school segregation case of *Ward v. Flood* to support its contention that the state endowed all administrators with broad discretion over admissions.[99] It was a feeble attempt, not only because *Ward* upheld an existing segregation statute, whereas California did not prohibit coeducation, but also because *Ward* required the establishment of separate schools for black students, whereas the law school made no such provision for women.[100] Not surprisingly, California's high court rejected the suggestion that *Ward* authorized the wholesale exclusion of women from public legal education.[101] Decades later, the same court referred to two other separate-but-equal common school rulings while ordering a state normal college to reinstate an expelled white student.[102] Similarly, the Pennsylvania judge who presided over the 1882 *Hill* case explained his support for the expelled white college student by citing two earlier rulings that ordered the enrollment of black students who had been barred from public elementary schools.[103]

Common school segregation rulings figured even more prominently in the *Stallard* fraternity case of 1882. In particular, Purdue's counsel cited the antebellum segregation ruling of *Roberts v. City of Boston* in an attempt to legitimize its administrative control of admissions.[104] *Roberts* rejected a suit filed by a black parent who argued that his daughter was inappropriately denied access to an elementary school.[105] In Boston, where school committee members made no attempt to hide their discriminatory intent, a lone common school was designated for African American pupils. Operated by a bigoted teacher, the Abiel Smith School was in poor physical condition (even a school committee member was "astonished" by its disrepair) and produced the lowest scores on citywide examinations. Some parents wished to preserve the segregated school, albeit with equal resources and a black teacher.[106] Rallied by Benjamin F. Roberts, other black Bostonians lobbied for desegregation. Roberts, whose commitment was fueled by his experience growing up in a biracial family, filed suit after his five-year-old daughter was compelled to attend the Smith School rather than a school closer to home.[107] Chief Justice Lemuel Shaw, consistent with his earlier support for school authorities, upheld Boston's segregation policy after reasoning that district officials possessed broad discretionary power to "arrange, classify, and distribute students." Justice Shaw noted that the "experience and judgment" of educators might also prompt them to form single-sex schools or remedial institutions. The opinion rejected the arguments presented by Roberts's lawyer, William Graham Sumner, who asserted that racial segregation violated the state's constitutional guarantee of equal protection. *Roberts*, a ruling that prefigured the core debate over this issue for more than a century, posited that segregation did not necessarily amount to unequal treatment.[108]

The lawyers for Thomas Hawley, the rejected Purdue applicant, countered *Roberts* by citing other common school discrimination rulings that favored black students. In total, ten out of the twelve cases cited in Hawley's brief concerned racial exclusion (the court's opinion would cite all ten).[109] Many were western cases, such as *Ward*, that ordered school districts to educate black students without necessarily requiring racial integration. In 1872, for instance, the Supreme Court of Nevada declared that public education was almost an "absolute right," and could only be denied on the grounds of "moral obliquity or mental incapacity." Although state law required segregation, the court ruled that white schools must enroll black students if districts made no other arrangement for their education.[110] More comprehensively, the Supreme Court of Illinois ruled that school officials could not discriminate, since the state legislature required all districts to educate black students.[111] After acknowledging the "large and discretionary powers" of school board officials, the opinion stated that a "school" serving just two students failed to satisfy a district's statutory obligation.[112] Thomas Hawley's brief argued that these cases established that denying education to a class of citizens constituted a violation of the Fourteenth Amendment.[113] Purdue's attorneys responded by claiming that the amendment applied to racial minorities, not white fraternity members.[114]

Ultimately, the Indiana Supreme Court agreed that these segregation rulings supported Hawley's claim. The court somehow concluded that *Roberts* only authorized schools to expel students but did not allow "invidious discrimination" at the point of admission.[115] Purdue's lawyers responded, in vain, by demonstrating the illogic of distinguishing between admission and expulsion in racial discrimination cases. "How farcical the right to admission would be," stated the university's fruitless petition for rehearing, "if the teacher could require a colored pupil to wash himself white as a condition of remaining in the school."[116]

Three decades later, when judicial enthusiasm for academic deference was intensifying, the Mississippi Supreme Court rejected *Stallard*'s interpretation of these lower school discrimination cases. In *Waugh v. University of Mississippi*, university lawyers argued successfully that *Roberts* and other prosegregation rulings instructed courts to defer to school admission policies.[117] The attorneys for J. P. Waugh, the excluded applicant, responded by invoking *Ward* and several other separate-but-equal decisions that emphasized the right to attend public schools.[118] When appealing the case before the United States Supreme Court, Waugh's counsel also mentioned that it would seem odd to permit discrimination against white fraternity members while forbidding discrimination against black citizens.[119] As indicated by this rhetoric, early disputes over the admission of white college students invoked school segregation cases in part because of their demagogic power. Yet common school discrimination cases also possessed some substantive relevance for all college access cases because they contained dueling arguments about the scope and limits of judicial deference toward educators. These cases highlighted tensions between student rights and academic discretion that would resonate with later challenges to collegiate authority.

Courts routinely apply principles derived from litigation in one context to disputes involving other contexts; *Plessy v. Ferguson*, to name a particularly famous example, upheld the constitutionality of segregated railroad cars but was regularly cited in school segregation cases.[120] Compared to the relationship between railroads and schools, lower and higher education cases seem intimately connected. Indeed, university attorneys rarely argued that elementary or secondary education cases were inapplicable to their domain. Still, the frequency with which lower school precedents appear in higher education cases is noteworthy given the significant legal and actual distinctions between these types of institutions. As noted by the Supreme Court, for example, universities naturally enjoyed somewhat greater authority over enrollment because their students attended on a voluntary rather than obligatory basis.[121]

Yet because of the lack of higher education precedents, the similarity of their governing statutes, and the blurred lines between the academic status of these institutions during the nineteenth century, attorneys on both sides of college access suits referred to elementary and secondary school case law. Although colleges could take comfort from a large pool of decisions that favored the authority of lower school officials, a small but significant number of prostudent common school rulings appeared in higher education briefs and opinions. These cases reflected the extent to which common law granted substantial power to parents (especially before the spread of compulsory education statutes), as well as the extent to which state education statutes promoted mass enrollment. The prominence of these lower school citations within college access cases helps to account for the fragility of academic deference during the nineteenth century. When colleges appeared roughly analogous to the "common" schools in which parents and students enjoyed significant rights, then judicial oversight of college admissions, expulsion, and tuition policies could certainly seem justifiable.

During the first half of the twentieth century, the jurisprudence of schools and colleges remained interconnected. However, rather than fueling controversy, lower school case law became more consistently deferential and encouraged courts to rule in favor of higher education officials in almost all cases. Twentieth-century courts referred to the older rulings that limited the discretion of school officials only when they adjudicated state university desegregation suits. With the important exception of these racial discrimination cases, analogies to common school rulings no longer undermined the authority of college faculty and administrators. By the start of the First World War, American courts agreed that students surrendered a significant degree of personal freedom at higher and lower schools alike. Decades later, in the wake of the 1960s, both types of institutions would once again become vulnerable to student-initiated litigation. As I discuss in this book's conclusion, parallels to lower schools returned to threaten academic autonomy during the late twentieth century, a recurrence that underscores the deeply rooted and ongoing challenges faced by proponents of judicial deference to higher education.

2

Admissions

Whereas late-twentieth- and early-twenty-first-century courts have entertained a steady procession of challenges to admissions policies at state universities, these suits were relatively scarce prior to the civil rights movement.[1] Yet despite their modest quantity, the substance of these cases illustrates how early legal constraints on academic authority ultimately gave way to a more deferential judicial climate, a pattern that is consistent with the expulsion and tuition rulings examined in subsequent chapters. In particular, the first hundred years of admissions litigation highlights the extent to which courts shifted from restrictive to permissive interpretations of the statutes that governed access to public universities.

In the nineteenth century, the high courts of California and Indiana regarded these statutes as relatively rigid limits to the discretion of academic officials. The two courts agreed that public institutions of higher education could not reject entire categories of students without explicit legislative authorization. During the early twentieth century, amid greater appreciation for academic authority and increasing doubts about the ideal of the open-access flagship, other courts allowed public universities to devise admission restrictions without the express approval of legislators. While this transition consisted of cases with statutory contexts that differed from the earlier California and Indiana decisions, twentieth-century judges emphasized, in general, that enrollment at a public institution of higher education was akin to a privilege granted by academic experts instead of an entitlement conferred by state officials.

These decisions reverberated through subsequent college access suits because they redefined enrollment as a quasi-judicial enterprise rather than a mechanistic or bureaucratic procedure. Since legislatures continued to directly or indirectly determine the entrance requirements of state universities, these cases had only a moderate impact in the short term; then as now, the admissions policies of public institutions reflected a combination of legal, political, demographic, financial, and academic factors. Nevertheless, these rulings urged courts to defer to university admissions policies unless they blatantly violated specific statutes or constitutional provisions. This revision eventually dominated the jurisprudence of admissions in the twentieth century, though it did not put an end to public disputes, especially with respect to racial exclusion or inclusion. Ultimately, the history of admissions litigation indicates that the principle of judicial deference has been a shifting and often contentious basis for academic authority.

Judicial Oversight of College Admissions, 1860–1910

During the nineteenth century, law, custom, and a scarcity of well-prepared students prevented most public as well as private colleges from enacting substantial admission requirements. As I discuss in the next chapter, black students were formally excluded from most southern institutions and hardly welcomed by most northern ones.[2] Yet for white applicants, entrance requirements typically consisted of semiformal and forgiving examinations in classics, basic mathematics, some philosophy, and perhaps elementary science. After the Civil War, many colleges began to implement tests of English grammar and composition, geography, history, and some additional math and science. In 1892, the National Education Association attempted to standardize these requirements by promoting four options for high school curricula, each of which contained similar core subjects along with varying kinds and quantities of foreign languages.[3] However, the vast majority of colleges were unable to uphold even these modest standards without inviting unsustainable enrollment decreases or unwelcome political scrutiny.[4]

As a result, most white applicants were able to enter the schools of their choice, especially because institutions often permitted nondegree or part-time students to attend if they were ineligible for regular admission. Colleges also offered "conditional" enrollment to unqualified applicants and invited them to remediate their deficiencies. Although this method of admission was a source of some embarrassment, half of first-year students even at institutions such as Harvard, Yale, Princeton, and Columbia were admitted conditionally as late as 1907.[5] Enrollment in remedial or "preparatory" courses often matched or exceeded attendance in regular college offerings.[6] These flexible entrance policies served the interests of most faculty and administrators, who hoped to expand enrollment either for the sake of institutional survival or because large enrollment was, at the time, equated with prestige.

Nevertheless, nineteenth-century legislatures still felt compelled to restrict the discretionary powers of state universities in order to ensure access for white students (as discussed in the next chapter, some northern legislatures also ordered state universities to accept black applicants after the Civil War). While these statutes can seem perfunctory by modern standards, they still limited institutional authority and, on rare occasions, prompted judicial intervention. For example, many states banned admissions discrimination against religious minorities. This language appeared in the founding legislation of numerous state universities as well as within the constitutions of Arizona, Nevada, Texas, and Wisconsin. Public university administrators tended to embrace these prohibitions, which provided important symbols of their duty to serve all state residents. The charters of roughly half of private colleges contained similar clauses.[7] As I discuss later in this chapter, these laws failed to prevent some universities from discriminating against Jewish applicants. Yet the mainstream of American higher education professed to support religious tolerance, at least in theory.[8]

In contrast, statutes designed to increase access for rural white students were less compatible with academic culture. In response to the lack of high school education in rural districts, these laws limited the academic entrance requirements of state universities.[9] Populists and other agrarian leaders advocated for these limits and lobbied against any substantial modifications to admission standards that might "discriminate" against disadvantaged rural students.[10] Influenced by legislators' interest in representing their districts, the founding laws of state universities routinely acknowledged these concerns by requiring regional diversity. For example, Pennsylvania State Agricultural College (now Pennsylvania State University) was directed to enroll a student body that reflected county population levels.[11] Legislators obligated the regents of the University of California to seek geographically proportional enrollment so that the entire state could "enjoy equal privileges" at the Berkeley campus.[12] In 1872, two years after designating the University of Missouri a land grant institution, the state legislature capped the number of students per county and stipulated that this quota could be exceeded only if other counties fell short of their allotments.[13] Without specifying that Cornell University needed to seek exact proportionality, the New York legislature required the land grant institution to admit students "without distinction as to rank, class, previous occupation, or locality."[14] Although these laws did not formally ban entrance requirements, they directed state universities to prioritize regional access.

These expectations sometimes frustrated faculty members, who tended to be more concerned about unprepared freshmen and less concerned about the geography of access. Professors often looked forward to the day when they could end remedial programs, even if those closures would lead to lower enrollments from rural counties or agitate critics who accused colleges of favoring privileged urban youth.[15] Statutes that prohibited the rejection of applicants with minimal levels of preparation reflected these tensions between politicians and professors. In the 1860s, for example, legislators rejected a proposal that would have enabled Illinois Industrial University (now University of Illinois) to increase its entrance standards.[16] Kentucky legislators forbade the state land grant college from rejecting any student who had obtained a common school education.[17] A Texas act prohibited state normal colleges from rejecting students who were inadequately prepared in Latin or algebra.[18] In Kansas, the state agricultural college could not even deny admission to students who had been expelled from other schools.[19] These statutes signaled the widespread belief that virtually all white applicants were entitled to enter a state college or university.

This perspective was often codified with sweeping legislative or constitutional language. The Indiana Constitution of 1816, which directed the state university to be "equally open to all," provided one of the more absolute statements of this sort of obligation.[20] The founding legislation of public universities in other states contained comparable phrases. When the Ohio legislature established the Ohio Agricultural and Mechanical College (now Ohio State University), it stipulated that the school would admit "all persons" over the age of fourteen.[21] State constitutions often sent similar messages by requiring that public education of some sort be made available for all residents under the age of twenty-one. The Texas constitution, for example, specified that "public schools" (including the state university and state agricultural college) must be accessible to every young person.[22]

Typically, these laws were understood to reserve some discretion for faculty and administrators. Yet the extent of this authority remained unsettled, and academic leaders sometimes bristled against statutory restrictions. Though these laws lacked the enforcement mechanisms of later federal civil rights statutes, they communicated the expectations of legislatures, whose good favor was courted by state universities during each appropriation season. Public colleges and universities indirectly sought to limit the extent of this legislative authority by influencing state attorneys general, seeking representation within departments of education (which sometimes determined admissions requirements), and lobbying to revise state constitutions.[23]

Many legislatures, however, continued to obligate public universities to employ "mechanical" admissions procedures that automatically offered seats to all applicants who fulfilled certain basic criteria. State universities responded by promoting "admission by certificate," a system that enabled faculty to raise standards indirectly by influencing the curricula and graduation requirements of local high schools. Originating at the University of Michigan during the 1870s, the certificate system guaranteed admission to students who completed the college-preparatory track of any high school that had been accredited by university faculty. By the turn of the century, the majority of college students gained admission in this manner. Although the certificate system empowered state universities to shape high school curricula, faculty tired of the burdensome responsibility and eventually ceded authority over accreditation to state officials or regional associations. Having abdicated control over high school standards, state colleges were still compelled to accept all graduates of accredited college-preparatory tracks.[24]

Thus access to public higher education was institutionalized as a bureaucratic process, rather than a quasi-judicial exercise involving the discretion of professors or administrators. During the late nineteenth century, judicial interpretation of the statutes governing state universities reflected this attitude toward college access. In both of the admissions rulings reported in this era, a mechanical vision of admissions triumphed over discretionary policies that excluded certain categories of applicants.

Foltz v. Hoge

Foltz v. Hoge, the first of these decisions, compelled Hastings College of the Law to admit women students.[25] Hastings was an affiliate of the University of California (UC), an institution whose founding legislation merely required applicants to be morally upright residents over the age of fourteen. In 1879, Clara Foltz and Laura deForce Gordon argued that they were entitled to attend Hastings because this statute did not authorize UC to discriminate on the basis of sex. Ultimately, the California Supreme Court intervened on behalf of the two students and, in the process, rejected the college's attempt to defend its discretionary power over admissions.

Although women's enrollment had increased since the Revolutionary era, they attended college at roughly half the rate of men at the time of the *Foltz* suit. Whereas southern states tended to operate separate colleges for women, most eastern and western state universities gravitated (sometimes reluctantly) toward coeducation during the 1870s. The Morrill Act of 1862 had been silent on this topic, providing neither a guarantee of women's rights nor a directive to exclude women from land grant institutions. In some instances, women were compelled to demand access to these state colleges and universities.[26] Once enrolled at coeducational public institutions, women frequently encountered discrimination, such as exclusion from extracurricular activities or discouragement from enrolling in science or engineering courses.[27] This bigotry persisted despite the passage of legislation in some states that guaranteed access for women and men "on equal terms."[28]

In California, the governing board of the state university voted to accept women students in 1869, its first year of operation, and proudly reported that women made up a quarter of the undergraduate student body.[29] The college of law, however, was less receptive to women. The only law school operating west of Iowa, the college opened in the fall of 1878 as a UC affiliate funded by a large gift from Judge S. Clinton Hastings.[30] When Foltz and Gordon arrived in January of 1879, college authorities hesitantly processed their registration. Some students responded to their arrival by mimicking the women whenever they coughed or adjusted their seats. After enduring three days of this hazing, Foltz and Gordon learned that the board of directors had decided to revoke their admission. Judge Hastings, who served as the school's first dean, was concerned that the women would distract their classmates (he considered seating them in separate sections—a proposal that the *San Francisco Chronicle* mockingly compared to a Turkish harem).[31] After initiating her lawsuit, Foltz attempted to continue attending lectures but was physically barred by other students. One professor informed Foltz that she had "no rights in the matter at all." Needless to say, Foltz objected to this characterization and framed her case as an effort to determine whether Hastings was "a private institution or a public one."[32]

Foltz's petition was part of a wider campaign for women's access to the legal profession. The case transpired only a decade after women first enrolled in American law schools and gained admission to the bar in some states.[33] Foltz herself operated a pioneering practice (she had developed an interest in law while composing a lecture on women's rights) and lobbied to authorize the admission of women to the California bar. Reportedly, she entered the governor's office without an appointment and rescued the bill from a stack of rejected proposals. Although a law degree was not a requirement for attorneys in this era, Foltz and Gordon (a journalist and suffragette) hoped to attract more clients by earning formal credentials from Hastings.[34]

The resistance that Foltz and Gordon encountered at the college stemmed from a widespread assumption that women were ill suited for participation in the combative realms of law, commerce, or politics. During one of Foltz's earlier trials, for instance, a district attorney warned the jury that a woman lawyer would appeal to their emotions, since she could not be expected to employ formal reasoning. The attorney accused Foltz of being "ambitious" and wanting to "show off." Undeterred by either Foltz's abilities or the passage of the bill establishing the right of women to practice law in California, the lawyers representing Hastings College also attempted to persuade a district court judge that female lawyers were "revolting," that they would have unfair influence over juries, and that the delicate sensibilities of womanhood were "surely not qualifications for forensic strife."[35] In light of this context, *Foltz* is best known as a victory for women's rights.

However, the suit was also an important episode in the contested development of academic deference. Both sides in the case understood that the two students sought to limit the discretionary powers of an academic governing board. Representing themselves in district court, Foltz and Gordon argued that public colleges were obligated to admit women unless legislators explicitly authorized their exclusion.[36] The court ruled in favor of Foltz and Gordon, who were soon disappointed to learn that the college was appealing the case to the California Supreme Court.[37] Foltz's supreme court brief bolstered her earlier argument by contending, in general, that broad declarations of accessibility in California's school laws limited administrative authority in the absence of any particular statute to the contrary.[38]

In response, Hastings's lawyers claimed that the members of a college governing board should be able to "exercise their best judgment." The board claimed that it was entitled to exclude "any and all persons" whose enrollment could be "useless to such persons themselves, or detrimental to said college, or likely to impair or interfere with the proper discipline and instruction of the students."[39] Hastings's lawyers asserted that the state should defer to academic authorities unless a charter or statute expressly limited these powers. Moreover, they claimed that Hastings was not subject to the statutes governing the public university as a whole because the law college was privately endowed. As an ostensibly private college, Hastings could lay claim to the landmark *Dartmouth* case of 1819 and enjoy substantial immunity from state oversight.[40] Regardless, Hastings's brief argued that a governing board composed of respected members of a "great and conservative profession" should enjoy "wide and enlightened discretion" over admission standards. The lawyers maintained that the governing board ought to be insulated from external pressures in order to ignore "clamor" and "innovations which, by whatever insidious influences promoted, might lower its standards or endanger its usefulness."[41]

Hastings's lawyers also argued a broader point about the nature of college enrollment: they suggested that institutions of higher education were *inherently* entitled to establish selective admissions policies. "No person can claim a strict legal right to be admitted," stated the brief, because "the very idea of a college implies the power to fix the qualifications and limit the number of students." The lawyers added that it was "absurd" to suggest that applicants could challenge the board's judgment. Citing *Dartmouth* for the second time, the brief reminded the court that Justice John Marshall had ruled that no individual student had a "vested right" to attend college.[42]

The California Supreme Court rejected this analogy to *Dartmouth* and upheld the lower court ruling that favored Foltz and Gordon. In particular, the decision rested on the finding that Hastings must abide by the same permissive statute that governed admission to the rest of UC. Although the university's founding legislation stated that the faculty of an affiliated law school would maintain control of "immediate government and discipline," the court determined that the legislature did not intend for this language to apply to fundamental enrollment policies such as a ban on women. The decision was also consistent with the prevailing sentiments of California's political leaders. After the briefs were presented but before the court issued its judgment, the state's constitutional convention reaffirmed that women were entitled to attend UC (the court still based its decision on UC's statute rather than these convention results).[43]

Although UC's founding legislation and this statewide support for women's rights were the decisive factors in *Foltz*, the opinion also emphasized the traditional accessibility of public higher education. Whereas Hastings had argued that colleges were inherently selective, the court maintained that the governing boards of public institutions could not unilaterally establish admission policies that excluded entire categories of students. Initially, the decision conceded that no individual student enjoyed a "strict legal right" to admission and agreed that applicants could be rejected for "any sufficient reason." However, *Foltz* concluded that the members of a state college governing board lacked "unlimited" authority to "exclude every one who does not possess some qualification arbitrarily selected by them." To some extent, this judgment merely reflected a logical interpretation of Hastings's founding statute, which gave the college control of certain elements (such as curriculum) but did not specifically mention admissions. The court reasoned that powers not expressly granted to Hastings remained subject to the laws governing all of UC.[44]

Yet *Foltz* also indicated that the court appreciated the customary accessibility of state colleges and universities. The opinion stated that there was nothing "in the nature or purpose" of a public institution that empowered its governing board to exclude broad swaths of students who met UC's statutory entrance requirements.[45] Hastings could reject applicants who seemed especially unfit for instruction, but the college was otherwise obligated to admit eligible students in a mechanical fashion. Although the core of the decision interpreted a particular statute and protected a particular class of students, the court agreed with Clara Foltz's broader argument about academic deference by ruling that categorical exclusions from public colleges required explicit legislative authorization. According to the decision, governing boards could not write their own admissions policies because that level of discretion clashed with the very nature of public higher education.

State ex rel. Stallard v. White

Three years afterward, the Indiana Supreme Court cited *Foltz* in an opinion that more emphatically prioritized accessibility rather than academic authority. *State ex rel. Stallard v. White*, which ordered Purdue University to admit fraternity members, echoed *Foltz*'s conclusion that access to public higher education could not be denied to a category of students without the consent of the state legislature.[46]

Many nineteenth-century college administrators objected to fraternities because they seemed to promote intemperance and class snobbery. In their original antebellum form, these organizations attracted few poor rural students, who tended to be financially and socially repelled by fraternity culture. After the Civil War, when fraternities became even more tightly linked to elitism and academic underachievement, extracurricular rivalries between "Greeks" and unaffiliated "barbarians" dominated student life on many campuses. In 1890, three-fourths of college presidents told the National Education Association that sororities and fraternities exerted an unhealthy influence at their institutions. According to one scholar, most college administrators considered Greek organizations to be "the incarnation of dissipation and profligacy."[47]

At Purdue, President Emerson White attempted to exterminate fraternities and nearly destroyed the university in the process. In the spring of 1876, when White assumed the presidency, the university was two years old and enrolled just sixteen students. At a time when the nation was still emerging from a devastating economic panic, Purdue struggled to establish itself as a viable institution of applied higher education.[48] Yet White moved aggressively to ban fraternities, undeterred by this fragile context. In 1877, he persuaded Purdue's trustees to require applicants to sign a statement promising that they would disavow membership in "any so-called Greek or other college secret society." Violators of the promise faced expulsion. According to a former student, White's background in common school administration predisposed him to focus on student conduct with the fervor of a "principal of a backward graded school." He maintained strict social regulations and lowered students' grades for cursing, smoking, drinking (or even mentioning alcohol), whispering, or poor posture. Allegedly, White once chastised a professor for riding a bicycle. Students were also required to secure permission if they wished to visit the town of Lafayette after sunset.[49]

White's hostility to Greek organizations was not based solely on moral grounds. He was also concerned that Purdue, Indiana's public agricultural and mechanical institution, might evolve into a traditional college. White worried that Purdue could lose its way and become "choked by customs, practices, and other hindrances copied from the classical system, many of these being poor imitations of the stale mummeries of the aristocratic university of Oxford and Cambridge." He interpreted the Morrill Act as a mandate to focus predominantly on utilitarian subjects and predicted that fraternities would infect Purdue with a "classical and professional spirit" that could overpower the egalitarian "industrial spirit" of the land grant campus.[50]

Of course, the antifraternity policy was unpopular with many incoming students, especially those who had already joined Greek organizations while attending other schools. Some of these applicants signed the statement but continued to participate passive-aggressively in secret societies. A student named Thomas Hawley opted for open defiance and challenged the policy in court (since Hawley was a minor, the suit was filed in the name of his guardian, Samuel F. Stallard). Active in a fraternity that was affiliated with a college he'd previously attended, Hawley asked a circuit court judge to rule that a public university could not reject residents just because they refused to sign an antifraternity statement. Hawley and his attorneys had some reason to believe that the policy would be invalidated, because nineteenth-century jurists were trained to invalidate "class legislation" that harmed (or aided) particular groups rather than the entire public.[51] Hawley's counselors contended that Purdue's policy violated fraternity members' Fourteenth Amendment right to equal protection of the law. They also argued that the state constitution of Indiana required public schools to accept all students on equal terms. Similar to the attorneys who represented Hastings College in the *Foltz* case, Purdue's lawyers responded by asserting that no student had an "absolute legal right" to enrollment. They also suggested that the equal protection clause of the Constitution only prohibited discrimination against African Americans.[52]

Issued by Judge D. P. Vinton, the circuit court ruling endorsed the principle of academic deference and refused "to set limits to the inherent and necessary powers" of Purdue's governing board. Judge Vinton determined that the fraternity ban did not violate Hawley's right to equal protection because it was required of every applicant. The opinion also stated that Indiana's constitutional requirement for schools to be "equally open to all" should not be interpreted literally, but rather as a protection of all eligible residents as defined by the state legislature. Judge Vinton concluded that Hawley's right to attend Purdue depended on his obedience to regulations set by university trustees unless those policies were "plainly and palpably wrong." The ruling deferred to university authorities because they were "more likely to know what bylaws are necessary and proper to conduct and manage an institution of learning than a court."[53]

President White was so enthusiastic about this outcome that he encouraged Hawley to appeal to the Indiana Supreme Court in order to settle the question even more authoritatively.[54] Yet to White's dismay, the state's high court exhibited less deference to academia. Purdue's attorneys continued to stake much of their argument upon the notion that university officials were the most competent judges of student qualifications. Their brief characterized the antifraternity policy as the product of careful deliberation by scholars who had studied the regulations employed by other institutions. They likened the policy to an entrance examination and argued that it was a reasonable application of the university's power to exclude unsuitable students.[55]

In an opinion written by Judge William Ellis Niblack, the Indiana Supreme Court rejected this premise and refused to defer to Purdue's governing board. First, *Stallard* distinguished between on-campus discipline (the domain of the university) and admissions policies (the domain of the legislature). "The admission of students in a public educational institution is one thing," stated the opinion, "and the government and control of students after they are admitted, and have become subject to the jurisdiction of the institution, is quite another thing." Judge Niblack reasoned that law and custom limited administrative authority over admissions policies, whereas college officials exercised more complete control over internal discipline.[56] The laws and customs to which the judge referred included a decade-old statute that empowered the state board of education to manage admission-by-certificate systems for Purdue as well as Indiana University. Passed in 1873, this statute essentially stripped both state universities of their authority over entrance standards.[57]

This context helps to explain why *Stallard* not only defended the rights of fraternity members but also supported a broader rationale for judicial intervention. Although Hawley's attorneys argued that fraternity membership was comparable to the sort of religious or political affiliations that were protected by the constitutional right to equal protection, this aspect of their brief did not figure prominently in the opinion.[58] Instead, the ruling emphasized the mechanical admissions procedures employed by public universities. Judge Niblack concluded that Hawley "had the right to be admitted" because he was an Indiana resident who met the minimal entrance requirements outlined by the state legislature. According to the court, Purdue's founding statute virtually guaranteed admission to all such residents who possessed "reasonably good moral character," were free of "contagious or loathsome disease," and lacked any serious "mental or physical infirmity."[59]

In total, *Stallard* referred to enrollment as a "right" five times. According to the court, this right could only be denied if a state university had no room for additional students or if an applicant was lacking in "preliminary studies." Even in these two scenarios, the right was merely "postponed" until seats became available or until the applicant became better prepared. Judge Niblack concluded that the fraternity ban conveyed an "utter disregard of the fundamental ideas upon which our entire educational system is based." In support of this expansive interpretation of student rights, the opinion cited *Foltz* and several opinions that protected access to elementary and secondary schools (as discussed in the preceding chapter).[60] Albeit somewhat extreme, this comparison reflected the conventional assumption that accessibility was essential to the mission of a state university.

Stallard also echoed the populist impulses of late-nineteenth-century political life. In particular, the opinion may have reflected ongoing hostility stemming from the Democratic Party's antagonism toward state funding for higher education. Many Democrats had opposed the Morrill Act, which only became law after the Civil War disenfranchised the predominantly Democratic congressional delegations of the Confederate states. Purdue was situated in the district of a Republican congressperson, in part because Indiana Democrats had voted against the act. Therefore, it is worth noting that Judge Niblack was a prominent Democrat, whereas Judge Vinton (who sided with Purdue in the district court proceeding) and Judge William Allen Woods (who dissented from the high court's decision) were Republicans.[61] Purdue was also vulnerable to the Democrat's anti-elitist criticism because farmers' children were underrepresented on campus, whereas students from the town of Lafayette attended in disproportionate numbers. President White exacerbated these tensions by advocating for more rigorous entrance requirements despite the likelihood of a negative impact on rural enrollment.[62] One of Thomas Hawley's lawyers scolded President White for failing to realize that "the humblest of the students who have been driven from Purdue University because they would not surrender their rights as citizens . . . is his peer in all the courts of the land."[63] These comments suggest that the anti-elitism of late-nineteenth-century politics may have limited the extent to which judges were willing to defer to academic authorities.

Ultimately, Purdue barely survived White's resistance to *Stallard* and the political context that it embodied. At first, White stubbornly claimed that the opinion was still a victory for the university because it upheld Purdue's authority to ban fraternity membership among matriculated students. White continued to attack fraternities by prohibiting members from receiving honors and engaging in other campus activities. Eventually, he resigned after profraternity legislators threatened to withhold the university's appropriation. According to a former student, White's fraternity campaign relegated the university to the legislature's "doghouse." Hostile legislators temporarily froze Purdue's funding and, in the process, delayed appropriations for all state agencies. The university was able to borrow some funds but was late paying faculty salaries. Soon thereafter, faculty opposition to fraternities faded, and the organizations received official recognition.[64]

When viewed out of context, *Stallard* may seem like a "bizarre" exception to the doctrine of academic deference.[65] Indeed, the court essentially told Purdue that it was obligated to admit a student even if his subsequent expulsion was virtually certain. In his dissenting opinion, Judge Woods pointed out the absurdity of drawing a sharp distinction between the university's authority over admissions and its authority over internal discipline.[66] Furthermore, the ruling cast a member of an elitist fraternal organization in the role of a humble everyman. Yet to dismiss *Stallard* as an outlier is to overlook an important point. The case illustrates that the impulse to champion access to higher education was so powerful that it could rival the power of academic authority and justify an almost nonsensical decision.

The Rise of Academic Deference, 1910–60

By limiting administrative authority over admissions, both *Foltz* and *Stallard* reflected a nineteenth-century vision of college enrollment that emphasized access rather than selectivity. During the first decades of the twentieth century, these assumptions about accessibility receded alongside the underlying demographic and institutional circumstances that had originally encouraged universities to adopt minimal entrance requirements. The capacity of public universities to welcome nearly all applicants came under pressure from rising enrollments that began to outpace state funding. In addition, the increasing availability of public secondary education gradually ended the presumption that students could flow directly from common schools to institutions of higher education. Eventually, the development of regional state colleges and public junior colleges allowed flagship universities to raise their standards while still asserting that some form of public higher education remained open to virtually all students.

This erosion of the customary drivers of accessibility coincided with changes in judicial attitudes toward higher education that paralleled, and perhaps facilitated, support for new admission standards at state flagships. Even before the development of more rigorous entrance requirements, judges began to redefine public higher education as something closer to a privilege than a right. A series of cases, including the first college access ruling delivered by the United States Supreme Court, signaled that judges would no longer challenge the admissions policies of public universities as long as they did not violate the specific wording of statutes or constitutional provisions. In contrast, *Foltz* and *Stallard* had determined that public colleges could not implement any major changes to admission policies without explicit legislative or constitutional authorization.

Two rulings handed down in 1913 heralded the emergence of this more deferential approach to admissions law. First, a California appeals court allowed the state university to require applicants to be vaccinated against smallpox regardless of their religious objections. In *Williams v. Wheeler*, the court concluded that UC was entitled to regulate public health in the absence of legislation to the contrary. In contrast with *Foltz*, which prevented Hastings College from excluding women without approval from the California legislature, *Williams* determined that UC could ban unvaccinated students even without legislation to that effect. The contexts of *Foltz* and *Williams* differed significantly because courts tended to give state officials broad authority to protect public health. However, *Williams* exhibited a conspicuous level of deference toward academic authorities, because a statute passed in 1911 had specifically directed schools to exempt conscientious objectors from vaccinations. *Williams* skirted this statute by somehow reasoning that the conscientious objector provision indicated that the vaccination law was not primarily a public health measure (which would have fallen under the state's police powers and outranked UC's authority). In essence, the court's respect for UC trumped the will of the legislature. Whereas *Stallard* had bent over backward in support of student access in 1882, *Williams* contorted to defer to university officials in 1913.[67]

A Mississippi Supreme Court ruling issued that same year also revealed the judiciary's new deference toward admission policies. This case, styled *University of Mississippi v. Waugh*, essentially "reversed" *Stallard* by upholding a ban on fraternities at all state colleges and universities.[68] Yet although the dicta of *Waugh* directly clashed with *Stallard*'s emphasis on college access, it is important to recognize two other distinctions that help to explain the different outcomes of these suits. First, state lawmakers enacted the Mississippi ban, whereas Purdue administrators prohibited fraternities without legislative approval.[69] The litigant in *Stallard* could assert that Purdue's policy was inconsistent with state law, whereas the fraternity member who sued the University of Mississippi (UM) faced the taller hurdle of challenging a statute on equal protection grounds.[70] This argument ran counter to the judicial tendencies of the era: the United States Supreme Court rejected the vast majority of equal protection challenges to state laws, especially when those laws purported to increase public safety.[71] The Mississippi suit also clashed with the routine judicial endorsement of statutes, state agencies, and independent licensing boards that governed admission to professional schools or set professional standards.[72] Jackson H. Ralston, the attorney representing UM, highlighted this analogy between the fraternity ban and other accepted forms of state regulation. A Progressive reformer who framed the case as a conflict between the public interest and the power of privileged fraternity members, Ralston also argued that the ban did not violate state or federal guarantees of equal protection because it applied to all applicants in the same manner.[73] Speaking for the Mississippi Supreme Court, Judge Robert Burns Mayes agreed that the antifraternity statute did not discriminate against fraternity members as a "class." "The act in question is not class legislation," the ruling stated. "It is quite the reverse, and seeks to destroy the possibility of the existence of any class at the educational institutions."[74]

The second significant distinction between the contexts of *Stallard* and *Waugh* is that Purdue's policy antagonized the university's political rivals, whereas the Mississippi fraternity ban enjoyed the support of influential officials who had campaigned against university elitism. In a state that had the nation's highest rate of illiteracy, UM provided an attractive target for the populist rhetoric of Governor James K. Vardaman and State Senator Frank "Wool Hat" Burkitt.[75] Fraternities became a focal point for these attacks after one student accused a chapter of rejecting him on account of his humble origins and after another student claimed that privileged classmates were allowed to violate fraternity regulations with impunity. In 1906, Governor Vardaman seized the opportunity to reconstitute UM's governing board, which in turn hired a new chancellor to "popularize" the university. Six years later, the legislature abolished fraternities and secret societies at UM and every other state-supported school. Perhaps because this animosity toward fraternities was associated with a broader critique of higher education, UM professors came to the defense of these organizations and protested in vain against the notion that Greek life encouraged a "spirit of snobbishness." A student lawsuit was unlikely to prove any more successful than these faculty objections because several judges on the state's high court were Vardaman's appointees. Since the fraternity ban was so closely associated with the governor, *Waugh* should not be interpreted as a pure victory for academic authority.[76]

But even though these legal and political contexts were critical factors in *Waugh*, the ruling also embodied a perspective on public higher education that differed fundamentally from *Stallard*'s emphasis on college access. Like the lawyers who represented Purdue three decades earlier, Jackson Ralston argued that students were never "entitled" to attend UM. Ralston assured the court that administrators were capable of identifying applicants who would be detrimental to the campus without discriminating against any particular class of students (he neglected to mention racial segregation).[77] In contrast with the Purdue case, the state's high court agreed that public higher education was a privilege rather than a right. More specifically, the court ruled that rejected students had no claim to procedural due process because they had no property rights at stake. Concluding that the Mississippi constitution did not protect rebellious applicants, the judgment described college access with a statement that would reverberate through subsequent rulings: "the right to attend the educational institutions of the state is not a natural right. It is a gift of civilization, a benefaction of the law."[78]

In its first-ever college admissions ruling, the United States Supreme Court upheld *Waugh* and thereby endorsed this characterization of public higher education.[79] The court concluded that even if fraternity members were considered a distinct class, the equal protection clause did not prohibit distinctions that were "obvious and rational." The opinion, written by Justice Joseph McKenna, stated that the ban's justification seemed reasonable enough because fraternities could potentially distract students from their studies. An admission requirement designed to eradicate fraternities could conceivably promote the essential purpose of the institution. The court also rejected Waugh's due process argument by characterizing admission as a "conditional" rather than "absolute" right. "It is very trite to say that the right to pursue happiness and exercise rights and liberty are subject in some degree to the limitations of the law," concluded Justice McKenna.[80]

The legal controversy over fraternity bans subsided soon afterward, and *Waugh* would come to be seen as a relatively insignificant decision in the annals of the Supreme Court.[81] However, in the context of higher education law, *Waugh* remained an important precedent for a half century.[82] Issued at a time when flagship universities stood on the threshold of greater selectivity, the ruling put the Supreme Court's imprimatur on a right-privilege distinction that limited students' legal protections until the 1960s.[83] *Waugh* marked the beginning of a five-decade span in which institutions prevailed in virtually all college access suits aside from desegregation cases.[84] Unless confronted with blatant violations of the rights of African American students, judges would be extremely reluctant either to invalidate admissions statutes on constitutional grounds or to question administrative interpretations of those statutes. Since *Waugh* established that students, in general, had no basic "right" to higher education, state universities did not need to seek precise legislative approval or adhere closely to constitutional prohibitions against unequal protection or lack of due process.

It is important to note that very few public universities had the luxury of selecting among a pool of qualified applicants when *Waugh* was decided, and even fewer legislatures were keen to allow academic selectivity. Predictably, it was elite private universities that pioneered the development of selective admissions. In particular, Columbia University began to require an eight-page application form, interviews, and psychological tests after World War I (motivated in large part by the institution's desire to limit the number of Jewish students).[85] Lawmakers in most states continued to forbid public institutions from raising academic entrance standards or requiring any sort of subjective measurements of student qualifications. Many states continued to give full control of their admission-by-certificate procedures to secondary school administrators. Ohio even granted automatic accreditation to high schools in towns that had more than five thousand residents, thereby guaranteeing admission for all seniors who completed the college preparatory curricula of those schools. Legislators even pressured the University of Wisconsin into providing probationary admission to students who had graduated from *un*accredited high schools.[86]

Yet in the years after *Waugh*, public institutions started to call greater attention to the competing virtues of quantity and quality. Traditionally, state universities had accepted most applicants and regarded the first two years of enrollment (rather than the initial admissions process) as the time for weeding out weaker students.[87] This practice began to seem wasteful between 1915 and 1930, when rising enrollment outstripped state funding and caused per-pupil expenditures to fall by 50 percent. Faculty questioned whether mechanical methods of admission, such as the certificate system, squandered scarce funds on students who were likely to flunk out. Aided by new quantitative methods of educational measurement, those public universities that were not restrained by statutes contemplated requiring applicants to have a minimum grade point average or high school class rank. Even land grant institutions implemented new standards despite their special legal and historical commitments to accessibility. By 1930, thirteen land grant colleges or universities required minimum examination scores, and a dozen of them rejected applicants whose high school rank fell below a certain cutoff (usually the bottom quartile).[88]

In contrast to the tenor of *Stallard*, state university officials began to consider selectivity, rather than accessibility, to be a precondition for their service to the public interest. This perspective was bolstered in subsequent decades by the proliferation of regional state colleges (many of which evolved out of teacher-training schools) that could educate students who were rejected by flagship universities.[89] A few legislatures revised state laws to reflect these changes. For example, South Carolina lawmakers authorized public colleges and universities to limit enrollment based on academic qualifications.[90] Whereas many legislatures preserved significant barriers to academic selectivity, *Waugh* guided later judicial decisions that deferred to university-imposed entrance requirements. In the absence of a more specific statute, judges became unlikely to interpret vague phrases about remaining "equally open to all" as real limitations to the discretion of state university officials.

Indeed, courts sided with colleges and universities in all six of the reported nondesegregation admissions cases adjudicated between *Waugh* and the 1960s. Three years after *Waugh*, the Supreme Court of Missouri allowed a school superintendent to implement a new admissions requirement at a public teachers college. The superintendent instructed the college to reject applicants who failed an entrance examination or graduated in the bottom third of their high school class. Although three judges dissented, the majority opinion stated that the court was "at a loss" to understand the student's attorney, who had claimed that these requirements were inappropriate for a public school. The ruling held that colleges, unlike elementary schools, were empowered to establish admission standards—though the court noted that it might invalidate a policy that admitted only the highest-scoring applicants rather than all students who achieved some minimum passing mark.[91] Not surprisingly, rejected applicants who challenged private institutions fared no better. In 1937, the New Jersey Supreme Court authorized Rutgers University to reject applicants to its school of education even if they passed the institution's general entrance examination (although Rutgers housed New Jersey's public agricultural and mechanical programs, the university as a whole remained private until after the Second World War). The court ruled that admission decisions were quasi-judicial in nature and rightfully under the control of "an ancient institution of higher learning."[92] Ten years later, an Illinois court determined that Northwestern University could revoke an offer of admission because its bulletin stated that students could be denied for "any reason."[93]

As indicated by the aforementioned *Williams* vaccination ruling, applicants who claimed to be victims of religious discrimination also found that they had limited legal recourse during the first half of the twentieth century. In 1952, the Washington Supreme Court ruled against a Christian Scientist student who refused to submit to a chest X-ray as part of the state university's admissions process. The court ruled that the threat of tuberculosis took priority over the student's right to free exercise of religion. Although the university was not explicitly authorized by statute to regulate public health, the court determined that this responsibility was an implied power granted to the institution by the legislature.[94]

Even when state law offered explicit protections to minorities, deferential attitudes toward academia discouraged robust enforcement. In response to advocacy by the American Jewish Congress (AJC), the National Association for the Advancement of Colored People (NAACP), the Congress of Industrial Organizations, and various Christian groups, New York State passed a Fair Educational Practices Act (FEPA) in 1948 (Massachusetts and New Jersey followed soon thereafter).[95] The law endowed an office of fair educational practices with quasi-judicial authority to review student complaints.[96] The AJC soon became frustrated with the reluctance of the New York office to examine institution-wide enrollment patterns. Instead, the state administrator focused narrowly on individual allegations, most of which were dismissed when colleges claimed that students were rejected because of social or academic failings, rather than anti-Semitism or racism.[97] Seven years passed before the New York Fair Educational Practices office supported a single petition.[98]

According to the AJC, the Massachusetts Fair Educational Practices office also exhibited a great deal of deference toward university officials. The AJC worried that the state's administrator emphasized "conciliation" in order to appease college presidents who had strenuously opposed passage of the act. Later, when the attorney general of Massachusetts determined that the practice of asking applicants to include photographs violated the law, the head of admissions at Harvard University continued to protest the act's infringement on "the proper freedom" of higher education. Perhaps influenced by this pressure, the office pursued just one formal petition in response to the seventeen complaints it received during the early 1950s. The AJC believed that students were being discouraged from proceeding with their cases. The organization was also disappointed that the state office did not require schools to preserve admission data or reveal their procedures and only "suggested" that colleges change potentially discriminatory catalog statements.[99]

This sort of deferential attitude also swayed a Texas court that heard the most prominent midcentury challenge to the exclusion of white women from a state university. In 1958, Lena Ann Bristol and Barbara Tittle filed suit after being rejected from the Agricultural and Mechanical College of Texas (now Texas A&M University).[100] The institution's governing board and most of its students opposed coeducation, though Bristol and Tittle received some support from faculty, the local press, and the student newspaper (its editor was subsequently asked to resign by the leader of A&M's student government).[101] Bristol later recalled being harassed in church by fellow congregants, including one who declared, "How dare you think you can get into A&M?"[102] Initially, a lower court sided with Bristol and Tittle. Reminiscent of *Foltz*, the court concluded that the governing board could not ban women without the express authorization of the state legislature. The ruling also suggested that such a law would have violated the applicants' constitutional right to equal protection. Since the college had educated small numbers of female students (typically the wives and daughters of professors) as recently as 1934, the exclusion of the petitioners seemed arbitrary. The opinion also emphasized the broadest possible justification for striking down an admissions requirement: sex segregation did not promote the "public interests" of state residents. Finally, the court took a cue from desegregation cases by speaking out against the impossibility of "separate but equal" higher education.[103]

The Texas Court of Civil Appeals reversed this decision with an opinion that showed unmistakable (though perhaps unconscious) traces of *Waugh*. The court concluded that judges should defer to administrators unless an admissions policy was prohibited by a "plain, certain and positive law." The court determined that the legislature granted "discretionary authority" to the college's governing board and never objected to the all-male tradition when it passed appropriation bills or revised higher education statutes. A senate resolution directing the college to admit women had been tabled by a nearly unanimous vote just a few years earlier. Consistent with legal trends since the Progressive Era, the court also noted that there was a "strong inclination to adopt and follow the construction given a statute by an administrative agency." In addition, the opinion stated that the college's military training requirement meant that it was reasonable for the institution to classify applicants according to sex, especially when women had access to seventeen other public colleges and universities in the state. Unlike *Foltz*, the ruling rejected the argument that the college was a branch of the University of Texas and therefore obligated to abide by the coeducational policy that governed the flagship campus in Austin.[104] Whereas *Foltz* and *Stallard* had taken their cues from the traditional accessibility of public higher education, the Texas court emphasized the extent to which deference toward academic officials and other administrative agents had become conventional during the early twentieth century.

From 1860 to 1960, college admissions cases interpreted a variety of statutes, constitutional provisions, and common law precedents. When viewed together, these suits indicate that judicial deference toward the admissions policies of state universities intensified during the early twentieth century. Whereas two earlier state court rulings had prevented universities from excluding entire categories of students without legislative authorization, judges began to favor institutional authority as a matter of course. This deferential period was bookended by two United States Supreme Court cases: *Waugh* in 1915 and *Sweezy v. New Hampshire* in 1957. In *Sweezy*, which protected a professor's right to political expression, Justice Felix Frankfurter penned an oft-cited concurring opinion that urged courts to defer to universities when considering questions about admissions procedures and other academic policies.[105] A few years after *Sweezy*, a New York court confidently observed that judges would honor the "administrative discretion" of governing boards unless the circumstances of an admissions case left no room whatsoever for the exercise of that authority.[106]

As demonstrated by *Foltz* and *Stallard*, courts had not always embraced this deferential stance. Scholars have underemphasized this unsettled phase of college access jurisprudence and suggested instead that virtually all nineteenth-century courts refrained from questioning admissions policies.[107] Yet we should not dismiss these early prostudent rulings as mere exceptions. Yes, *Foltz* responded to a blatant instance of discrimination and revolved around statutes that were specific to California. However, the court also emphasized that the very purpose of public higher education necessitated limits to the discretion of academic officials. *Stallard* could be characterized as a merely symbolic decision because the court permitted Purdue to ban students from joining fraternities after they were enrolled at the university. Yet the ruling also presumed that the function of a state university would be compromised if administrators enjoyed any more authority than the members of a local school board.

These decisions fell to the wayside after *Waugh* established, for a time, that public higher education resembled a privilege more than a right. This ruling accompanied a broader shift in which selectivity began to rival mass enrollment as the most conventional strategy for maximizing the public service provided by flagship universities. While this new vision of the selective public university increased deference toward college officials in the short term, it eventually prompted challenges from rejected white applicants who felt that flagship institutions abused their discretion in order to recruit racially diverse student bodies. As I discuss at the end of this book, these affirmative action cases targeted the principle of academic deference by arguing that state universities should return to earlier mechanical admissions procedures, albeit with more selective formulas based on test scores and grade point averages.

Yet from the 1930s through the 1950s, universities asked for judicial deference more often while defending racial exclusion rather than integration. The NAACP's early desegregation briefs, which I explore in the following chapter, were contested by state officials who invoked *Waugh* to justify administrative as well as legislative authority over discriminatory admissions policies. These suits illustrate how the discourse of academic deference was deployed for conflicting purposes over time. The success of the NAACP's campaign also demonstrates that the peak period of deference was short lived. By the 1930s, *Foltz*, *Stallard*, and other earlier cases that had constrained academic authorities reemerged as important (albeit indirect) antecedents for the students who sought to desegregate public institutions of higher education.

3

Desegregation

Although *Brown v. Board of Education* focused on elementary schools, a federal district court applied the ruling to a state university soon afterward.[1] Initially, segregated institutions of higher education had attempted to deflect *Brown* by distinguishing themselves from lower schools and claiming that the judiciary should defer to their greater expertise in the realm of admissions. In 1955, district court judge Morris Soper rejected this argument and ordered the University of North Carolina (UNC) to enroll three African American students. Yet Judge Soper still felt compelled to reassure faculty and administrators that universities could continue to evaluate the "necessary qualifications" of all applicants.[2] This reassurance signaled the extent to which higher education desegregation cases intersected with long-standing traditions of academic deference. Indeed, North Carolina officials responded to the federal ruling by employing UNC's discretion over academic standards in order to impede the process of integration. UNC began to require applicants to submit Scholastic Aptitude Test scores in 1958, knowing full well that this policy would have a disproportionate impact on the eligibility of black students.[3]

And yet legal scholars rarely situate the first phase of the university desegregation campaign within the arc of this older framework of academic deference.[4] This oversight is certainly understandable, because the core of desegregation suits asserted that the Fourteenth Amendment guaranteed access to equal (and ultimately integrated) public institutions of higher education. In landmark midcentury rulings such as *Missouri ex rel. Gaines v. Canada* and *Sweatt v. Painter*, debates about the principle of judicial deference were peripheral to arguments about the definition of equality and the constitutionality of segregation.[5] Nevertheless, desegregation cases also required judges to determine whether academia's traditional independence could insulate state universities against charges of racial bias. As discussed in the previous chapter, earlier admission cases involving white applicants questioned whether administrators could restrict access without explicit constitutional or statutory authorization.

This chapter will demonstrate that the first wave of university desegregation suits revisited these disputes. Prior to their frontal campaign against the separate-but-equal framework, civil rights lawyers referred to rulings that defined state university enrollment as akin to a right—a bureaucratic procedure rather than an act of quasi-judicial deliberation. Meanwhile, segregated institutions defended their administrative authority by citing decisions that defined enrollment as a privilege granted at the discretion of academic experts. These competing interpretations of admissions surfaced within the earliest desegregation suits, which tended to target universities in states that lacked precise statutory grounds for racial exclusion. A comprehensive legal history of college access, therefore, should contextualize desegregation cases within these debates over academic deference.

As in other categories of college access litigation, desegregation cases prompted debates about judicial deference in various legal contexts. Some cases emphasized arguments over the level of scrutiny that courts should apply when adjudicating constitutional challenges. Other cases revolved around the question of whether public universities could institute segregation without express legislative authorization. In both scenarios, universities asked courts to defer to their academic expertise. University officials solicited this deference in order to obscure racial bigotry; general affirmations of academic discretion prevented administrators from having to make direct arguments in favor of segregation. Meanwhile, civil rights lawyers challenged the doctrine of academic deference in order to bring discrimination more clearly into the light.

In this chapter I focus on the ways in which these disputes over college access and academic deference manifested in the first few university desegregation cases. The chapter does not provide an exhaustive account of desegregation, nor does it engage directly with the rich scholarly literature about the causes, strategies, and consequences of the National Association for the Advancement of Colored People's (NAACP's) legal campaign.[6] I do not mean to suggest that academic deference constituted the most important hurdle in the road toward *Brown* or the most decisive factor in the ruling's aftermath. Instead, I revisit the earliest higher education desegregation suits in order to highlight a previously underemphasized element of this story. In the process, I make the case for featuring desegregation rulings within the legal history of academic deference.

Booker v. Grand Rapids Medical College

The first reported college desegregation cases were litigated at the start of the twentieth century. In *Berea College v. Kentucky*, the first and more infamous of two early suits, the United States Supreme Court ordered an exceptional private college to abandon its commitment to racial integration in order to comply with a state segregation statute. Although the court's decision had the effect of contravening the principle of academic deference, this concept was not discussed in the opinion, which focused instead on the nature of the college's corporate charter.[7] Decided in 1909, one year after *Berea*, the comparatively obscure Michigan Supreme Court case of *Booker v. Grand Rapids Medical College* engaged more directly with debates about academic discretion.[8] *Booker* involved a number of legal questions, including arguments about whether a private college could be considered a state actor and whether the institution's catalog was contractually binding. Yet amid these disputes, the case also asked judges to determine if racial exclusion fell within the traditional domain of academic authority. In the process of addressing this question, the case was part of an ongoing clash over whether college enrollment approximated a right or a privilege.

Like most northern and western institutions of higher education, Grand Rapids Medical College neither officially excluded nor overtly welcomed African American students. Especially after the Civil War, most colleges in the North and the West were ostensibly open to black students, though few schools were particularly hospitable (some institutions allowed black students to enroll but excluded them from dormitories and other aspects of college life).[9] In Grand Rapids, President L. L. Conkey hesitated to admit Wesley D. McCoy and Felix D. Booker even though they had attended Kansas State Agricultural College and were more than qualified for acceptance into the school's veterinary program. Conkey was concerned because classmates had harassed the only previous black student at Grand Rapids until he withdrew. Conkey eventually acted on the advice of University of Michigan president James B. Angell, who recommended admitting McCoy and Booker while alerting them that their tuition would be refunded if "anything came up." McCoy and Booker attended for two semesters but were prevented from registering for their sophomore year after three classmates left in protest and others threatened to follow. At one point, a group of students danced around effigies of the two men, chanting "This is a white man's school" and "Lynch 'em if they don't keep out." Conkey, who was in the process of retiring, offered McCoy and Booker small consolation by assuring them that they had passed their exams and conducted themselves like "perfect gentlemen." The college's incoming president, who admitted to harboring "very bitter" feelings toward African Americans, simply informed the men that their classmates had protested and "the majority rules."[10]

McCoy and Booker hired an attorney who challenged their expulsion on several grounds. First, he presented the inverse of the argument that would be deployed by university lawyers in *University of Mississippi v. Waugh* (see chapter 2). The students' attorney warned that if Grand Rapids could discriminate against African Americans, then the college might be permitted to bar any other class of students as well. Next, the brief asserted that the Fourteenth Amendment protected McCoy and Booker against arbitrary expulsion. Even though Grand Rapids was a private institution, the students' lawyer maintained that the college was nevertheless a state actor because of its tax-exempt status, its state-approved corporate charter, and its accountability to the state superintendent of public instruction. As a quasi-public institution, the college would be obligated to abide by the amendment's equal protection and due process clauses. Moreover, the brief continued, all tax-exempt, state-sanctioned colleges should be "compelled to accept the public under reasonable limitations."[11]

At this point, the attorney for McCoy and Booker offered a broader argument against judicial deference toward the admissions policies of "public" colleges. Citing *State ex rel. Stallard v. White* (see chapter 2), the brief invoked the accessibility of nineteenth-century higher education and argued that the customary rights of qualified students superseded administrative authority. During the *Stallard* proceedings, after all, Purdue University had tried and failed to invoke racial segregation as an example of appropriate academic discretion.[12] Emboldened by *Stallard*'s endorsement of a "right" to admission, the lawyer maintained that Grand Rapids was obligated to educate McCoy, Booker, and all applicants who presented themselves "without disqualification." Although *Stallard* involved a state university, the brief suggested that the private medical college must also employ this mechanical approach to admissions because its corporate charter promised to promote education in Michigan. In the unlikely event that the court accepted this argument, which ran against the grain of permissive turn-of-the-century corporate law, then college officials could only reject applicants or expel students if they could identify a specific violation of a published institutional rule or state law. In addition to citing *Stallard*, the brief attempted to support this contention by mentioning two other rulings that reinstated students who were dismissed from state colleges, as well as a ruling that ordered a private college to conduct disciplinary proceedings prior to expulsion.[13]

Finally, the brief referred to two cases in which judges determined that contractual agreements (based on catalog statements) required colleges to award diplomas to all students who were in good standing.[14] Similar to most colleges in this era, Grand Rapids listed minimal admission requirements in its catalog—applicants merely needed to be eighteen years of age, have a common school education, and exhibit "good moral character." The only language regarding the requirements for continuing students emphasized attendance rather than achievement by stating that students needed to attend 85 percent of lectures and 90 percent of clinics and laboratory sessions.[15]

The college's counterarguments also cited a wide range of higher education cases, most of which emphasized academic discretion in general rather than racial segregation in particular. Initially, President Conkey had been reluctant to admit that race had been a factor in his decision to expel McCoy and Booker. He emphasized that he was not personally opposed to their enrollment, but he nevertheless claimed that a private college could reject students "arbitrarily" without having to provide a reason. He later testified that the college decided to expel McCoy and Booker because their continued attendance would be "unwholesome" and could jeopardize the institution's financial viability.[16] Grand Rapids stressed its private status and its monetary self-interest instead of arguing directly that segregation was constitutionally permissible. Because enrollment was a privilege rather than a right, argued the college, academic officials were authorized to consider a variety of factors when implementing admission policies.

The Michigan Supreme Court embraced this interpretation and ruled that private colleges could "discriminate by sex, age, proficiency in learning, and otherwise." Primarily, this broad formulation allowed the court to sidestep the particularly controversial and unseemly reality of racial discrimination. Yet in the process, *Booker* also emphasized the procedural question of whether courts could issue writs of mandamus against private colleges—a question that required the court to define the nature of college admissions.[17] Writs of mandamus were intended to order officials to perform ministerial or bureaucratic duties, such as granting a degree to a student who had met all published graduation requirements. These writs were not intended to overrule quasi-judicial decisions made by experts.[18] By defining enrollment as a discretionary rather than mechanical process, *Booker* concluded that private colleges could exclude black students on the basis of far-ranging academic authority.

Since *Booker* was the first reported segregation case filed on behalf of college students (*Berea* was filed by the college itself), the attorneys for both sides had no choice but to rely on precedents that did not involve allegations of racial discrimination. In addition, the college may have believed that the court would look more favorably on a procedural argument rather than a substantive argument in favor of segregation. Regardless, *Booker* foreshadowed the manner in which the NAACP's initial round of desegregation suits would ask courts to decide whether the enrollment of academically qualified applicants at state universities resembled a ministerial process (close to a right) or an act of discretion (essentially a privilege). When civil rights lawyers launched a concerted campaign against segregated higher education in the 1930s, they were compelled to argue that academic deference should not deter courts from policing admissions practices.

Pearson v. Murray

Under the leadership of Charles Hamilton Houston and Thurgood Marshall, the NAACP emerged as the intellectual and logistical center for the desegregation fight. Whereas some civil rights leaders had reservations about the fate of black teachers and the hostile environment for black students within white-majority schools, Houston, Marshall, and their colleagues believed that integration was the only effective strategy for securing equal educational opportunity.[19]

To this end, the first wave of NAACP higher education suits exposed the inequities of segregated schooling while laying the groundwork for a direct challenge to *Plessy v. Ferguson*, the nineteenth-century Supreme Court ruling that upheld the constitutionality of "separate but equal" facilities.[20] Houston hoped that litigation would force states to equalize funding for black schools, thereby making segregation prohibitively expensive as well as legally suspect. In the 1930s, graduate and professional education seemed like the logical starting point for this campaign because black students were blatantly denied entrance to these programs throughout the South. Some legislatures created scholarships that enabled black residents to attend northern graduate schools, but most southern states offered no graduate-level education to black students within their borders. It is well understood that graduate schools were less daunting targets than elementary schools for other reasons as well. Not only did graduate programs provide specialized training that was difficult to replicate in underfunded segregated settings, but elementary school cases raised greater fears about interracial contact and were more likely to jeopardize the jobs of parents whose children were named in the suits.[21]

However, it is also important to recognize that university officials could mount a legal defense that was unavailable to their elementary school counterparts. Institutions of higher education could appeal for judicial deference and contend that they were not obligated to enroll any particular applicant. This argument was designed to convert allegations of racial bigotry into murkier discussions of academic discretion. To counter these invocations of academic deference, civil rights lawyers referred to *Stallard* and other rulings that defined enrollment at a state university as a bureaucratic process that was intended to facilitate the education of all residents who possessed minimal statutory qualifications. The NAACP attacked academic deference because the concept emphasized the individual judgments of university experts and thereby distracted courts from the reality of systemic discrimination. If state universities were required to come out squarely in support of race-based policies, then the NAACP could demand equal facilities and eventually attack the constitutionality of segregation.

Disputes about the principle of academic deference emerged most clearly in *Pearson v. Murray*, a suit against the University of Maryland (UMD) Law School that resulted in the NAACP's first higher education victory.[22] Thurgood Marshall, who worked on the case from 1934 to 1936 with the assistance of Houston and William I. Gosnell, hoped that the strategy they developed for *Murray* would serve as a model for subsequent litigation.[23] By 1950, when they mounted the landmark *Sweatt* case, civil rights lawyers would be able to lean on the foundation provided by a number of previous desegregation victories. But no such precedents existed in the mid-1930s.

Indeed, the *Murray* brief stated that Marshall, Houston, and Gosnell had "been unable to find a case with facts exactly paralleling the instant case."[24] So instead the brief cited a number of elementary school rulings, as well as a few college admissions rulings that stripped state universities of the authority to exclude qualified students.

The UMD Law School, which had rejected nine black applicants between 1933 and 1934, was an especially attractive target for the NAACP because it operated in a border state that lacked a university segregation statute. Outside of the Deep South, most state universities were segregated on the basis of tacitly sanctioned discrimination, the inequalities of highly segregated lower school systems, and all manner of hostility toward black students. Although segregation in Maryland was not based on any written law, the state's legislature implied that black students were not welcome at public graduate schools when it passed a bill that funded students who wished to attend out-of-state programs. Marshall and Houston contended that these scholarships did not fulfill Maryland's obligation to provide equal higher educational opportunities, especially because the legislature had failed to appropriate sufficient funds for the scholarships. Furthermore, Marshall and Houston believed that judges would be especially sympathetic to a highly qualified plaintiff who wished to receive legal training. Donald Gaines Murray, an Amherst College graduate, clearly fit the bill. Houston, whose interest in cultivating black professionals had caused him to gravitate toward graduate school cases, emphasized that litigants should be exceptionally accomplished, not merely qualified. Six months after launching his practice in Baltimore, Marshall agreed to spearhead Murray's suit.[25]

The case focused primarily on determining whether either Maryland's out-of-state scholarship program or Princess Anne Academy (the state's historically black college) could provide a legal education that was equivalent to the training available at UMD. The case against Princess Anne was almost self-evident. The underfunded academy offered no law program and employed few faculty members with graduate degrees in any field.[26] Marshall had the good fortune to bring the case before a sympathetic Baltimore City Court judge who harangued the university's witnesses before ruling in Murray's favor. Judge Eugene O'Dunne listed several flaws in the university's case, including the fact that the scholarship offered to Murray did not cover the additional expenses of attending an out-of-state law school.[27] When UMD appealed the ruling to the state's high court, the NAACP responded by emphasizing a number of elementary school desegregation cases that obligated states to provide equal (though not necessarily integrated) education for African American students. Marshall, Houston, and Gosnell stressed that Maryland's scholarship program was a clumsy attempt to obscure the state's long history of unequal education funding with an initiative that failed to provide a legitimate alternative to the public law school. They also noted that Murray was already attending classes at the university when the appeals case was tried and reported facing no discrimination from students or faculty (the Maryland attorney general had tried to advance the date of the appeal in order to avoid this scenario).[28]

While the core of the NAACP's case focused on the insufficient alternatives that Maryland provided to black law students, a subordinate prong argued that courts should not defer to academic officials when they enacted discriminatory admission policies. In particular, Murray's lawyers emphasized that state universities were obligated to treat all applications in a standardized ministerial fashion. This aspect of the *Murray* brief may have been inserted as a response to the case of *Hocutt v. Wilson*, in which a court upheld the rejection of a black student who had applied to the University of North Carolina School of Pharmacy. Initiated by Durham attorneys in 1933 and supported in part by the NAACP, *Hocutt* failed for multiple reasons, including the applicant's underwhelming performance on the stand and a lack of wholehearted support from local black leaders. A North Carolina NAACP chapter voted against endorsing the suit and, more important, the president of the North Carolina College for Negroes would not submit the plaintiff's undergraduate transcript or provide a required recommendation because he worried that white legislators would retaliate by cutting funds for black higher education.[29] Yet the suit also failed because the court concluded that UNC possessed quasi-judicial power over admissions. If university enrollment was a discretionary (rather than ministerial) procedure, then student complaints were "not of a public character" and a court could not compel admission. The court indicated that it would defer to UNC's decisions as long as the university reviewed applications in "good faith."[30] In other words, academic deference enabled the university to sidestep a direct challenge to its discriminatory admissions policy.

This element of *Hocutt* may explain why Murray's lawyers revised their brief by adding two nineteenth-century college admissions rulings (*Foltz v.*

Hoge and *Stallard v. White*). Marshall and Houston anticipated that the University of Maryland would take a cue from UNC's defense and argue that enrollment was "a matter of discretion."[31] Houston would later warn another potential litigant that admission to UNC's medical school was subject to the "discretionary power" of administrators as long as they avoided mentioning segregation because its catalog stated that only the most qualified candidates would be accepted whenever the school received more than thirty-six applications.[32] Yet UMD's law school had issued no statement of this sort, and *Foltz* and *Stallard* both characterized state university enrollment as a mechanical administrative process rather than a matter of expert deliberation. As noted earlier, the *Stallard* court was also unmoved by university lawyers who argued for discretionary powers over admission by conjuring the specter of racial integration. During the *Foltz* proceedings, lawyers representing Hastings College had also suggested that denying administrators the authority to ban women would open the school to African American and Asian American students, an argument that was undoubtedly calibrated to intimidate California judges during an era of widespread xenophobia along the Pacific Coast.[33]

Foltz was particularly applicable to *Murray* because Maryland officials had attempted to draw a parallel between their authority to impose segregation and their authority to operate single-sex institutions. Thurgood Marshall pointed out that *Foltz* had determined that administrative authority did not ordinarily extend to bans on an entire class of applicants, such as women. He argued that *Foltz* had recognized the trustees' control over "certain routine matters in the college" but ultimately prevented the governing board from unilaterally excluding all female students. According to Marshall, the crux of *Stallard* was "practically the same."[34] Supported by these citations, the *Murray* brief asserted that every applicant who met the statutory requirements for entering a public university had a "right of admission . . . which the trustees or other officers [were] not authorized to abridge."[35]

Essentially, civil rights lawyers argued that public universities did not have the authority to categorically reject black applicants unless directed by a specific state law. *Foltz* and *Stallard* had each distinguished between proper administrative discretion over routine functions and improper discretion over matters, such as major admissions policies, that could only be determined by a statute or state constitution. The *Murray* brief also cited *Connell v. Gray*, a case in which a student's attorney invoked the threat of unbridled academic power while persuading the Oklahoma Supreme Court to invalidate a fee charged by the state's agricultural college.[36] Houston and Marshall concluded that these cases demonstrated that public universities could not discriminate against fraternity members, women, indigent students, or racial minorities without explicit legislative or constitutional authorization.[37]

During the appellate court proceedings for *Murray*, Houston underscored that Murray's suit would ascertain whether the administrators of a public university had an "inherent right" to create exclusionary admissions policies.[38] Without actually citing *Waugh*, the NAACP's brief implied that the University of Mississippi had won that decision only because of the existence of antifraternity legislation, and not because the Supreme Court deferred to the discretion of college officials. Perhaps mindful of this opinion, the *Murray* brief conceded that segregated state universities might be legal, but only when segregation was established by statute or constitutional provision. Instead, the policy that excluded Donald Murray had been based on a resolution passed by the UMD board of regents.[39]

Because Maryland law did not mandate segregation, civil rights lawyers and state officials emphasized competing interpretations of UMD's charter. The attorney general argued that the State of Maryland empowered UMD to determine admission policies because the school operated in the "nature of a private corporation." UMD had functioned as a private institution until it merged with the Maryland State Agricultural College in 1920, and, according to the attorney general, the terms of its original charter remained more or less intact. The attorney general asserted that the merger "did nothing to limit the privileges and rights of the board of regents . . . to admit students, reject students, or expel students."[40] The NAACP brief countered that public officials funded UMD and appointed its governing board. Furthermore, the charter mandated that the institution must operate "for the benefit of students from every county and every foreign denomination . . . according to their merit." Although this language might allow for a degree of selectivity, Murray's attorneys argued that its overall thrust directed UMD to admit students "on the most liberal plan for the benefit of students of every country and every foreign denomination."[41]

The NAACP's legal team assumed correctly that Maryland courts would define UMD as a public university. This definition allowed them to argue that the institution must abide by *Foltz* and *Stallard*, both of which suggested that admission should be a default response to all qualified applicants. At trial, Marshall emphasized that these decisions had stripped state university governing boards of significant authority over admissions.[42] Initially, Houston had considered a more cautious approach that would seek a good-faith review of Murray's application, rather than admission per se, in order to avoid possibly overreaching into "areas of discretionary power."[43] Yet ultimately their brief asserted that admission to UMD operated according to a simple ministerial process for all white students who possessed certain minimal academic qualifications (acceptance was virtually automatic) as well as all black students (rejection was entirely automatic). Indeed, the university president testified during the trial court phase that UMD's rejection of black applicants was "routine." Therefore both racial prongs of UMD's admissions process operated according to bureaucratic procedure rather than case-by-case deliberation. As a result, Murray's exclusion could not be considered part of the university's lawful arena of academic discretion; he would have been turned away regardless of his qualifications. And if Murray's rejection stemmed from a routine violation of state law, then a judge could compel his enrollment by issuing a writ of mandamus.[44]

The Maryland Court of Appeals agreed with the NAACP and ordered UMD to admit Donald Murray, who would go on to become an important civil rights attorney in his own right. The decision also prompted the state legislature to increase funding for in-state black higher education and out-of-state scholarships.[45] Penned by Chief Judge Carroll Bond, who had attended UMD in the 1890s (a short time after the university categorically excluded black students), the opinion focused on the Fourteenth Amendment and concluded that the state had failed to provide Murray with an equivalent form of legal education.[46] Nevertheless, *Murray* encouraged Houston and Marshall to continue arguing that the concept of academic deference was inapplicable to desegregation cases. Writing about a similar dispute in Virginia, for example, Houston stressed that the state university "*is* a public institution" and therefore subject to state statutes.[47] After *Murray*, the NAACP could be more confident that courts would not allow university governing boards to counter desegregation suits by claiming that they had inherent academic authority over enrollment.

Redmond v. Hyman

As *Murray* neared its conclusion, the NAACP began to pursue a similar, yet ultimately unsuccessful, suit that attempted to prevent the University of Tennessee (UT) from excluding black students unless authorized by statute.[48] The case came to the organization's attention when Houston received a letter from William B. Redmond, a college graduate who wished to attend the UT School of Pharmacy.[49] As in Maryland, civil rights lawyers focused on the Fourteenth Amendment while also making a secondary argument about UT's lack of administrative authority.

Yet in contrast with Maryland, which did not have a segregation statute, Tennessee legislators had appeared to forbid black students from attending the university. The NAACP nevertheless attempted to undermine that statutory basis for segregation by noting that the university had enrolled black students between 1869 and 1913 (albeit in a separate facility called Knoxville College). During those decades, UT officials referred to Knoxville College students as "our students," funded both campuses out of the same budget, and awarded the same diplomas. In 1913, the Tennessee legislature established a black agricultural and industrial college in Nashville, which was supposed to end UT's responsibility for black undergraduates, but which failed to provide equivalent graduate or professional training.[50] In order to establish that the university had an ongoing obligation to African American graduate or professional students, one of Redmond's lawyers highlighted that the UT governing board once proclaimed that "the doors of the state university should be thrown wide open to all persons from everywhere who were prepared to enter and enjoy the advantages here provided for them." The trustees went on to specify that the only requirement for admission to the university should be age, character, and "sufficient preparation."[51] Redmond's petition mentioned that the pharmacy school merely required applicants to be seventeen years of age and in possession of a diploma from an accredited high school. As a result, the registrar had a "plain ministerial duty" to review and accept his application. The NAACP's brief would also cite *Foltz* to underscore this point.[52]

Civil rights lawyers faced long odds when trying to convince a Tennessee court that the state had never authorized the segregation of UT's graduate and professional programs. The university president responded to Redmond's application by noting that the general assembly had mandated segregation in 1901 by passing a statute that criminalized interracial education in all settings. University attorneys also argued that Redmond's Fourteenth Amendment claim was inappropriate because federal courts had never considered higher education to be a privilege or property right that would warrant the amendment's protection.[53] The court agreed, while noting that Redmond had been encouraged by an out-of-state organization and had not exhausted all potential administrative remedies before filing his suit. The court also ruled that the only proper response to any unequal provision of graduate programs would be to petition the state to build additional segregated schools. Not only did the opinion embrace the university's interpretation of Tennessee's segregation law, but it also suggested that segregation could be maintained as a purely administrative policy even in the absence of such a statute. The court pointedly refused to interfere with the "discretion" of the board of trustees.[54] In large part because Redmond struggled academically at Fisk University during the course of the trial, the NAACP decided to not appeal the decision.[55]

Missouri ex rel. Gaines v. Canada

Instead of continuing Redmond's suit, the NAACP pursued *Missouri ex rel. Gaines v. Canada*, a Missouri case that also argued against the "inherent" authority of university administrators.[56] The suit was filed on behalf of Lloyd Lionel Gaines after he was excluded from the University of Missouri (MU) Law School in 1936. The case was more challenging than either *Murray* or *Redmond* because Missouri's historically black Lincoln University, from which Gaines had earned an undergraduate degree, was relatively well funded and could somewhat more plausibly offer separate but equal legal training. Furthermore, the Missouri legislature had appropriated more funding for its out-of-state scholarship program (though these grants still did not cover the additional costs of travel and living expenses).[57] Perhaps cognizant of *Murray*, Missouri's attorney general also did not emphasize academic deference but argued instead that (as in Tennessee) segregation was required by state law.[58]

Houston, along with attorneys Sidney R. Redmond and Henry D. Espy, challenged this interpretation by noting that Missouri's constitution referred to the segregation of common schools but not institutions of higher education. Without a constitutional mandate to segregate, the university could be vulnerable to a suit based on the permissive state laws pertaining to MU's admissions requirements. The lawyers argued that a nineteenth-century statute ordered MU to enroll all state residents between the ages of sixteen and twenty-five. Although the statute was revised in 1929 to authorize the governing board to require certain "scholastic attainments and mental and moral qualifications," race was still not mentioned, and an original reference to "all youth" remained in force. Echoing *Murray*, the NAACP's brief cited *Foltz*, *Stallard*, and *Connell* in support of the proposition that only specific statutory or constitutional language could justify the exclusion of students from a state university.[59]

After Missouri's high court ruled in favor of the university, Houston repeated this argument in a petition for certiorari to the United States Supreme Court. Citing *Murray*, the petition asserted that "the admission of a qualified citizen to a state university is not a mere privilege but a right."[60] This language challenged the "right-privilege distinction" that the court had endorsed in *Waugh* when it upheld Mississippi's fraternity ban. Indeed, during the state court phase of *Gaines*, Missouri's attorney general cited *Waugh* to support his contention that higher education was not the sort of property right that obligated institutions to provide due process for excluded students. Adjudicated in the era before racial classifications were subject to strict scrutiny, a degree of discrimination could be considered constitutional, especially if that discrimination affected access to a privilege rather than a right. In response, Houston asked the court to discard the right-privilege distinction and endorse the earlier state cases (*Foltz* and *Stallard*) that had limited university discretion over enrollment.[61]

It is fitting that *Waugh* would resurface in desegregation cases because it contained frequent references to racial discrimination, even though the suit itself concerned the exclusion of a white fraternity member from a historically white university. The pamphlet that initiated the challenge to Mississippi's antifraternity statute sought to capitalize on the demagogic fervor of James K. Vardaman's gubernatorial campaign by referring to the policy as a "Jim Crow law against whites."[62] The original brief filed on behalf of J. P. Waugh underscored this theme by stating that fraternity members were entitled to the same sort of "equal enjoyment of state institutions" that was granted "even to the negro and the mulatto." Waugh's brief noted that white fraternity members had not been provided with a separate "segregated" university after being banned from Ole Miss. For good measure, his attorneys submitted a supplemental brief that cited *Plessy* to support the claim that Waugh was entitled to "equal" (albeit potentially separate) access to public services.[63] Lawyers for the University of Mississippi sought to trump this racial provocation with more of the same. The university's brief asked how an institution could possibly exclude black students if it was not also authorized to ban fraternity members. "If the argument of the complainant is followed to its legitimate conclusion," wrote the attorneys, "the state has not the power to prohibit a Negro from entering the state university." The brief also cited the *Berea* ruling that upheld legislative authority over segregated higher education in Kentucky.[64]

To bolster their response to *Waugh* and the right-privilege distinction, Houston and colleagues added *Gleason v. University of Minnesota* to the section of their brief that argued against academic deference.[65] *Gleason*, which I discuss at greater length in the next chapter, concluded that public universities must provide students with some form of due process prior to expulsion. Since Lincoln University could not yet provide an equivalent legal education to African Americans in Missouri, the NAACP argued that this standard should apply to black students rejected from MU's law school. The petition also cited *Gleason* in support of the premise that a writ of mandamus could compel universities to educate all students who met their published standards.[66] Civil rights lawyers would later invoke *Gleason* for similar reasons during an unsuccessful attempt to desegregate the University of Missouri School of Journalism.[67]

Although the Supreme Court would rule that state law called for the segregation of MU (because a combination of statutes communicated that intent), a majority of justices determined that out-of-state scholarships did not relieve Missouri of the obligation to provide separate but equal education within its borders.[68] After the decision, Missouri legislators passed a $200,000 appropriation for graduate programs at Lincoln University. A new law school soon registered a few black students (while an interracial group of protesters picketed outside). Lloyd Gaines moved to Chicago and disappeared, leaving the NAACP with no choice but to pursue other cases.[69]

After *Gaines*, the NAACP no longer needed to emphasize that public universities had a ministerial duty to educate all students who met statutory admissions requirements. *Gaines* demonstrated that the Supreme Court would not defer to state university officials when they implemented the sort of total exclusion that would be unconstitutional if practiced by a streetcar company. *Stallard* and *Foltz*, which had never been at the forefront of the NAACP's argument, disappeared from the organization's briefs once *Gaines* established that public institutions of higher education could not simply appeal for deference in order to shield blatant violations of the Fourteenth Amendment.

This component of the NAACP campaign also vanished because the organization's next major desegregation suits were litigated in locales where segregation was indisputably required by state law. University officials in these states could claim that they were adhering to legislative or constitutional directives and lacked the discretion to integrate their institutions. In Oklahoma, for example, Ada Sipuel reported that the president of the state university actually seemed to oppose the state's segregation law and offered to document her rejection in whatever way would be most helpful for her suit.[70] In Tennessee, administrators also continued to emphasize their obligation to abide by state law in the decade after *Redmond*. Instead of invoking the spirit of deference, the university's president preferred to forward all questions about segregation to the state attorney general. In 1950, he advised UT's head of admissions to inform black applicants that segregation was the law of the state rather than a university decision.[71]

Despite this waning emphasis on the discretionary authority of university administrators, some defenders of segregated higher education continued to act as if they could influence federal courts by referring to enrollment as a privilege instead of a right. Most notably, the attorney general of Texas cited the right-privilege distinction while arguing (unsuccessfully) for the exclusion of Heman Marion Sweatt from the University of Texas Law School. The university's governing board had been so opposed to integration that it fired the institution's previous president for even suggesting that the state should increase funding for black colleges.[72] When faced with Sweatt's suit, the board reconsidered this stance and moved quickly to build some semblance of a segregated law school during the late 1940s. At the same time, the state attorney general argued that Sweatt did not have a case against the law school because, as indicated by *Waugh*, higher education was not a right protected by the Fourteenth Amendment.[73] The attorney general asserted that the Supreme Court had reaffirmed this interpretation in *Hamilton v. Regents of the University of California*, a 1934 opinion that cited *Waugh* while upholding a university's power to expel students who objected to compulsory military training.[74] When deciding *Sweatt* in 1950, the Supreme Court ignored this citation and simply ruled that the new black law school did not provide an equal education.[75]

Four years after the *Sweatt* decision, *Brown v. Board of Education* banned segregation in public elementary and secondary schools. And during the following year, the federal court case mentioned at the beginning of this chapter applied the decision to the University of North Carolina and other public institutions of higher education. By that time, black students attended public universities in every border state. Every state university in the Deep South enrolled at least one black student by the mid-1960s, though more substantial integration in most of these institutions occurred only toward the end of that decade, when the federal government began to enforce court orders with greater vigor.[76]

Yet even in the immediate wake of *Brown*, Louisiana officials clung to the hope that the right-privilege distinction might help to defeat a university desegregation suit. After the NAACP won cases against the graduate school of Louisiana State University (LSU) and several regional state colleges, the Louisiana legislature passed a law requiring applicants to public institutions to submit a "certificate of eligibility" signed by their former principals and superintendents.[77] When the NAACP sued to overturn this act, attorneys representing LSU and the state board of education cited *Waugh* as part of their unsuccessful defense. The state's brief declared that "an education in any particular state institution of higher learning is not a property right to which any person is entitled but a mere privilege conferred by the state." The United States Court of Appeals for the Fifth Circuit was unmoved by this argument and ruled that the statute was clearly designed to promote segregation by pressuring black school officials to withhold their signatures from the certificates of black students who wished to attend historically white institutions. The court concluded that legislatures could not grant this sort of discretion to school officials without outlining a clear standard for determining which students should be eligible for signatures.[78]

The right-privilege distinction continued to appear within civil rights cases as late as the 1960s. In the initial phase of *Dixon v. Alabama State Board of Education*, a district court judge cited *Waugh* when ruling against six black student activists who had been expelled from a state college. The judge referred to *Waugh* as confirmation that "the right to attend a public college or university is not in and of itself a constitutional right." As I discuss in the next chapter, a federal appeals court would ultimately reverse this ruling.[79] Finally, in 1963, as part of a last-gasp attempt to justify his defiance of a federal order mandating the enrollment of James Meredith, Governor Ross R. Barnett cited *Waugh* while contending that judges should defer to state officials when deciding suits filed against the University of Mississippi.[80]

After *Gaines*, federal courts rejected these arguments and consistently invalidated formal legal barriers to integrated higher education. In all, students won more than 80 percent (21/26) of reported college desegregation cases between 1930 and 1960.[81] Needless to say, these victories were not sufficient to secure desegregated, let alone equal, education. Many state university systems resisted full-fledged integration, and the admission of one or two students of color at historically white institutions rarely paved the way to enrollment at rates that reflected state demographics. The slow pace of these changes and the persistence of varied forms of educational inequity have indicated the need for political advocacy as well as perhaps for ongoing litigation.[82]

Nevertheless, midcentury desegregation suits constituted a remarkable challenge to institutional authority during an era in which American colleges and universities seemed otherwise almost immune from student-initiated lawsuits. To be sure, a case could be made for excluding desegregation cases from that broader trajectory of academic deference. Desegregation orders advocated for the rights of a discrete minority and did not necessarily challenge institutional authority over enrollment in general. Most desegregation suits, furthermore, targeted policies established by legislators rather than university officials. However, the earliest desegregation briefs encouraged judges to temper their deference toward academia while citing nineteenth-century cases that characterized enrollment as a ministerial process that virtually guaranteed access for all applicants who possessed minimal qualifications. In response, universities attempted to invoke deference as a tool of obfuscation that prevented academic leaders from having to make direct arguments in favor of segregation. Thus, these first desegregation cases differ from the later civil rights confrontations in which schools openly defended their discriminatory policies and courts considered questions of constitutional interpretation and enforcement head on.

Before engaging in that direct challenge to the sham of separate but equal education, civil rights lawyers first had to establish that public universities did not possess inherent authority over the fundamental contours of admissions. Never a main pillar of the legal assault on desegregation, this position was still an important element of the *Murray* and *Gaines* cases that laid the foundation for subsequent victories. Recognizing the role, however fleeting, played by earlier admissions rulings provides a deeper understanding of the first wave of desegregation suits and indicates the manner in which this campaign participated in a long-standing debate over academic deference.

4

Expulsion

Between 1860 and 1960, college students filed suit to challenge expulsions far more often than they contested admissions decisions or tuition policies.[1] Not only were expulsions particularly traumatic for students, but they also involved questions about due process and contracts that fell squarely within the traditional realm of the judiciary.[2] In addition to their sheer volume, these early expulsion suits also occupy an important place in higher education lore because they are routinely cited as contrasting background for *Dixon v. Alabama State Board of Education*, the landmark federal decision that marked a fundamental shift in the legal relationship between students and colleges.[3] The *Dixon* ruling, which overturned the expulsion of six civil rights activists, established that students at public colleges were entitled to due process under the auspices of the Fourteenth Amendment. Prior to *Dixon*, which was issued in 1961, only three reported expulsion rulings had even mentioned the due process clause—and two of those opinions were penned in the late 1950s.[4]

Instead, most early expulsion suits evaluated whether students received fair treatment according to the traditions of contract law, though some suits against public colleges invoked statutes that arguably set parameters for expulsion policies. Regardless, state appellate courts entertained dozens of expulsion cases before *Dixon* but failed to develop a coherent set of guidelines regarding the extent to which ordinary contractual norms should govern campus life at either public *or* private colleges. In 1963, one scholar characterized expulsion case law as "formless" because courts had not established consistent standards for either the substance or procedure of discipline.[5] In contrast to the post-*Dixon* landscape, nineteenth-century courts did not even unanimously grant greater latitude to colleges when they adjudicated cases challenging academic (as opposed to disciplinary) expulsions. The distinction between academic and disciplinary authority was relatively blurry during the nineteenth century because professors tended to be intimately involved with the supervision of student conduct. It was not uncommon for a college president to be the sole senior administrator aside from an absentee board of trustees, and professors often regarded character formation as a core element of their vocation.[6] Perhaps as a result, the likelihood of a student victory in academic and disciplinary suits was virtually the same between 1860 and 1910.[7] In both domains, some judges defined enrollment as a privilege that could be almost summarily revoked by institutions, whereas others defined enrollment as an ordinary contractual or bureaucratic status that obligated colleges to engage in some sort of disciplinary process prior to expulsion.

Because *Dixon* occurred in the midst of dramatic civil rights protests and resulted in an enduring revision to constitutional law, scholars have underemphasized this earlier debate. Since *Dixon*, it has become common to remark that earlier courts exhibited "nearly unanimous" or "overwhelming" deference to colleges regardless of whether students challenged the substance of institutional rules or the procedures of expulsion.[8] Yet contrary to these characterizations, students won almost half of reported expulsion cases before 1910.[9]

Although nineteenth-century courts did not consistently distinguish between deference to institutional/disciplinary authority and deference to professorial/academic authority, challenges to expulsions based on behavioral infractions or poor scholastic performance often involved different legal grounds. Therefore, in the first two sections of this chapter, I examine how early suits disputed the basis for disciplinary and academic expulsions, respectively. The chapter's final section demonstrates that judicial concern for due process did not evaporate during the middle of the twentieth century, when courts appeared to agree that students sacrificed certain rights in exchange for the privilege of higher education. Although students lost every single reported expulsion suit between 1910 and 1960, this apparent consensus was shaped by cases involving tensions over gender roles and political dissent as much as by support for collegiate authority in itself. Furthermore, supplementary comments in roughly half of the expulsion cases from this period indicate that courts still expected colleges to provide procedural safeguards such as a hearing or semiformal investigation. These cases reveal that the judiciary never unanimously regarded colleges as entities that could operate beyond the rules that governed ordinary commercial or public affairs. Even before *Dixon*, faculty and administrators struggled to persuade courts to confer exceptional status upon either private or state institutions of higher education.

Judicial Oversight of Disciplinary Expulsions, 1860–1910

Faculty and administrators have endured the misbehavior of impious, rebellious, and anti-intellectual students since the dawn of American higher education.[10] Conflicts between students and college officials may have intensified during the nineteenth century, when the center of student life shifted from the relatively academic precincts of the literary society to the rowdier atmosphere of the fraternity house. The narrowing age range of students over the course of the century may have exacerbated this clash of expectations. With fewer students younger than eighteen or older than twenty-two, college campuses incubated a concentrated form of oppositional youth culture. Intercollegiate athletics, for example, became a common flashpoint whenever administrators increased institutional supervision of scheduling, coaching, or officiating. Many students avoided serious academic commitments and denigrated studious classmates with epithets such as "bootlick."[11]

Some colleges, especially those closely affiliated with religious denominations, attempted to corral students by imposing strict discipline codes. A few college presidents were rumored to scan for misbehavior through the lens of a telescope or from behind dark glasses during chapel prayers.[12] More commonly, faculty and administrators loosely enforced bans on sins such as drinking or gambling as long as students acted with some decorum inside campus buildings. As early as the 1880s, a university president observed that professors no longer supervised student conduct outside of class. Another president reported that a judge advised him to overlook most legally permissible activities, such as smoking or card playing, and to forbid only those behaviors that directly impaired academic performance. By the turn of the twentieth century, most college presidents ceased to function as paternal authority figures; they no longer knew every student by name, taught a capstone course on moral philosophy, or exerted much direct influence over campus conduct. Whereas colleges had once ranked students according to a combination of their behavior and academic performance, most began to focus exclusively on the latter. The emergence of the modern university, with its emphasis on scholarly production and graduate education, further discouraged administrators from monitoring student life.[13]

Regardless, institutions continued to expel students who committed serious offenses. But even though faculty and administrators felt entitled to dismiss students, the judicial response to expulsion was somewhat inconsistent. Expulsion cases often invited judicial interpretation because the charters of private colleges and the establishing statutes of public colleges tended to be silent or imprecise when it came to defining and punishing student misconduct. Only in rare cases did nineteenth-century charters or statutes provide any details regarding disciplinary procedures or consequences. The founding legislation of the Washington State Agricultural College was more specific than most, just because it stated that the institution could only impose "reasonable" penalties.[14] The charter of Warsaw College in Kentucky was highly unusual because it limited expulsion to cases of "persistent" disobedience.[15] The charter of Douglassville College in Texas was also an outlier because it required faculty to give "repeated admonitions" prior to suspension or expulsion.[16] Precise discipline statutes remained rare during the early twentieth century, although some legislatures instructed colleges to ban hazing.[17] Yet aside from these antihazing statutes, judges continued to have few guidelines with which to evaluate the appropriateness of collegiate discipline.

The development of a consistent approach to expulsion suits was also complicated by disagreements about whether writs of mandamus could apply to private institutions. Some courts held that these writs could compel private colleges to reinstate students based on implied contractual agreements or charters granted by the state, while others ruled that the writs were inapplicable to private colleges because they were only intended to compel public officials to perform ministerial responsibilities.[18] Along with fundamental disagreements about the extent of institutional discretion, this question contributed to the unsettled pattern of judicial responses in early expulsion cases.

Scholars may have overlooked this variation because the first reported expulsion ruling, *Pratt v. Wheaton College*, clearly defined higher education as a privilege and strongly championed the authority of colleges to determine the substance of disciplinary rules during the nineteenth century.[19] As was typically the case with denominational institutions, the regulation of student conduct was integral to the mission of Wheaton College, a school established by Wesleyans twenty-five miles west of Chicago. Wheaton's founders attempted to create a utopian community that, according to President Jonathan Blanchard, could hasten the emergence of heaven on earth. To this end, Blanchard prohibited travel, smoking, drinking, billiards, marriage, desecration of the Sabbath, or promulgation of sacrilegious theories. The college's catalog assured families that its faculty would "exercise a parental and moral oversight of the character and conduct of students." Blanchard also enforced a ban on secret societies, which he believed to be inherently unchristian. In 1866, after being expelled for joining the Good Templars, Edwin Hartley Pratt challenged this ban in a suit that ultimately reached the Illinois Supreme Court.[20] Blanchard's son-in-law, James Philemon Stoddard, believed that the devil had encouraged outsiders to prompt Pratt's suit.[21] Even though the Good Templers was a temperance organization (and therefore largely compatible with the college's values), Pratt's membership jeopardized the survival of the fledgling institution by questioning its authority to regulate student behavior.

The Illinois Supreme Court agreed that Wheaton could ban secret societies. Judge Charles B. Lawrence sympathized with Blanchard's claim that these organizations tended to "withdraw students from the control of the faculty." More important, he stated that courts should defer to college officials unless a policy clearly violated "good morals" or an essential "law of the land." *Pratt* assured colleges that they could limit rights that students would otherwise enjoy as citizens. Pratt's enrollment, after all, was voluntary and could reasonably entail the loss of certain rights, especially within a private institution. Judge Lawrence believed that it would be "absurd" to prevent a college from restricting student rights, including "the legal right to marry, or to walk the streets at midnight, or to board at a public hotel." In a classic endorsement of a college's power to govern students in loco parentis, the court concluded that it had "no more authority to interfere than [it had] to control the domestic discipline of a father in his family."[22] This concept had deep roots, stretching back to the English tradition of authorizing private tutors to employ corporal punishment. According to subsequent American case law, teachers enjoyed broad powers over their students and, like parents, could rely on a wide range of disciplinary tactics.[23]

The first reported case of its kind, *Pratt* is routinely cited as a representative statement of traditional academic deference.[24] Three decades later, the Illinois Supreme Court reaffirmed that students temporarily surrendered many of their rights when they enrolled in college. In that particular case, a student had been expelled after he objected to compulsory chapel attendance at a state university. Similarly, a New York court refused to intervene in 1893 when a student was denied a law school diploma after he protested the institution's decision to have a bishop preside over commencement ceremonies.[25]

Yet *Pratt* has become a somewhat outsized symbol of the historical prevalence of in loco parentis.[26] The *Pratt* ruling endorsed administrative authority over the substance of a college's rules, but it did not discuss student demands for procedural due process. These demands formed the core of many of the expulsion cases that students won before 1910.[27] Although *Pratt* indicated that academic authorities might be immune from most student suits, other courts acted as if enrollment was an ordinary contractual relationship that endowed students with the right to some degree of due process prior to expulsion.

Commonwealth ex rel. Hill v. McCauley, the next reported expulsion case after *Pratt*, pioneered this approach to disciplinary expulsion suits.[28] Decided in 1887, *Hill* marked the culmination of years of discord at Dickinson College.[29] Like many colleges in the nineteenth century, Dickinson was divided between students who honored official expectations and those who defined themselves in opposition to adult culture. Whereas President James Andrew McCauley praised the religiosity of the student body and credited Young Men's Christian Association prayer meetings with achieving "a general quickening of the spiritual life of the college," many students expressed something close to contempt for the "old fogies" who ran the institution. The student editors of the *Dickinsonian* noted that pranks during chapel ceremonies had become "alarmingly frequent" and complained about classmates who objected if anyone praised a professor or criticized a rowdy student. In particular, the editors expressed concern about the tendency of students to shelter rule breakers from college authorities. "Although it is right to discourage the sneak and the toady," the newspaper stated, "we should also try to prevent the violation of college laws." The editors tried to dissuade classmates from indulging in the "foolish custom" of knee-jerk antiauthoritarianism.[30]

This culture clash fueled the incident that precipitated Hill's suit. In the fall of 1886, a student attended a recitation despite the fact that classmates had disabled the college bell (a maneuver that was intended to delay the start of classes). Making matters worse, the student reminded the professor that he had forgotten to assign homework. According to the *Dickinsonian*, this student "was laboring under the delusion that faculty control affairs here." Classmates responded with merciless hazing, prompting

President McCauley to suspend eight perpetrators. When McCauley convened the faculty to gather additional evidence, indignant students howled and jeered outside until someone tossed a rock through the president's office window. A professor and a janitor identified sophomore John Martz Hill as the culprit. Hill denied throwing the stone but was nevertheless expelled after he reportedly "turned white" when questioned.[31] Like Pratt's suit against Wheaton College, Hill's case threatened Dickinson's viability. McCauley reported that newspaper coverage of the incident drastically suppressed enrollment.[32] The student newspaper felt compelled to dispute the perception that Dickinson was "on the eve of final dissolution" or that students exercised "almost unlimited control" of the campus.[33]

In contrast with his counterpart in the *Pratt* case, Judge William F. Sadler determined that student rights were not "entirely suspended" when they enrolled in a private college. Even though Judge Sadler was a Dickinson trustee, his opinion struck a populist note by declaring that he paid close attention to Hill's story because the courts should remain forever "open to the meanest and humblest." Judge Sadler acknowledged that Dickinson's charter endowed the school with a certain degree of authority over student conduct, but he emphasized that the college was nevertheless beholden to the "ordinary duties and obligations" of contractual relationships. He concluded that applying a more permissive standard to colleges would wrongly suggest that expulsion was less important "than many matters for which redress is daily sought and obtained in legal tribunals." The opinion cited cases that challenged the substance of school regulations as well as the "regularity" of their proceedings. All of these rulings concerned common schools, implying that Judge Sadler exhibited no special deference toward institutions of higher education. He concluded that accused students were entitled to something akin to a trial (Hill had been merely summoned by the faculty and asked to make a statement), including the opportunity to question witnesses and present their own evidence.[34]

Hill foreshadowed the increasing role of contract law in subsequent expulsion cases. Contracts emerged as the dominant legal structure for regulating financial affairs in the late eighteenth and early nineteenth centuries, when the scope and complexity of commerce overwhelmed the capacity of direct legislative oversight. Over time, contractual logic emerged as a common framework for defining a wide range of social as well as commercial relationships.[35] By the late nineteenth century, contract law formed the core of the legal relationship between students and colleges, particularly at private institutions. Although students seldom signed formal agreements, enrollment came to be seen as an informal contractual arrangement. The growing scale of higher education, the increasing prominence of research universities, and the decreasing presence of very young students also promoted this shift.[36]

A deferential spirit still encouraged some courts to place the burden of proof entirely on any student who alleged that colleges had failed to honor their contractual obligations; a few judges even empowered colleges to resolve their own contractual disputes.[37] However, other rulings indicated that the principles of contract law could justify oversight of expulsion policies if colleges failed to adhere to basic principles of fair play. Some of these rulings reflected the influence of progressive legal scholars who advocated revising contractual principles in order to protect the interests of weaker parties.[38] As jurists began to examine whether particular contracts simply reified unequal power dynamics, expelled students sometimes received sympathetic treatment in court.[39]

In particular, courts could choose to view catalog statements as mutually binding obligations even if colleges had clearly intended for these publications to simply explain institutional policies. In 1891, a New York court established this practice by ruling that the course requirements listed in a medical school catalog served to guarantee that compliant students would earn degrees unless the institution could cite a specific violation of institutional policies. In *People ex rel. Cecil v. Bellevue Hospital Medical College*, the school had argued that it could withhold diplomas at will. The court disagreed after concluding that "absolute and arbitrary" expulsions exceeded the scope of the school's discretionary power. A pharmacy journal applauded the court for standing up to an "autocratic faculty," while also predicting that the ruling would "doubtless commend itself as perfectly sound to everyone outside of Bellevue College." It should be noted that *Cecil* provided students with an extremely thin layer of protection (colleges merely needed to state a reason for expulsion). Nevertheless, the ruling pointed the way toward considering contract law as a source of more significant procedural rights for students.[40]

A decade after *Cecil*, a Maryland court agreed that students were contractually entitled to remain enrolled in college unless they disobeyed a published rule. The court overturned the expulsion of a University of

Baltimore student who had been dismissed for making late payments and for taking a part-time course load. Not only did the court observe that the university had not explicitly prohibited these practices, but it also signaled that it would interpret broad catalog statements in light of the institution's customary practices. The ruling noted that it had been the "general usage" of the university to accept tuition in installments and to operate during the evening hours for the benefit of self-supporting students. While grounded in the conventions of contract law, this determination also reflected the court's sense that expelling students on these grounds would contradict the university's traditional purpose. The court noted that the institution had been specifically established to serve students such as the petitioner, who supported his sister while studying "as diligently as the discharge of his other duties might permit."[41]

Two other courts ruled against students on procedural grounds but nevertheless endorsed the notion that contract law could protect against expulsion without cause. In 1906, the Supreme Court of Wisconsin concluded that a writ of mandamus was an inappropriate remedy for a student at a private college yet stated that anyone unjustly refused a diploma could sue for breach of contract.[42] As I discussed in the preceding chapter, the Michigan Supreme Court adopted a similar stance while ruling against two African American students in 1908. The court appeared to encourage the students to sue for damages based on the quasi-contractual "understanding" that students who passed their courses should not be dismissed without some other reasonable explanation.[43]

Even when colleges cited an acceptable cause for expulsion, courts often indicated that students were contractually entitled to some form of investigation or hearing. Although an Ohio court ultimately rejected a suit by a student who claimed that his former university should have conducted a standard criminal trial, the ruling emphasized that students should not be dismissed unless a disciplinary process included careful evaluation of all evidence and provided students with "every fair opportunity" to prove their innocence. Issued in 1901, the opinion stated that the institution had met this standard when it relied on informal proceedings to expel this particular student, who had been arrested twice, failed multiple classes, fought with classmates, and carried a revolver.[44] During the following year, a New York court communicated a similar expectation while also ultimately ruling in favor of a college. The court defined the student-college relationship in contractual terms (citing *Cecil*) and noted that judges were entitled to overrule university authorities in the case of "unjustified" discipline—a somewhat lower threshold than the "arbitrary" or "perverse" standards that many later courts would apply. Ultimately, the court found ample justification for expulsion because the university had gathered testimony from multiple witnesses and invited the accused student to address a faculty meeting, an opportunity that the court interpreted as an adequate substitute for a formal hearing.[45]

Although judges deferred to collegiate disciplinary policies more often than not, they rarely regarded higher education as an endeavor that should be exempt from ordinary contractual standards. Not only did judges occasionally reinstate students if their expulsion appeared to have been ordered without cause, but dicta within cases that were decided in favor of institutions often indicated that students were entitled to some form of disciplinary procedure. Either because they did not distinguish between colleges and other sorts of institutions or because they recognized higher education's import for students, courts tended to view enrollment as a contractual relationship that entailed certain due process rights.

Judicial Oversight of Academic Expulsions, 1860–1910

Typically, courts are presumed to intervene more readily in disciplinary cases because they resemble criminal trials and therefore fall squarely within the traditional expertise of the judiciary. Academic expulsion suits, in contrast, ask courts to reconsider evaluations made by professors who have far more experience in their respective fields.[46] In 1901, for instance, a New York court reasoned that academic failure should be determined entirely by faculty members and rejected the petition of a student who argued that he had performed adequately at a private medical college. The court concluded that it was simply "in the nature of things" to leave these decisions to the experts. The opinion stated that a writ of mandamus could not apply to a case of academic failure because colleges were "quasi judicial" bodies endowed with "ample discretion" to interpret the powers granted by their corporate charters. Furthermore, the court noted that it would never "re-examine" students because judges were not competent to question academic evaluations. The court concluded that the law "leaves the subject where it belongs—with those qualified to master it."[47] Similarly, a Pennsylvania court ruled the following year that it would only override a college's decision to deny a diploma if the action was not merely "wrong" but clearly "perverse." This judgment was particularly telling because it concerned a student whose diploma had been endorsed by the faculty and then revoked by the board of trustees.[48]

However, other early courts were willing to limit the academic discretion of college professors and administrators especially (but not exclusively) when they worked at public institutions. While judges refrained from expressly challenging the substance of academic judgments, they sometimes intervened if the grading process or the consequence stemming from poor grades seemed erratic, inconsistent with past practices, or at odds with state law.[49] For example, the Supreme Court of Nebraska ruled in 1908 that a student at Lincoln Medical College was contractually protected against "arbitrary and capricious" evaluations of her examinations. In response to the college's assertion of absolute authority over academic standards, the court countered that this sort of "autocratic right" could lead to unacceptable outcomes for students who paid tuition and studied diligently for four years but then incurred "the ill will of one professor." The court suspected that the student was expelled because she became pregnant. Even though her pregnancy caused her to miss some classes, the opinion noted that the college's football players had greater rates of absenteeism and other students had graduated with weaker academic records, including some who missed their final examinations altogether. The court also censured three professors who refused to return the student's completed examinations, thereby violating "an unwritten law" that failing students should be allowed to inspect their papers. In contrast to courts in other jurisdictions, Nebraska's high court questioned the rectitude of the student's grades and even listened to testimony of doctors from outside of the college who were asked to review her work. The court concluded that the professors had exhibited "bias and prejudice" and dominated the school "as absolutely as ever Caesar did his empire."[50]

Although it was unusual for courts to express this sort of criticism toward the substance of academic evaluations at a private college, multiple courts raised procedural questions about academic expulsions from public colleges. These rulings did not challenge the fairness or accuracy of faculty grades but rather prohibited state institutions from expelling students on any academic grounds whatsoever. Citing specific statutes as well as the traditional accessibility of public colleges, courts sided with students in four out of the five reported academic expulsion suits brought against state schools before 1910.[51] The first of these rulings reinstated a student who had been expelled after earning low marks at a normal school operated by the City of Cleveland. Although it had been customary for the normal school to dismiss struggling students whenever there was excess demand for seats, the court concluded that all students who met the standard of admission were entitled to remain as long as they complied with published school rules. Issued in 1899, the ruling repeatedly invoked the *Stallard* fraternity case (see chapter 2) to justify its intervention. While the court acknowledged that courts should defer to academic grading practices, it asserted that expulsion should be subjected to more vigorous scrutiny. "There is no right more sacred than the right to admission to the public schools of the state," declared the opinion. The court saw no reason why the institution should not have to adhere to Ohio's common school statutes, which prohibited expulsions except after a hearing and a two-thirds vote by a governing board.[52]

The Supreme Courts of Nebraska and California also reinstated students and limited the academic discretion of public normal schools. Citing *Stallard*, Nebraska's high court prevented a state normal college from expelling a student in 1898 even though the student had attended the institution and failed to earn a degree for nearly a decade. Although a statute authorized the governing board to regulate enrollment, the institution had not published explicit rules and simply informed the student that his continuing presence was contrary to the "interests of the school." The governing board had argued that these decisions had the "character of an adjudication" and therefore could not be reversed by a writ of mandamus. Yet the court disagreed, stating that enrollment amounted to a ministerial process consisting of "naught but the registration of the pupil."[53] California's high court arrived at a similar conclusion four years later and compelled a state normal school to reenroll a student who had failed his teaching practicum. The court ruled that the institution's founding statute did not authorize its governing board to infringe upon a student's right to enrollment unless it could show cause. Because the statute did not mention a threshold for performance, the court concluded that there was no limit to the number of times a student could register for courses. This conclusion was bolstered by the testimony of an instructor who reported that other struggling students had been allowed multiple attempts to pass the practicum. The court determined that professors lacked the power to expel a student "simply because in their judgment he will never make a successful teacher."[54]

To some extent, these normal school cases reflected the intermediate status of teacher education institutions at the turn of the twentieth century. The ruling against the Cleveland normal school, in particular, stemmed from the court's invocation of a common school statute. However, the principles that emerged from these suits also figured prominently in *Gleason v. University of Minnesota*, a ruling that ordered the reinstatement of a student at a flagship university. The Minnesota Supreme Court not only affirmed earlier decisions that had required some form of due process for students expelled on account of disciplinary infractions, but it also severely limited the ability of Minnesota's public colleges to expel students because of academic failure.[55]

Gleason originated as a dispute between students and faculty over control of the university's athletics program. Whereas students had initially managed sports teams, a national movement to reform college football prompted the University of Minnesota and most other institutions to transfer control to administrators and faculty. Led by John L. Gleason, a popular law student and president of a defunct athletics board, students argued that extracurricular activities should remain outside the sphere of faculty power. Gleason organized rallies and participated in a debate with a professor who chaired a new faculty-led athletics committee. According to a reporter, Gleason relished the role of provocateur and "flaunted the flag of defiance in the face of the faculty." Gleason and his supporters also campaigned in favor of several rule changes that had been proposed by the "Big Nine" athletic conference, including an increase in the number of football games and a liberalization of student eligibility rules. A classmate of Gleason's recalled that the university's governing board wanted to "crucify" him. When he attempted to enroll in courses during the fall of 1907, Gleason received a notice that the board of trustees had expelled him because of academic deficiency and "certain insubordinate acts."[56]

Gleason sought the counsel of George Leonard, a graduate of the university's law school and an ally of the Knights of Labor.[57] Leonard's initial petition asserted that Gleason was entitled to a disciplinary hearing in which he could hear evidence and defend himself against these vague charges. In response to the charge of academic inadequacy, Leonard echoed the arguments of the earlier normal school cases, declaring that every state resident was entitled to attend the university even if he or she had already failed multiple subjects. Leonard's brief cited *Stallard* and maintained that the "right" to pursue higher education was "vital to democratic governance."[58] The attorneys representing the university responded with the standard assertion that a writ of mandamus could not apply to a quasi-judicial academic decision (though their brief acknowledged that the *initial* enrollment of qualified students might be ministerial and nondiscretionary). The university's brief also emphasized that trustees were entitled to a certain amount of deference because they were "men of character, fitness, and responsibility."[59]

The Minnesota Supreme Court rejected the university's argument and ordered Gleason's reinstatement. Regarding his alleged disciplinary infractions, the court ruled that Gleason was entitled to some degree of due process and observed that the institution had never before expelled a student without notice and a hearing (including cross-examination of witnesses). With respect to Gleason's alleged academic shortcomings, the court forbade expulsion except in cases where the evidence indicated that a student was "in all respects unworthy to be retained." Similar to the earlier normal school cases, *Gleason* emphasized that the university's founding statute did not explicitly empower trustees to expel failing students. The court also noted that the reenrollment of failed students was such a common practice that it amounted to a formal rule. Gleason's rejection would be an arbitrary denial of this right unless the university could demonstrate that he exhibited "persistent inattention and failure to take advantage of his opportunities." In general, *Gleason* determined that students had a "prima facie case" for reenrollment as long as they pursued their studies "in good faith."[60] The ruling combined the due process requirements that courts had occasionally imposed on private colleges with the constraints on academic expulsion that limited the discretionary power of state normal schools.

Although *Gleason* never achieved the prominence of *Pratt*, it was not an unprecedented outlier. *Gleason* represented the culmination of two strands of earlier rulings that challenged institutional authority over disciplinary and academic expulsions. Looking back at these cases from the vantage point of the 1920s and 1930s, legal scholars observed that earlier courts had used a range of different standards to define the meaning of an "arbitrary" expulsion.[61] Indeed, when dicta are taken into consideration, three-quarters of these early judgments mentioned that courts might limit institutional discretion.[62] This era of expulsion law suggests that the spirit of academic deference competed with a set of countervailing principles grounded in a mixture of contract law, state statutes, and customary practices.

Expulsion in the Era of Academic Deference, 1910–60

In 1911, the dean of the University of Illinois College of Law predicted that judges would suffer "embarrassment" if they attempted to override decisions made by professors or academic administrators. According to the dean, faculty and college officials possessed "habits of thought, study, and life" that rendered them especially competent to make wise determinations. Courts should adopt a "hands off" policy, concluded the dean, "except in clear cases of abuse of discretion."[63] Two decades later, a contributor to the *Journal of Higher Education* was confident that courts had become "loath to impugn the motives of a college faculty."[64] Indeed, expulsion case law coalesced in support of institutional policies and academic judgments after 1910, putting an end to the level of inconsistency that had characterized these rulings during the late nineteenth and early twentieth centuries. Before 1910, students had a fighting chance of winning reinstatement, especially if their expulsion clashed with catalog language, statutes, or past practices. After 1910, judges deferred to college officials in all reported expulsion cases up until the *Dixon* ruling. Although the extent of this deference was not as absolute as indicated by these results, students lost every suit regardless of whether the cases involved disciplinary infractions or academic failure, and regardless of whether their suits targeted private or public institutions.[65]

This shift was particularly dramatic in cases that challenged academic dismissals from state colleges. Perhaps signaling increased respect for scholarly expertise and institutional standards, a number of jurisdictions rejected *Gleason* by ruling that public colleges were entitled to expel students on account of inadequate academic performance. In 1931, an Ohio court allowed Miami University to bar a failing education student from reenrolling for another term. To some extent, the circumstances of the case differed from earlier academic expulsion rulings because a particular statute allowed the university to require teaching candidates to meet supplementary academic standards. Yet dicta within the opinion also disagreed with the broader spirit of *Gleason* by endorsing a more exclusive vision of public higher education. After quoting a dictionary definition of "university," the ruling stated that accommodating subpar students would run counter to the essential nature of an institution of higher learning.[66] The following year, a Texas court allowed the state university's medical school to expel students who failed to exceed certain academic benchmarks. Citing the *Waugh* fraternity case (see chapter 2), the court concluded that it was reasonable for the school to require students to meet "a standard of excellence."[67]

This new tolerance of academic expulsion coincided with a broad campaign to increase the efficiency of state universities. Beginning in the early twentieth century, social scientific studies of public university systems routinely encouraged flagship institutions to focus on high-performing students while redirecting ill-prepared students to regional colleges or two-year colleges.[68] Ultimately, some states revised their higher education statutes in order to remove potential barriers to academic expulsion. For example, California empowered its public colleges to expel subpar students in 1953.[69] Epitomized by California's "Master Plan" of 1960, increasingly hierarchical networks of state colleges and universities may have encouraged courts as well as legislatures to allow flagship institutions to exercise greater authority over academic expulsions.[70]

Judges also exhibited more deference toward college officials when resolving challenges to disciplinary expulsions. The case of *Gott v. Berea College*, which is sometimes cited as the representative example of all early expulsion cases, actually marked the intensification of deference during the twentieth century.[71] Filed in 1913 by a restaurant owner, the suit challenged a college regulation that prohibited students from patronizing off-campus establishments. In court, the institution justified its policy by stating that it needed to protect "inexperienced" rural students who moved to Berea's more urban setting. The Kentucky Court of Appeals agreed that the college was responsible for the welfare of its students and could therefore enforce "any rule or regulation" that a parent might adopt. The court stated that colleges had full discretion over disciplinary matters unless a rule was "unlawful or against public policy."[72] *Gott* echoed *Pratt* by endorsing institutional authority over the content of collegiate rules, but unlike that earlier decision, it heralded a half century of judicial deference toward the procedure as well as the substance of expulsion policies.[73]

To some extent, the streak of institutional victories that followed *Gott* simply reflected the degree to which colleges had adapted to earlier rulings by implementing a semblance of procedural due process. During the era between *Gott* and *Dixon*, there were no reported cases in which students were expelled entirely without cause or any form of hearing. In addition, the expansion of judicial deference corresponded with the development of clearer limits on the due process obligations of all manner of institutions. Between 1914 and 1921, the United States Supreme Court established that individuals expelled from various associations were not entitled to full-fledged adversarial hearings. The court noted the impracticality of providing elaborate proceedings for each case and concluded that the judiciary should not require any "particular measures" or "establish ideal systems" for other organizations.[74] These decisions encouraged state courts to grant wide latitude to all academic governing boards that had implemented any modicum of disciplinary procedure. American higher education had developed enough prestige, size, and complexity to make an especially persuasive argument on behalf of this sort of deference.[75]

College administrators may also have been able to make more credible arguments on behalf of their discipline codes because of the rebirth of institutional attention to student life that transpired during the 1920s and 1930s. Previously, colleges invoked the principle of in loco parentis to justify their authority, but they rarely cited specific reciprocal responsibilities for student well-being.[76] Yet during the early twentieth century, some administrators responded to the emergence of the impersonal research university by reemphasizing student life as a venue for inculcating virtue. Colleges built new dormitories, encouraged extracurricular activities, and expanded the role of deans and counselors in order to promote desirable behavior and combat psychological "maladjustment," a concept that was becoming the primary explanation for student attrition.[77]

Despite these administrative efforts, there was no shortage of student misconduct during the 1920s and 1930s. Institutional regulation of fashion, parties, visitors, and outings remained common sources of contention. If anything, students and faculty became more distanced from each other as a result of decreased contact outside of class and the proliferation of an especially insular form of youth culture.[78] In case after case, courts sided with colleges whenever these disciplinary clashes culminated in litigation, even when colleges provided a bare minimum of due process. The *Yale Law Journal* concluded that student rights "retrogressed" during this period, noting that students had been entitled to some form of hearing prior to World War I, whereas colleges were permitted to expel students without providing much justification in subsequent decades.[79]

This phenomenon emerged clearly in *Barker v. Bryn Mawr College*, a case that upheld an expulsion despite imprecise charges and cursory proceedings during the early 1920s.[80] The suit was filed on behalf of Margery Barker, a student from rural Indiana who had struggled to qualify for admission to Bryn Mawr.[81] Margery was asked to leave during her sophomore year after she allegedly stole thirty dollars from a classmate. Margery had attracted suspicion because she changed her alibi and was known to habitually enter other students' rooms when they were not present. Ultimately, Margery was found in possession of a marked two-dollar bill, which she claimed to have received as change from a taxi driver. The college never formally charged Margery with theft, opting instead to dismiss her on broader grounds. According to President M. Carey Thomas, Bryn Mawr was entitled to expel "undesirable" students without a formal hearing, especially if their transgressions were personal in nature. President Thomas informed Margery's mother that the college had expelled dozens of students for reasons ranging from disease and insanity to mere social awkwardness or "queerness."[82] Like other administrators at elite women's institutions, President Thomas was determined to maintain Bryn Mawr's reputation during an era when the college was bracing for a backlash against women's suffrage.[83]

Although eventually decided in favor of Bryn Mawr, Margery's suit revealed the persistence of some disagreement about whether colleges were required to justify expulsions. Margery's lawyer was so convinced that Bryn Mawr had violated the basic spirit of fair play that he agreed to represent her pro bono. A colleague of the attorney agreed that Margery had a strong case because she had been convicted in a "star chamber" without the opportunity to question her accusers.[84] Similar reasoning motivated the Bryn Mawr alumni association of Chicago to ask President Thomas to conduct a hearing.[85] The *New York Times* also sympathized with Margery and wondered why the college failed to present "direct and formal charges."[86] Yet the Supreme Court of Pennsylvania ruled that the college (because of language in its catalog) was entitled to absolute control of enrollment.[87]

Whereas Bryn Mawr had prevailed in large part because of its private status, judges also upheld the expulsion of students who had not received a hearing before being dismissed from the University of Maryland (UMD).[88] This case, styled *Woods v. Simpson*, concerned two students who had been expelled for a series of small infractions in 1924.[89] Discord between Vivian Simpson, Virginia Flanagan, and university administrators stemmed from their efforts to establish a chapter of Chi Omega, a sorority with a rebellious reputation.[90] Simpson had already fallen out of favor with school officials by violating fashion norms, failing to sign out when leaving campus, and "insolently" refusing to greet Dean of Women Adele Stamp when they crossed paths.[91] Simpson referred to herself as the campus "Bolshevik" and discouraged other students from following dorm policies, which she considered "ridiculous and silly."[92] Simpson reportedly told classmates to "rebel against the rules."[93] Meanwhile, Virginia Flanagan earned the enmity of Dean Stamp because she avoided social events, neglected to clean her room, and snuck into a secluded section of the library with a man.[94] Ultimately, President Albert F. Woods expelled both students after he suspected that they were responsible for a salacious *Washington Post* article that accused faculty members of sexual impropriety.[95]

Citing the *Waugh* fraternity case, the university's legal team argued that the institution was authorized to bestow or revoke the privilege of attendance.[96] The attorneys representing Simpson and Flanagan countered by invoking *Gleason* and asserting that a public university could only expel students after conducting a hearing and presenting evidence of a major infraction.[97] Flanagan had previously objected to a lack of due process when she was banned from student housing, asking President Woods to clarify whether "a dormitory resident may be ejected, without a hearing, at the discretion of the Dean of Women."[98] A lower court judge sided with the students and ruled that the university neglected to conduct a proper investigation and based its conclusion merely on the refusal of the students to discuss the newspaper article. The judge remarked that "the thing began to disgust me" after he observed that the two students had strong academic track records.[99] Yet upon appeal, Maryland's high court concluded that the students' misdeeds amounted to a serious threat to campus discipline, which fell within the purview of the university in almost all circumstances.[100]

In 1928, a New York appeals court also endorsed an expulsion that occurred with negligible procedural safeguards.[101] At first, a lower court sympathized with a student named Beatrice Anthony, who claimed that Syracuse University could not expel her without providing an opportunity for her to mount a defense. The judge emphasized the importance of higher education and opined that students were entitled to "the elementary right of notice and opportunity to be heard." Furthermore, he characterized the student-university relationship as contractual in nature and ordered Syracuse to justify expulsions in relatively precise terms.[102] Yet a state appellate court reversed this decision after determining that the university was not obligated to divulge the reason for an expulsion. *Anthony v. Syracuse* placed the burden of proof entirely upon the student, noting that a catalog statement empowered Syracuse to expel students on any grounds.[103]

Gender, Dissent, and Deference

Although *Barker*, *Woods*, *Anthony*, and other expulsion cases from the 1920s and 1930s appear to exhibit almost complete confidence in university administrators, the extent of this deference seems less complete when their social context is considered. Many deferential rulings from this era may have been influenced as much by exogenous tensions as by the notion that colleges were entitled to exercise broad discretion over enrollment. Although most of these cases included some discussion of expulsion procedures, they tended to emphasize the substance of student rebellion in terms of the behavior of young women or the expression of dissenting political convictions.[104]

The *Woods*, *Barker*, and *Anthony* cases highlight how anxiety over the rapid evolution of gender roles could contribute to the outcome of expulsion suits. Women students, whose numbers had been growing steadily for decades, constituted just under half of all college enrollment during the 1920s, yet they were the focus of all eight reported expulsion cases between 1923 and 1931.[105] Increasing supervision on campus reflected widespread concerns about student conduct, and young women attracted disproportionate attention whenever they embraced new political rights and personal freedoms. According to historian Barbara Solomon, college presidents were "bedeviled and challenged" by women students, who frequently resented and sometimes resisted institutional attempts to regulate fashion, dating, and smoking.[106] The appearance of these tensions within so many midcentury expulsion cases calls into question the extent to which these rulings reflected principled support for deference to higher education itself.

For example, a Michigan Supreme Court ruling from 1924 upheld the expulsion of a woman who smoked cigarettes in public and rode in a car while seated on a man's lap. While the opinion endorsed the concept of academic deference, it also considered whether it was appropriate for the state normal college to ban cigarettes when male students could smoke freely at the neighboring state university.[107] Women smokers were controversial during the 1920s; the practice was becoming a romanticized symbol of liberation, while also retaining an earlier association with sexual promiscuity.[108] Ultimately, the court concluded that it was reasonable for a college to enforce special rules to govern the conduct of "1,400 girls of tender years." The ruling praised the college's dean of women for displaying "a motherly interest" in the expelled student and for "upholding some old-fashioned ideals of young womanhood."[109] Similarly, the *Anthony* ruling supported the right of Syracuse administrators to expel a student after interviewing her sorority sisters and determining that she was not "a typical Syracuse girl."[110]

The *Woods* case provides an especially vivid example of how tensions over social norms undermined legal protections for women students during the 1920s. *Woods* focused on students who disobeyed policies that were meant to regulate sororities, organizations that were closely associated changing sexual mores. A boom in sorority membership during the decade emerged as a symbol of the sometimes-unwelcome increase in women's enrollment and of the dilemmas that coeducation presented to administrators.[111] When Vivian Simpson and Virginia Flanagan started a chapter of Chi Omega, the University of Maryland was just four years removed from the graduation of its first female student. Along with many other institutions, UMD had implemented a series of rules "generally accepted as proper and desirable for women," imposing curfews, requiring chaperones, and placing restrictions on playing phonographs. President Woods also notified students that the dean of women had "absolute authority" to discipline students who smoked, used "coarse" language, or failed to maintain tidy rooms.[112]

Simpson and Flanagan regarded Chi Omega and its lawsuit as part of a campaign for equal rights. Prior to Chi Omega's founding, UMD's two sororities had rejected women who were deemed too "fast." The start of the sorority coincided with other demands for full participation in UMD student life. Students petitioned, for example, to create a women's rifle team. Upon Simpson's suggestion, the Women's Student Council suggested that a constitution should be drafted to clarify the rights of women on campus.[113] In particular, Simpson objected to a rule requiring women to turn their lights off at 10:30 p.m. She argued that she should be able to study late into the night in order to keep pace with male classmates, who faced no such restriction.[114] In response to this dimension of the case, the Prince George's County Federation of Women issued a statement of support for the students and demanded a "square deal."[115]

During their trial, most of the charges arrayed against Simpson and Flanagan related to violations of gender norms. For example, one classmate who differed with the two students referred to Chi Omega as an "Amazon-hued" sorority.[116] In preparation for the suit, the dean of women collected evidence about Simpson's habit of embarrassing other residents of her dormitory by talking to their dates while wearing a kimono.[117] Flanagan's roommate also complained that she smoked, swore, and dressed "immodestly."[118] Other students accused Flanagan of being "unladylike."[119] The *Washington Post* article that was the catalyst for their expulsion touched a nerve by accusing certain UMD officials of getting "mushy" with coeds.[120] Ultimately, Maryland's high court ruled that maintaining proper decorum was a delicate task that required special expertise, "especially in dealing with girl students."[121]

The extent of judicial deference in interwar expulsion cases was also likely magnified by the prevalence of suits featuring radical students who sought reinstatement based on alleged violations of their constitutional rights. Students lost all of these cases, not solely because courts deferred to academic authorities, but also because judges generally did not protect students' freedom of speech prior to the Second World War.[122] Before the war, students who stepped outside of mainstream political or religious expectations were quite vulnerable to persecution and unlikely to find redress through the courts.

The most transparent example of this sort of ruling occurred when a New York court endorsed the expulsion of Leon Samson, a pacifist who attended Columbia University during World War I.[123] College campuses, like American society in general, exhibited little tolerance for antiwar protest in this era. Indeed, most colleges welcomed the Students' Army Training Corps, a program that temporarily transformed campuses into training facilities for officers and technical experts.[124] Samson, whom the *New York Tribune* mocked as "the most anti-militaristic student to ever start a riot," had already been dismissed from the City University of New York for protesting American mobilization.[125] Columbia expelled Samson after he told a meeting of the Collegiate League for Peace and Harmony that Americans should rebel against the draft, the "dollar war," and "the American Kaiser." The meeting, which featured an address by Emma Goldman, ended when officers of the National Guard and the New York City police department blocked the exits and interrogated suspected draft dodgers.[126] While the court recognized that Samson had a contractual relationship with the university, it ruled that his conduct threatened Columbia's "discipline, good order and fair name" and thereby violated an implied term of their agreement. The opinion, however, spent more time asserting that "love of country" was a fundamental purpose of higher education. The court concluded that the university was entitled to expel Samson because "the poison of his disloyalty" could corrupt the student body.[127]

After the armistice, New York courts remained unsympathetic to radical students. A judge ruled against a student who was expelled from Albany Law School for making "socialistic and seditious utterance and propaganda calculated to injure the standing and reputation of said school." Although the student denied the charges, classmates told administrators that he had befriended a Socialist assemblyman, criticized the war, read a book entitled *Socialism, Sovietism and I.W.W-ism*, and declared "to hell with the American government." The court ruled that it was appropriate for institutions of higher education to expel students who expressed political beliefs that were "unpatriotic, revolutionary and anarchistic."[128]

American courts also sided with colleges when they expelled students who objected to military training requirements. Christian pacifists spearheaded protests against compulsory military courses on a number of campuses during the 1920s and 1930s.[129] A suit challenging the expulsion of these protesters reached the Maryland Supreme Court in 1933, when a student petitioned for reinstatement to UMD. Although the student claimed to be a conscientious objector, the court ruled that the university could disregard this status because it was a privilege bestowed by Congress, not a constitutional right. The court ruled that the expulsion did not violate the student's First Amendment right to religious expression, his Fourteenth Amendment right to equal protection, or a section of UMD's charter that prohibited a "sectarian or partisan" admission tests or requirements of any "particular plan of religious worship."[130] One year later, the United States Supreme Court also ruled against Christian students who had refused to register for a compulsory course in military science at the University of California. Although the opinion stated that students were not entitled to Fourteenth Amendment protections because college enrollment was voluntary, the court also indicated that it was particularly inclined to rule against pacifists because all citizens owed a duty to "support and defend government against all enemies."[131]

Even though American mobilization against fascist adversaries encouraged greater protection of free speech during World War II, judges continued to endorse the expulsion of radical college students.[132] In 1949, for example, a court upheld the dismissal of a Michigan State University student who organized a meeting featuring a Communist speaker.[133] During an era when colleges were scrutinized for evidence of "un-American" activity, students were well aware of the risks associated with taking unpopular political stances.[134] Courts continued to offer little protection for these students during the late 1950s, well after the peak of McCarthyism. For example, a Florida court supported the expulsion of an atheist from the University of Miami's education program in 1958. "It seems obvious," stated the court, that universities should expel education majors who promoted "fanatical ideas" that could injure schoolchildren.[135]

If we bracket cases involving gender norms, political dissent, or religious iconoclasm, it becomes easy to detect an undercurrent of support for the procedural rights of expelled students even during this peak period of academic deference. In 1930, Harvard Law School professor Zechariah Chafee Jr. provided scholarly heft to this sentiment in an influential essay about due process. Disturbed by the violations of civil liberties that occurred during World War I, Chafee argued that citizens were entitled to robust protections even within colleges and other private associations. Inspired by Progressive revisions to contract law, Chafee offered a nuanced interpretation of private associations by noting that some were more consensual than others. He reasoned that vitally important organizations, such as colleges, must honor the unstated expectations of their members. This proposal contrasted with earlier arguments for student rights, which tended to emphasize the standard contractual nature of private college enrollment rather than the high stakes associated with the college degree itself. Chafee concluded that it was unlikely that parents or students ever believed that an "autocratic" power to expel students could be "inherent in the nature of an educational institution." He argued that every association should adhere to its own rules, operate without malice, and follow the "principles of natural justice." Chafee looked favorably upon early rulings, such as *Cecil*, that had reinstated students who were expelled without cause.[136] Most strikingly, Chafee believed that the state's interest in education empowered courts to overturn summary expulsions even if the catalog of a private college expressly rejected due process. "Even if an association desires to operate like an army," he wrote, "the state may not sanction this wish . . . depend[ing] on the value which the community sets on the purposes of the association." In the case of colleges, in particular, Chafee suggested that "an institution which professes to prepare youth for life in a democracy might wisely give them an example of fair play."[137]

Whether motivated by these principles or merely by the lessons communicated in earlier student victories, the colleges that were involved in midcentury expulsion suits tended to measure up to Chafee's standards. Most of the students who lost expulsion cases between 1910 and 1960 had experienced fairly substantial disciplinary procedures regardless of whether they attended public or private institutions. Reflecting upon this era, one legal scholar concluded that dicta indicated that most colleges had developed a "judicial or quasi-judicial standard" for expulsion.[138] For example, the Supreme Court of Montana endorsed the expulsion of a student in 1927 because the state university had allowed her to speak before a disciplinary committee. The student had been expelled for hosting parties that lacked proper chaperones for women. Although the court reasoned that a formal trial (with cross-examination) would be impractical, it suggested that judicial intervention would be warranted if a university did not point to a published rule, interview witnesses, and provide proof of wrongdoing.[139] Similarly, a Massachusetts court ruled against a student only after determining that her college's disciplinary process "did not by any act or word seek to limit her opportunity of explanation or justification of her conduct."[140] When two University of Tennessee medical students were expelled for selling examination questions, the state supreme court also praised the institution's extensive disciplinary procedure. First, a student committee heard testimony from the accused and other witnesses. Next, the students were granted a "rehearing" that was attended by the university president. Finally, the president asked a subcommittee of trustees to preside over an appeals process that included the students' legal counsel.[141]

These expectations intensified in the years leading up to *Dixon*. The National Student Association, an umbrella group of student government organizations, asked colleges to honor a "Student Bill of Rights" in 1947. The document stated that the two-way "contractual . . . obligations and responsibilities" of students and colleges should be communicated prior to registration.[142] While the significance of these demands was probably more symbolic than real, new state laws indicated that administrators of public colleges could no longer assume that courts would defer to their treatment of rebellious students. That same year, California legislators felt compelled to specify that junior colleges had the authority to expel students for "continued willful disobedience, open and persistent defiance of the authority of the teacher, habitual profanity or vulgarity." In Louisiana, a 1950 statute that authorized the expulsion of "subversive" students still required a hearing with representation by council and cross-examination of witnesses.[143] More prominently, the Supreme Court signaled that all individuals were entitled to procedural due process in cases of noncriminal adjudication. In 1951, the court ruled that organizations could not be designated as communist threats to national security without first participating in a hearing.[144]

An increasing procedural emphasis can also be detected in scholarly responses to two rulings that upheld expulsions during the 1950s. An editor of the *Stanford Law Review* strongly objected when a Massachusetts court sanctioned the expulsion of a Brandeis University graduate student who had complained about the amount of his fellowship. In 1958, three years before *Dixon* ruled that public colleges must provide due process, the editor speculated that liberal interpretation of the state action principle might someday obligate private colleges to do the same.[145] When an Illinois court approved the expulsion of a student who had not been allowed to present evidence or see the evidence arrayed against him, Harvard Law School professor Warren Seavey responded with an article that was ultimately cited in *Dixon*. Seavey famously quipped that college students were at least entitled to "the protection given to a pickpocket." He cited the *Hill* decision against Dickinson College (which perhaps accounts for the appearance of this case in the *Dixon* opinion) and argued that students should be able to respond to their accusers. Seavey repeated Chafee's belief that colleges owed students "natural justice" even in the absence of any particular constitutional or contractual grounds. He found it "shocking" that "a state educational institution, which can function properly only if our freedoms are preserved, should not understand the elementary principles of fair play."[146]

The last major expulsion case prior to *Dixon* reveals the degree of procedural due process that students could expect even before the onset of the campus rights revolution. The case concerned a Brooklyn College student who was expelled after accusing administrators of committing "vile indecencies" during the course of his two previous suspensions. In 1959, a federal court rejected the student's claim that his right to due process had been violated, but only after it determined that he had been granted an array of hearings, meetings, and appeals. Furthermore, even this lengthy process did not satisfy one of the judges, who argued in a dissenting opinion that *Brown v. Board of Education* established that education was a right worthy of robust constitutional protection.[147] By 1960, therefore, students could reasonably expect courts to require colleges to conduct at least a semiformal hearing prior to expulsion.

Whereas American courts continued to defer to colleges when faced with academic expulsion suits after 1960, *Dixon v. Alabama State Board of Education* increased judicial oversight of disciplinary expulsions by anchoring the procedural rights of public college students to the United States Constitution. The ruling, delivered by the United States Court of Appeals for the Fifth Circuit, ordered the reinstatement of six Alabama State College students who had been expelled for protesting segregation at the lunch counter of a county courthouse. According to the college president, the students were dismissed for "conduct prejudicial to the school and for conduct unbecoming a student or future teacher in the schools of Alabama, for insubordination and insurrection, or for inciting other pupils to like conduct." *Dixon* defined college education as akin to personal property and, therefore, ordered state colleges to honor the due process clause of the Fourteenth Amendment. Never again could public colleges or universities expel students on account of their conduct without clear charges and some form of disciplinary proceeding.[148]

Yet although *Dixon*'s constitutional interpretation was unprecedented, the opinion invoked a tradition of expulsion oversight that was articulated by *Hill* in 1887, affirmed by *Gleason* in 1908, and evident in the dicta of other cases throughout the first half of the twentieth century.[149] To be sure, *Dixon* represented a major development in the history of academic deference by replacing the contractual and customary grounds for due process with a stronger constitutional basis. However, *Dixon* also participated in an older and more general debate about whether higher education was closer to a right (requiring robust judicial oversight of the disciplinary process) or a privilege (requiring negligible procedures and little external supervision).

The actions of Alabama State College fell far outside the boundaries of this debate as it stood in 1961. A survey of seventy-two state universities conducted just after *Dixon* found that 84 percent of these schools provided hearings prior to expulsion, 74 percent allowed students to cross-examine witnesses, and 70 percent permitted students to have legal representation during these proceedings.[150] The politics of racial bigotry may explain why administrators failed to provide the degree of due process that had been recommended in previous rulings and already existed on the ground at most other institutions. The testimony of state officials indicated that administrators were motivated by a desire to suppress support for the civil rights movement as much as by any particular concern for campus order. Indeed, Alabama State College typically conducted disciplinary hearings but attempted to argue that its officials could bypass this practice whenever circumstances demanded speedy action.[151]

Of course, the legal requirements for private colleges were less intense than the obligations of state colleges that were beholden to statutory prohibitions against academic expulsion, the customs of public education, and (after *Dixon*) the Fourteenth Amendment. Yet a number of decisions involving private colleges compelled administrators to honor catalog language as well as fundamental expectations of fair play. The reverberations of *Dixon* and the trends that it embodied also pressured private institutions to bolster their disciplinary procedures on their own accord. In general, the ruling signaled the demise of in loco parentis—an analogy between collegiate and familial authority that, in the words of one legal scholar, no longer seemed appropriate to "the modern, nearly-mature college student and the modern, impersonal university."[152] Instead, the student-college relationship was defined more often by rights predicated on contracts, statutes, and constitutional provisions. According to a federal ruling issued soon after *Dixon*, referring to higher education as a privilege rather than a right had become a "mere play upon words."[153]

5

Tuition

Nineteenth-century state university leaders routinely celebrated the ideal of free higher education. For example, Colonel Ashbel Smith pledged that the University of Texas would be "emphatically the poor boy's university" when he dedicated the institution's cornerstone. Indeed, the Texas constitution guaranteed tuition-free enrollment to all eligible students.[1] In those states that permitted tuition, legislators still expected public universities to provide free or inexpensive access in exchange for periodic appropriations. These efforts were driven by democratic ideals as well as the reality that few students could afford to pay for much more than room and board. However, starting around the time of Colonel Smith's declaration, increasing numbers of state universities began to charge tuition in order to cope with rising enrollments and the expense of constructing modern facilities. By the 1920s, substantial tuition rates were no longer unusual at public institutions of higher education.[2]

During this transitional period around the turn of the century, the tuition policies of public universities were vulnerable to student-initiated lawsuits that invoked earlier statutory or constitutional mandates. Students won five out of the six tuition suits reported before 1910.[3] However, as in cases involving admissions and expulsion law, twentieth-century courts eventually deferred to institutional authority and rejected suits that invoked ambiguous constitutional or statutory language. Judges also united in favor of a narrow definition of "tuition" that allowed for the introduction of "fees" even at those state colleges that were required to be tuition-free. As a result, students lost nine out of the twelve tuition cases reported between 1910 and 1960.[4] Since tuition policies have a relatively tenuous connection to academic expertise (compared to admissions and expulsion policies), one might expect judges to exhibit less deference in this domain. Yet twentieth-century courts nevertheless permitted institutions to increase tuition or fees as long as state laws did not expressly forbid these charges. When this permissiveness is contrasted with the greater extent of nineteenth-century oversight, judicial deference toward tuition policies appears to be contested and historically contingent rather than preordained.

This chapter also highlights how academic deference, as a legal argument, engendered awkward rhetorical tensions regarding the public missions of state universities. Since the students who filed tuition suits typically asserted that free higher education was justified by its contribution to the common good, universities found themselves arrayed against this premise when they argued in favor of administrative independence. As documented in the second half of the chapter, two state courts actually opined that the return on investment for individual graduates was more significant than any indirect contributions to a broader public mission. Citing the legal doctrine of "public purposes," these courts invalidated tax-supported scholarship programs after determining that their recipients did not necessarily advance the interests of the state as a whole.

Judicial Oversight of Tuition, 1860–1910

In the nineteenth century, most state lawmakers and academic leaders agreed that public higher education should be free or extremely inexpensive. Those legislatures that allowed tuition often encouraged public institutions to lower their rates. For example, the founding statute of the University of Minnesota directed its governing board to end tuition "as soon as . . . the income of the university fund will permit." North Carolina lawmakers instructed the state university to stop charging tuition "as soon as practicable" (which turned out to be never).[5] A few states provided more wiggle room. New York, for instance, simply required Cornell University to charge the "lowest rates of expense consistent with its welfare and efficiency."[6] Nevertheless, each of these laws provided grounds for student-initiated suits if institutions charged their own "fees" rather than tuition, or if administrators seemed insufficiently dedicated to lowering costs.

Of course, these laws applied only to state colleges and universities; typically, private institutions could set prices as they saw fit.[7] As one would expect, public higher education was also significantly less expensive than private higher education. At the turn of the twentieth century, private college students paid between $100 and $160 a year, whereas public college students usually paid less than $40.[8] Yet even some private colleges operated with constraints related to their tax-exempt status. California legislators exempted Stanford University from paying property taxes as long as the school did not charge tuition to state residents. In Alabama, Bailey Springs University was exempted from state and county taxes as long as it granted sixty full scholarships a year.[9]

Private colleges were also required to honor their contractual obligations. In 1861, the Supreme Court of Illinois ordered Illinois Female College to pay a father who had purchased a "perpetual scholarship" and sought a refund when the school required nonresidents to live in campus housing (the faculty wished to prevent students from socializing in a nearby town). The court ruled that the scholarship amounted to a contract, which could not be amended retroactively to include the expense of dormitory fees.[10] Similarly, the Supreme Court of Louisiana ruled that Tulane University could not charge a matriculation fee to the recipients of scholarships that had been established for residents of New Orleans.[11]

Courts also held state universities accountable to contractual obligations that limited their flexibility with respect to tuition. Ruling that a catalog statement amounted to a contract, the Supreme Court of Missouri ordered the state university to exempt current students when it increased tuition at its law school in 1895. Observing that the parties were not "on equal terms," the court rejected the notion that students were simply free to walk away if the university set a higher price.[12] Engineering students were keen to suggest that this ruling required the university to freeze their tuition too. Reluctant to cede control over tuition rates, the governing board turned to local attorneys, who advised the trustees to regard catalog statements as binding contracts with each class for the duration of their time on campus.[13]

In contrast with these contractual disputes, which simply obligated colleges to observe ordinary commercial practices, other early tuition suits were more intimately associated with debates over the nature of higher education. These suits sought to prevent public universities from generating new sources of income without direct state authorization. In particular, students challenged governing boards that had instituted new "fees" as a strategy for circumventing statutory or constitutional limitations on "tuition." Sensing that legislatures might never provide adequate support, state university leaders had good reason to seek this enlarged authority over revenue. During the late nineteenth century, fees for incidentals, laboratories, libraries, and diplomas became commonplace. Even the University of California added a laboratory fee in 1895, despite the fact that its leaders had proudly refused to charge tuition.[14]

By the 1920s, American courts agreed that public universities could charge these fees or raise tuition as long as they were not explicitly prohibited from doing so by state law. Yet between 1880 and 1915, three challenges to the distinction between "tuition" and "fees" resulted in one decision that favored institutional discretion, one decision that limited administrative authority, and one decision that fell somewhere in the middle—a mixed record that is consistent with the overall fragility of academic deference in that era. Not only were these cases shaped by different statutory and political contexts, but they also indicated how different courts responded to broader arguments about whether tuition undermined the public mission of the state university.

In the first reported challenge of this sort, the Supreme Court of Wisconsin granted the state university ample room to interpret the statute that governed its tuition policy.[15] Passed in 1848, the act that founded the University of Wisconsin (UW) instituted a twenty-dollar tuition charge and instructed the school to become tuition-free as soon as possible. Disappointing returns from the state's land grant investments prevented the legislature from following through on this goal until 1876. However, falling interest rates and persistent mismanagement of the land grant prompted the governing board to enact a four-dollar "incidentals fee" in order to avoid running a deficit. Encouraged by the campus newspaper, which editorialized that the fee violated "the spirit if not the letter of the law," students objected to the new policy. Two hundred students formed an Anti-Tuition League, while Edward B. Priest, a forty-year-old senior who planned to become a lawyer, withheld his payment and filed suit.[16]

Litigated in 1881, the case of *State ex rel. Priest v. University of Wisconsin* examined whether the board of regents possessed an implied power to enact fees that were not prohibited by the legislature. The statute of 1876 prevented the university from charging a fee for "admission," but it did not mention any alternative charges. Priest's counsel, supported by testimony from the state attorney general, argued that the legislature had intended to establish a free university. He stated that the regents possessed the authority to govern the institution but lacked the authority to increase its own revenue. Priest's attorney defined UW as part of a statewide system of free common schools, noting that appropriations for the university and other public schools were discussed in the same section of Wisconsin's constitution. He asserted that fees would transform the university into an aristocratic institution. The brief concluded by stating that access to higher education should be considered a public good rather than a private commodity because the graduates of UW endeavored to provide "the best possible services to the state."[17]

UW countered by arguing that the legislature's ban on "tuition" only applied to charges that were directly related to instruction (e.g., teacher salaries or educational equipment). Therefore, the statute did not prevent the regents from raising funds for heating, lighting, and campus maintenance. The university's brief pointed out that institutions had distinguished between fees for tuition and incidentals since the founding of Oxford and Cambridge, where students traditionally paid one fee to the university for access to facilities and another fee to their tutors for instruction. More broadly, the attorneys argued that a student should not depend entirely on state largesse, quipping that the state might as well "feed and clothe him, do his washing, shave his adolescent beard and buy him a new silk hat." UW also asked the court to defer to its governing board, which it characterized as an illustrious body that would never "exhibit any tendency to extortion." Invoking the concept of in loco parentis, the brief described the regents as "guardians" who ought to be able to determine the proper amount to charge students. After all, the legislature had endowed the governing board with the "necessary or convenient" authority to achieve the university's goals.[18]

The court sided emphatically with the university. *Priest* reasoned that since UW had charged a variety of admission and incidental fees prior to 1876, the legislature would have banned each of those fees by name if it had intended to guarantee free higher education. *Priest* also determined that the board of regents was a corporate body that could enact new fees "except as expressly limited" by the legislature. In response to the students' claim that the law did not mention incidental fees, the court noted that regents were entitled to a certain amount of deference and "trust," especially since "it would be altogether impracticable to prescribe by statute the numerous and varying duties of such a board."[19] In general, corporate charters were subjected to very permissive interpretation by courts during the late nineteenth century.[20]

Despite this ruling, state universities remained susceptible to the argument that tuition would compromise their ability to serve the public as a whole. This point of view prompted the Supreme Court of Kansas to order the University of Kansas (KU) to stop charging a library fee in 1895.[21] KU's founding legislation, passed in 1864, had authorized a ten-dollar admission fee and a tuition rate of thirty dollars, while ordering the institution to eliminate all charges as soon as circumstances allowed.[22] Just two years later, KU ended tuition for its arts and sciences students, though it continued to levy other assorted fees. This arrangement persisted until 1889, at which point the legislature formalized a ban on tuition.[23] Soon thereafter, KU's board of regents authorized a new library fee. Students reacted by forming a "protective association" that organized a boycott against the fee and explored the possibility of legal action.[24] The board disregarded these protests, although Chancellor Francis H. Snow worried that John Little, the state's Populist attorney general, might regard the library policy as a violation of state law.[25] Indeed, Little ultimately asked KU to discontinue the fee.[26] To counter the attorney general, KU hired D. M. Valentine, an attorney who had previously been elected to the state supreme court on a Republican ticket.[27]

In contrast with *Priest*, a full-fledged Populist movement backed the KU suit, which came to be titled *State ex rel. Little v. University of Kansas*. Although Populists did not always champion college students, they often sided with young people who challenged powerful organizations.[28] Populist legislators also tended to support appropriations to state colleges and universities on the condition that they remain free to students. H. S. Clarke, a Populist member of KU's governing board, tried in vain to undo the new library fee. Another Populist sympathizer predicted that allowing KU to establish its own fees would result in the exclusion of "every poor boy or girl in the state." The state's leading Populist newspaper exclaimed that charging students to attend a public institution was "an exhibition of asinine stupidity" that would create a "property caste" and violate the principle of equal protection before the law.[29] In response, the state's leading Republican newspaper argued that it was unfair to tax all residents in order to fund free higher education for relatively few students. Moreover, free higher education might promote insidious socialist notions and undermine the ideal of personal responsibility.[30]

Colored by this clash between Populist and Republican perspectives, *Little* provided different answers to the questions that had been at the core of *Priest*. Like the earlier Wisconsin suit, *Little* examined whether KU had the authority to charge fees that were not authorized by the legislature. Similar to the case made by the University of Wisconsin, KU contended that the statute requiring "free" admission did not preclude fees that were not directly related to classroom instruction. Valentine told the court that the library fee was intended to replace worn books and fell squarely within the board's routine managerial authority.[31]

Judge Stephen H. Allen, a self-educated Populist who had defeated Valentine in the election of 1892, rejected the notion that the library fee could be distinguished from other sorts of fees. "If the regents may collect $5 for the use of the library," he asked, "why may they not impose fees for walking in the campus?" Judge Allen maintained that the legislature had appropriated funds for the university in order to facilitate tuition-free access. The board could not raise additional resources "unless expressly authorized to do so by law."[32]

Second, *Little* determined that KU's financial accessibility affected its service to the state. Since the suit took the form of a quo warranto action (claiming that a public office was overstepping its statutory authority), *Little* required the court to pass judgment on the broader question of whether the library fee was a private concern of KU students or a matter of general public interest. If the fee only affected students, then those individuals should have filed instead for injunctive relief. KU's attorney argued that the students needed to pursue a private action because only those who refused to pay the fee were excluded from the library. Judge Allen disagreed. *Little* characterized KU as the "crown" of a public school system that provided more "certain and unalloyed" public benefits than any other function of state government. "The public maintains the institution," Judge Allen continued, "not for the special advantages conferred by it on particular individuals, but for the great advantage accruing to the state." When the board of regents implemented a fee that could prevent poor students from attending the university, it was manifestly a matter of public interest.[33]

Similarly, though less absolutely, the Supreme Court of Oklahoma ordered the state's agricultural and mechanical college to stop charging a five-dollar fee in 1912.[34] Intended to support extracurricular activities, the fee may have appeared to be a relatively minor expense to college officials, including President James H. Connell (who otherwise tended to promote financial accessibility during his tenure).[35] Yet the fee seemed illegal to a student named Ruth Gray and her attorney Freeman E. Miller, a former English professor at the college and poet laureate of the state. Echoing *Little*, Miller pointed out that the legislature had never authorized the board to impose fees. He argued that a fee was the equivalent of an admissions requirement, whereas state law only specified that applicants must be Oklahoma residents between the ages of twelve and thirty. Miller also objected to the beneficiaries of the fee, especially the Young Men's Christian Association (YMCA) and various athletic programs. He contended that a state institution should not support a religious organization or force poor farmers "to contribute to the expense of sending long-haired football sluggers around the country." In general, Miller warned that college officials tended to "arrogate to themselves practically the right to make laws" and asked the court to remind the college of its obligation to abide by the law just like "the humblest and most ignorant" citizen in the state.[36] The college's brief for this case, which was titled *Connell v. Gray*, also paralleled UW's and KU's arguments in *Priest* and *Little*. It asserted that the fee was not "tuition" because it supported extracurricular activities (in addition to the YMCA and athletics, it was intended to fund student literary societies and the college newspaper). Moreover, in contrast to their counterparts in Kansas, the Oklahoma legislature never mandated tuition-free higher education.[37]

Judge Robert Lee Williams, a former minister who would soon be elected governor, granted an injunction to stop the fee but employed reasoning that was more amenable to administrative authority than *Little*. In *Connell*, Judge Williams agreed that using student fees to fund the YMCA violated the separation of church and state. More broadly, he accepted the argument that the college could not impose a fee "as a condition precedent to entrance." However, the ruling supported the college's claim that the legislature had not banned every student expense *after* enrollment. The court found that the college could charge students for required uniforms and collect refundable deposits to protect against property damage.[38]

On one hand, *Connell* championed the right of Oklahoma residents to enjoy free higher education as long as they fell within the required age limits. As noted in chapter 3, this aspect of the ruling attracted the attention of Thurgood Marshall and Charles Hamilton Houston when they argued that African American residents were entitled to public higher education within their home states. Yet the distinction between charging fees before and after enrollment would prove to be largely symbolic. *Connell* authorized the college to institute fees as long as they were not explicitly defined as a prerequisite for admission. In practice, the ruling was closer to *Priest* than *Little*.

Tuition in the Era of Academic Deference, 1915–60

Indeed, *Priest* proved to be far more influential than *Little* over the long run.[39] As early as 1903, the legal scholar Roscoe Pound was confident that fees would survive suits predicated on "tuition" bans.[40] Pound's prediction was accurate—state universities won all seven cases that challenged tuition or fee increases between 1915 and 1960.[41] Technically, the influence of *Priest* reflected the belief that university leaders were entitled to raise revenue except in cases where they violated clear legislative or constitutional edicts. More generally, *Priest* also prevailed over *Little*'s argument regarding the legal implications of a state's interest in cultivating educated citizens.

In 1916, just four years after *Connell*, the Supreme Court of Washington State signaled the solidification of this consensus by rejecting another attempt to challenge tuition and fees at a public university.[42] Since 1893, the Washington legislature had required the state university to operate on a tuition-free basis for all qualified residents (enrollment more than doubled in 1894).[43] Yet as legislative appropriations lagged behind the growth of the student body, the university was forced to hold classes in attics, cellars, and outbuildings. The board of regents even refrained from advertising the institution in hopes of decreasing enrollment.[44] In 1915, the legislature allowed the university to raise funds for the construction of two buildings by charging a ten-dollar entrance fee and a tuition fee of ten dollars per semester. A group of students led by former law student Mark M. Litchman contended that the new law violated the state constitution.[45]

A veteran of the Spanish-American War, Litchman had worked as a sailor before returning to school to become "a lawyer for the hoboes." "My tramps over land and sea," Litchman told a friend, "have given me both a heart and a viewpoint for the underdog." He joined the Socialist Party and started a practice in Seattle that specialized in defending union members and political activists.[46] Litchman may have been drawn to the University of Washington by the opportunity to study with Professor J. Allen Smith, who argued that the founding fathers and the Supreme Court had served the interests of property owners.[47] The popularity of Smith and other Progressive scholars attracted the ire of conservative legislators in the state. During the same biennial session that reintroduced tuition, the Speaker of the House referred to the university as "a hotbed of socialism" and threatened to eliminate its appropriation unless the governing board dismantled the departments of social science and political economy.[48]

Litchman's arguments against the tuition law reflected this broader ideological clash. His brief in the case, which was styled *Litchman v. Shannon*, alleged that students who could no longer afford to attend the university were being excluded "because of their class and condition." Litchman argued that this exclusion conflicted with the university's constitutional mandate to be "open to all." He also asserted that tuition and fees were inconsistent with another provision in the state constitution that required public schools to operate "without distinction or preference on account of race, color, *caste*, or sex." Finally, he suggested that the law violated the state's guarantee of equal protection because the fees did not apply to students at the state agricultural college in Pullman. Aside from these constitutional claims, Litchman declared that the university should err on the side of accessibility as a matter of public policy because of the state's interest in training "an enlightened, intelligent, and educated citizenship." At stake was nothing less than "the stability of a free government."[49]

Although he expressed sympathy toward the ideal of free higher education, Judge Oscar R. Holcomb penned an opinion that rejected Litchman's argument. Judge Holcomb, who often took positions to the left of his colleagues, determined that the constitutional language regarding free education only applied to lower schools. In *Litchman*, Holcomb reasoned that the practice of charging students prior to 1893 revealed that lawmakers, including the members of two constitutional conventions, had never intended to guarantee free tuition in perpetuity. The ruling stated that *Little* was inapplicable because KU's governing board had initiated the library fee without legislative approval.[50] As formulated by a local newspaper, *Litchman* concluded that the constitutional mandate to be "open" did not require a university to be "free."[51]

This sort of interpretation heralded a steady increase in fees at state universities in the years following World War I, when inflation and enrollment increases combined to stress institutional budgets. By the middle of the 1920s, fees at some public institutions approached the tuition rates charged by some private colleges.[52] Confident in the constitutionality of fees in the wake of *Litchman*, Washington legislators endowed the university's governing board with the authority to increase or establish fees in 1919. Ten years later, the university president told students that he would have to reduce enrollment, dismiss faculty, or stop purchasing supplies unless the school increased fees. A dean cited *Priest* while reassuring the governor that an additional "fee" was more palatable than a "tuition" hike.[53] Although *Little* had temporarily restrained KU's governing board, the Kansas legislature authorized fees in 1902 (soon after returning to Republican control) and enacted steady increases during the 1920s.[54] In Virginia, the legislature required the state university to collect a minimum of forty dollars from each student in 1926, only two years after it had limited the institution to a *maximum* charge of the same amount.[55] And whereas Texas lawmakers had celebrated the lack of tuition at the state university and criticized the "excessive" fees at other state colleges as late as 1927, they authorized several new charges just six years afterward.[56]

By the end of the 1930s, tuition and fees had become widely accepted at public institutions of higher education in states with and without express legislative or constitutional approval for these charges. The onset of the Great Depression pushed greater numbers of students to take out loans to cover these costs. Although he championed a wide range of social welfare programs, even President Franklin Roosevelt believed that the government was not obligated to provide financial support "just because a boy wants to go to college."[57] This policy shift coincided with rulings that continued to uphold administrative authority over tuition at public colleges. In 1932, the Mississippi Supreme Court allowed a public teachers college to charge tuition. As in *Litchman*, the court concluded that institutions of higher education were not beholden to a provision regarding "free public schools" in the state constitution.[58] Twelve years later, the Supreme Judicial Court of Massachusetts ruled that another public teachers college could impose tuition, even though the legislature had only authorized charges for nonresidents. The court found no constitutional obstacle and determined that tuition policy fell within the college's authority over "general management." Epitomizing the spirit of deference, the court stated that the matter should be "left in the hands of those best qualified to do so by reason of intimate knowledge of the details of administration." Drawing on an emerging principle of administrative law, the opinion also cited a precedent that allowed the state Department of Public Health to chlorinate municipal water supplies without direct legislative approval.[59]

Using similar reasoning, state courts permitted administrators to enact a number of other miscellaneous fees. Twenty years after *Connell*, the Supreme Court of Oklahoma allowed the governing board of the state university to fund a student union building and football stadium by requiring students to pay an activities fee.[60] In 1934, the Supreme Court of Montana also sanctioned a student fee that defrayed the cost of a student center. The ruling suggested that the court might have rejected a fee that directly funded instruction but took no issue with a fee devoted to extracurricular activities.[61] That same year, the Supreme Court of Georgia allowed the state university to collect fees that were earmarked for construction of dormitories and a gymnasium. The court stated that it would only question a governing board if presented with evidence that proved an obvious "abuse of discretion." The ruling instructed lower court judges to scan statutes for specific limits to the university's authority rather than looking for express authorization for every policy.[62] When a student attempted to contest a student union fee in Texas, a state court also had "no difficulty" upholding the policy, especially because it considered attendance to be a privilege rather than a right.[63]

Yet it is important to note that these regular increases to tuition and fees did not mean that states objected to subsidizing public higher education.[64] The proportion of state budgets dedicated to higher education remained static between 1932 and 1957, but the absolute level of funding increased by a factor of eight.[65] These subsidies raised the stakes attached to the practice of charging preferential rates to state residents. The distinction between in-state and out-of-state tuition was predicated on the rationale that residents or their families not only paid state taxes but also were more likely to remain after graduation and use their education for the benefit of the state.[66] Although residency was tangential to the case, *Priest* had sanctioned the practice of in-state tuition as early as 1882. The decision encouraged courts in other jurisdictions to defer to residency distinctions as long as they were defined in some reasonable fashion.[67] In

1922, the Supreme Court of California cemented judicial support for this practice by ruling that a nonresident surcharge did not violate the state's constitutional guarantee of equal protection. The court concluded that the University of California's out-of-state tuition policy amounted to a reasonable "exercise of discretion."[68]

However, in something of an exception to the supremacy of academic deference in this era, public institutions lost each of the three other residency cases that were reported during the first half of the twentieth century. An Ohio court ordered the University of Cincinnati to define a student as a municipal resident (a status that conferred tuition-free education) in 1901 and again in 1954. The first decision emphasized the intentions of two recent migrants, while the latter decision ruled that a student could be a resident of Cincinnati even if he was not a citizen of the United States.[69] And in 1960, the Supreme Court of Idaho rejected the state college's practice of labeling students who had been born elsewhere as nonresidents regardless of how long they had lived in the state.[70] Yet these results did not necessarily trouble administrators, who did not always relish their power to determine residency status. One state university registrar confessed that it was not only burdensome to enforce a nonresident tuition policy but also antithetical to his school's interest in recruiting a large and diverse student body. Another administrator reported that his obligation to be on the lookout for dishonest residency claims was "the bane of [his] existence."[71]

Aside from the specific practices invalidated in these residency cases, administrative (and legislative) authority over tuition policies withstood all reported challenges from 1915 to 1960. Whereas *Little* and *Connell* had limited the ability of state universities to institute new charges, every subsequent ruling condoned tuition increases and other miscellaneous fees. In the process of deferring to these policies, courts tacitly agreed that the collective public benefits of free higher education did not justify restrictive interpretations of the laws governing tuition and fees.

Scholarships

Needless to say, state universities continued to champion their service to the public and (outside of the courtroom) never argued that this element of their mission was overshadowed by the advantages enjoyed by individual graduates. Yet in two revealing scholarship cases, one litigated during the 1890s and the other during the 1910s, state courts endorsed that very perception. Skepticism about the public benefits of free higher education lay at the core of these rulings—both of which invalidated scholarships programs after concluding that they did not serve the state as a whole.

In the nineteenth century, many state universities reserved a number of scholarships to students hailing from each county or legislative district.[72] According to the legal norms of the time, these tax-supported scholarships could only pass muster if their recipients performed concrete services that benefited the general public. This relatively narrow perspective on taxation developed in the wake the Panic of 1873, which precipitated increasingly strict rulings about the kinds of "public purposes" that could be the proper beneficiaries of tax revenue. Promulgated by Judge Thomas M. Cooley of the Michigan Supreme Court, this doctrine evolved out of decisions that invalidated municipal bonds issued to railroad companies. Judge Cooley's influential treatise on the limits of legislative authority concluded that these bonds failed to provide a *direct service* to the *entire population* of those jurisdictions. This definition of public purposes flourished in part because it combined conservative antiredistributive ideology with Jacksonian concerns about elitist misuse of state funds. The doctrine was intended to prevent the state from serving the interests of the masses or the interests of plutocrats, rather than the public in its entirety.[73]

In the realm of taxation, the public purposes doctrine found its most important early expression in the United States Supreme Court case of *Loan Association v. City of Topeka*, which thwarted subsidies that had been granted to a construction company. "To aid private enterprises and build up private fortunes," stated the court, "is none the less a robbery because it is done under the forms of law and is called taxation."[74] Issued in 1874, the decision epitomized the desire of nineteenth-century jurists to stamp out "class legislation" that favored particular segments of the population.[75] Although the public purposes doctrine could apply to the privileged as much as to the disenfranchised, courts tended to express particular revulsion toward social welfare policies. Because Cooley had argued that "public" expenditures should be defined according to "settled usage," the doctrine promoted the invalidation of any new areas of state responsibility.[76]

Although ultimately accepted as appropriate recipients of tax revenue, state universities initially posed a special challenge to the judges charged with interpreting the public purposes doctrine. By definition, appropriation bills for institutions of "higher" education could be considered class legislation because they directly benefited small segments of the population. As I mentioned in the first chapter, even high schools encountered critics who argued that only elementary schools provided the sort of universal service that merited state funding.[77] It is not surprising, therefore, that public colleges faced similar challenges. For example, periodic suits contested appropriations to the Kentucky Agricultural and Mechanical College until the early twentieth century.[78]

To those who questioned whether legislatures should fund public colleges in the first place, scholarship programs that served a fraction of the student body seemed like obvious examples of class legislation. Some commentators suggested that free tuition, in general, approximated a morally corrosive form of socialism. For example, University of Nebraska president E. Benjamin Andrews believed that free tuition may have been necessary during the infancy of public higher education but had been "abused" by subsequent generations of disengaged and ungrateful students.[79] Scholarships set aside for a subset of students could seem especially problematic because they could stigmatize recipients or create a class of dependent "weaklings."[80] Others worried that scholarships were susceptible to becoming currency for political patronage or a scheme for recruiting athletes.[81]

Yet whereas general state scholarships could be challenged on the grounds that they directed public funds to individual beneficiaries, financial aid programs that rewarded *direct* public service were almost universally accepted as valid uses of tax revenue during the late nineteenth and early twentieth centuries. For example, despite the potential violation of the boundary between church and state, legislatures routinely subsidized the education of students who intended to enter the ministry. In Kentucky, where scrutiny of public funding had been particularly intense, legislators authorized the state university to waive tuition for any student who trained to lead a "white religious denomination."[82] The legislature of North Carolina directed the state university to admit ministry candidates free of charge (children of ministers enjoyed the same benefit).[83] Some private colleges also discounted the tuition charged to these students. The writer Walter Hines Page, for instance, switched to the tuition-free divinity school of Randolph-Macon College when he found himself unable to pay the bill for the college's arts and sciences program.[84]

Another common, and relatively uncontroversial, form of scholarship provided free higher education to veterans or their children. These programs started with efforts to assist soldiers who were wounded in the Civil War. Virginia began to offer free enrollment in the state university to disabled soldiers even before the end of hostilities.[85] Illinois created scholarships to compensate the children of veterans, especially those whose parents were injured or deceased. New York continued to provide financial aid to the children of Civil War veterans for three decades.[86] Scholarships for World War I veterans were also common.[87] These programs survived two legal challenges in which courts ruled that expressing public appreciation and promoting patriotism were legitimate uses of tax revenue.[88] During World War II, the United States Congress essentially nationalized these state programs when it passed the GI Bill.[89]

Many states also subsidized the higher education of teachers without facing serious legal objections. After all, teaching was a relatively low-paying profession that provided a direct service to virtually the entire population. New York State sought to increase the supply of instructors by providing free higher education to students who agreed to teach after graduation.[90] This policy spread to other states during the nineteenth century and eventually encompassed tuition at state colleges and normal schools.[91] In 1881, North Carolina revised an earlier scholarship law in order to require recipients to teach for a period equal to at least half the time that they attended the state university. The statute also required candidates to provide an affidavit from a witness affirming that they possessed the "capacity for usefulness."[92] Some programs, such as scholarships for native Alaskans, intended to recruit teachers to serve particular communities.[93]

Scholarships for agricultural students, another common beneficiary of state subsidies, were also never subjected to a reported suit.[94] To some extent, these scholarships simply reflected the clout of rural legislators. The Morrill Act of 1862 also prompted state colleges to recruit agricultural and mechanical students.[95] For example, one of the first appropriation bills for the Texas state agricultural and mechanical college included a scholarship for one student from each legislative district, provided that half studied agriculture and half studied the mechanic arts.[96] These sorts of scholarships were justified by their supposed contribution to a state's economic development. As characterized by the Massachusetts legislature, the "principle benefits" of an agricultural college were presumed to flow to all the farmers in the state rather than merely to the graduates themselves.[97] In contrast, the study of law or medicine was typically presumed to be a relatively self-serving pursuit that was unworthy of direct public support. In an antebellum suit, a professor at Indiana University believed that it was safe to assume that a county scholarship program would not apply to law students.[98] Indeed, most state colleges that did not charge tuition for agricultural or liberal arts students still required payments from students in legal or medical departments, and colleges with limited numbers of scholarships were often directed to exclude students in those professional schools.[99]

An additional category of scholarships emerged during the early twentieth century in order to prevent future demands for state support. In 1912, New Jersey legislators voted to waive tuition charges for blind students who could not afford to attend college. During the next decade, seven more states followed suit. These statutes, which were a part of a broader shift toward "assimilationist" disability policies, were intended to impart skills that would enable graduates to become financially self-sufficient. Following the First World War, federal programs for wounded veterans further broadened public support for students with disabilities.[100]

Supporters of scholarships for ministers, veterans, teachers, farmers, or the disabled could reassure taxpayers that these programs encouraged direct service to the state, paid for past services, or prevented public dependency. Yet the legal rationale for the most common form of state scholarships was based on a more diffuse sort of public value. These scholarship programs assisted a limited number of students per county on the basis of locally administered examinations. The fundamental goal was to promote college access—courts in New York and South Carolina even ruled that students who were already enrolled in any form of higher education (including normal schools or remedial classes) were precluded from receiving this type of support.[101] Yet in order to satisfy the public purposes doctrine, universities had to persuade courts that these scholarships provided broad-based benefits rather than just promoting the welfare of individual beneficiaries, no matter how poor or meritorious. Whereas the legal distinction between public and private goods had been relatively blurry during the mid-nineteenth century, these categories became more distinct in Gilded Age courtrooms.[102] At the same time, the primary emphasis of American higher education was shifting from civic to vocational training.[103] By the

1920s, even a journal that usually disseminated progressive educational views considered the personal economic benefits of college to be more substantial than the public services provided by graduates.[104]

At the turn of the century, this perspective ignited a lawsuit that temporarily halted state scholarships at the University of Missouri (MU).[105] The scholarship program had been established in 1895 in response to the lack of regional representation in MU's student body—the university failed to attract any students from dozens of counties.[106] Legislators hoped that they could address this imbalance by providing full scholarships to one student per county (although the state assembly had abolished in-state tuition in 1872, MU continued to charge entrance and incidental fees). The scholarship program was funded by new taxes on estates, corporate charters, and patent medicines.[107]

MU president Richard Jesse was concerned that the scholarships would obligate the university to accept students who could not meet its academic standards. A former state legislator encouraged Jesse to embrace the scholarship program in order to increase MU's popularity within assembly districts that had previously sent few students to the campus. He acknowledged that large numbers of students might stress MU's facilities but advised Jesse to let the university's adversaries do the dirty work of undoing the law.[108] Similarly, a trustee recommended that Jesse "let things drift, and be tolerably blind and deaf." Jesse agreed to remain silent despite haphazard local implementation of the program. County judges, who were supposed to supervise examination and selection procedures, sometimes administered flimsy tests or indulged in nepotism. Contrary to the requirements of the scholarship law, some recipients were clearly able to pay their own fees. One county court simply refused to participate in the process.[109]

President Jesse would not have to look the other way for long, because a suit filed on behalf of two estates invalidated the scholarship program three years after its passage. The legal team representing the estates included the Missouri Supreme Court judge William Muir Williams, who recused himself from the case in order to contest the law. Judge Williams and his colleagues based their suit on the public purposes doctrine by arguing that the estate tax transferred state funds "into the pocket of some gentleman who is attending the state university." Taxing one citizen for the benefit of another, they suggested, was the equivalent of theft.[110] In keeping with prominent authorities on the subject, the brief contended that taxation could only be justified if it provided direct benefits to the state. The attorneys cited a series of cases in which courts struck down subsidies for businesses that claimed to provide residual public benefits in the form of increased employment and tax revenue. In Kansas, a court even ruled that the state could not allocate tax revenue to provide drought relief to farmers.[111]

In contrast with financial aid for veterans or teachers, the brief continued, the county scholarships failed to require recipients to provide particular public services. As a result, their education might simply further "their own private and individual advancement and benefit."[112] If the scholarships were limited to paupers who might otherwise strain the social fabric, then perhaps an argument could be made in favor of their public purpose. Otherwise the law devoted state funds to privileged individuals so that they could receive an "elegant and ennobling" education free of charge.[113] Finally, opponents of the law repeated a common ideological critique of financial aid by claiming that the nation's "glory" resided in the ability of poor students to work their way through college. The brief also added a new wrinkle to this argument by suggesting that easing the path to college for students who earned high scores on the county examinations unfairly increased their advantages compared to "their less favored fellow citizens."[114]

Despite his personal reservations, President Jesse asked former governor William "Gum-Shoe Bill" Stone to defend the scholarship law. Stone had represented the southwestern region of Missouri and had been nominated by Democrats in order to attract support from the state's agrarian counties. He was a graduate of MU, yet he continued to dress in a folksy manner while inveighing against railroad companies, the gold standard, and urban elites. As governor, Stone had supported the university to the point where Jesse privately considered him to be "a source of comfort and a tower of strength."[115] Stone's brief began to counter the opposition's charges of socialistic "paternalism" by reminding the court that Thomas Jefferson had supported university scholarships.[116] Next, Stone argued that American institutions and property rights would be more secure in a society "where the talent of no class is debarred from higher education."[117] Conceding that some scholarship recipients might fail to promote the interests of the state, the brief asserted that MU would be more "effective for the people" as a whole if it cultivated a Jeffersonian "aristocracy of talent" that was immune to demagoguery.[118] President Jesse had once made a similar case on behalf of the "indirect" yet "almost boundless" trickle-down benefits of higher education (such as the political, commercial, and cultural leadership of alumni) when he thanked the state for its assistance in the wake of a campus fire.[119]

Perhaps influenced by the participation of Judge Williams or by President Jesse's unenthusiastic response to the law, the Missouri Supreme Court rejected Stone's argument and declared the scholarship program unconstitutional. In a ruling titled *State ex rel. Garth v. Switzler*, the court concluded that the scholarships did not promote a public purpose as defined by the traditional functions of state government. The court cited *Loan Association v. Topeka* and Cooley's treatise in order to support its determination that "indirect" public benefits did not justify the expenditure of state funds. Thus, no matter how beneficial the state university might be, the new estate tax was invalid because it favored certain individuals without requiring direct service to the state. Absent any such reciprocal requirements, the scholarships amounted to a "pure and simple gift of public money by the state to private individuals for their own private use."[120]

Garth also repeated the petitioners' discussion of state overreach and condemnation of public regulation. The court promised to strike down any statute that "maximizes the government" while stifling "all motive for individual effort and laudable ambition." The opinion praised the State of Missouri for providing a free common school education and then informing young people that it would spend no more for their "private benefit."[121] A local newspaper announced that *Garth* had branded the scholarship law as "pure paternalism."[122] The legislature, however, simply passed a new version of the scholarship law that was modified to withstand constitutional scrutiny.[123] *Garth* resulted in only a momentary break in the program and did not dissuade other states from continuing or enacting these types of scholarships after the turn of the century.[124]

Still, county scholarships were dealt another temporary blow in the fall of 1917, when the Kentucky Court of Appeals struck down a similar policy.[125] As mentioned earlier, public higher education had endured regular challenges to state appropriations in Kentucky. Nevertheless, the legislature provided scholarships to the University of Kentucky (UK) for a small number of students from each congressional district beginning in the 1880s.[126] As in Missouri, the head of the state university opposed the law. President Henry S. Barker and UK's governing board commissioned an internal report that criticized the program for causing a "regrettable drain" on resources. The committee also believed that the scholarships were subject to political influence and alienated students whose applications were rejected. It is also possible that Barker's opposition to the program was fueled by a rivalry with James K. Patterson, his long-serving predecessor who frequently criticized Barker's leadership and pointedly refused to vacate the presidential mansion.[127] Regardless, Barker, who had previously served on the state's court of appeals, filed suit to invalidate the scholarship law.[128]

Barker argued that the scholarship program violated two elements of Kentucky's constitution. First, he claimed that the scholarships caused UK to illegally classify students into two groups by charging some and educating others for free. Second, Barker repeated the argument that had proved decisive in *Garth*—that the scholarships used tax revenue to grant special privileges to individuals in violation of the state's constitutional prohibition against making such awards "except in consideration of public services."[129] A circuit court judge rejected both of these prongs. He ruled that the scholarships classified students on the reasonable basis of merit and promoted the public good by raising the level of education within the state. Invariably, the judge concluded, college graduates would directly or indirectly become the teachers and leaders of Kentucky.[130]

Barker appealed the decision and urged the higher court to demand a stricter definition of public service. He conceded that most graduates, while capable and "well meaning," did "no more than they ought to do and no more than the public expects them to do." Indeed, every citizen provided a benefit to the state simply by leading "a life of honesty, diligence, industry, and patriotism" regardless of whether or not they studied at UK. Barker contended that tax-supported scholarships for individuals must require concrete or exceptional services in return. For example, scholarships could be earned by performing "heroic deeds," such as serving in the military. Truly brilliant students might win scholarships if they exhibited "inventive genius or great mental endowment" that was likely to translate into unusual benefits for the state. Aside from these instances, Barker maintained that scholarship recipients must teach in a public school or perform other specific civic functions.[131]

The attorneys who represented the scholarship recipients argued that the program had been a core part of the state's rationale for supporting a university. During Kentucky's constitutional convention of 1890, advocates for public higher education responded to those who sought to devote all funding to the common schools by pointing out that a certain percentage of college students could attend the institution on a tuition-free basis.[132] The students' representatives also stated that it was reasonable to distinguish between poor and wealthy students rather than depriving some youth of an education "for the sole reason that it can not be granted to all."[133] They claimed that invalidating the scholarships on those grounds would also jeopardize the legality of subsidies for teaching candidates or students with disabilities.[134]

The appellate court sided with critics of the scholarships and reversed the lower court's decision. The court agreed that the program provided special privileges to students without requiring that they serve as "benefactors" to the public in the strict sense outlined in Barker's brief. The opinion cited pensions for Civil War veterans as an example of the sort of specific and direct public service that could justify tax-supported benefits. The court also noted that many UK students did not even study agriculture or the mechanic arts, subjects that were presumed to be most likely to promote economic development. The opinion acknowledged "some difficulty in defining 'public services' as here used, with a satisfactory degree of precision" but concluded that common law suggested that public funds could only reward past services rather than future potential.[135] Two years later, the same court ruled that UK's agricultural extension program contributed to a valid public purpose because it generated wealth for the whole state rather than "a few favored boys" from each county.[136]

These scholarship rulings proved to be atypical and short lived. The public purposes maxim that had been at the heart of both decisions was rarely interpreted in such a strict fashion by the turn of the twentieth century, when state courts became more accommodating toward government spending for public works and other purposes.[137] By the 1920s, when thousands of land grant college students had already benefited from county scholarships, few Americans would have thought to question their constitutionality. The Great Depression and the Second World War encouraged even more judicial tolerance of state expenditures.[138] Although race-based programs and the balance between merit-based and need-based scholarships have been subjects of contemporary debate, twenty-first-century legislators and judges remain unlikely to doubt that scholarships, in general, are a permissible use of tax revenue. The practice of charging tuition and fees at state universities has also become an ordinary feature of American higher education. Courts united in favor of greater flexibility for administrators during the early twentieth century, while legislatures revised the statutes that had presented potential obstacles to tuition and fees.

Yet although the earlier objections to fees and scholarships no longer have traction, these cases demonstrate that judicial deference toward higher education was less than absolute. Secondly, these suits indicate the uncomfortable extent to which public universities found themselves advocating for deference by implicitly or explicitly arguing that free higher education did not necessarily benefit the state as a whole. In the process, these perceptions contributed to the justification of new fees while also jeopardizing two scholarship programs. Altogether, these early tuition cases indicate that academic deference, in itself, provides an incomplete summary of legal history as well as an occasionally problematic rationale for institutional authority.

6

Child Support

In the spring of 1953, a father told a Michigan trial court that he would only pay for his children's college tuition if he could continue to enjoy "their affection and their company." A trial court judge rejected this reasoning and ordered the father to support his college-bound daughter even though she had sided with her mother during their divorce proceedings. The judge concluded that the daughter's stellar grade point average justified an extension of child support until the age of twenty-one.[1] If this case had transpired three decades earlier, the outcome would almost certainly have been different. Traditionally, American courts had ruled that questions related to college tuition should be left to the discretion of parents. Paying for schooling beyond the primary level was always a choice, never an obligation.[2]

Then, beginning in the 1920s, judges began to consider whether to order divorced middle-class parents to pay college tuition and related expenses. Some courts started to mandate additional child support if they believed that college was a "necessary" expense for particular young people. Since child support was intended to approximate predivorce financial circumstances, these suits required courts to predict, in effect, whether a child had been on a college-bound trajectory prior to the dissolution of his or her parents' marriage.[3] During the midcentury decades when college became a defining feature of middle-class America, courts adopted increasingly lenient standards for making this determination. In the process, courts reevaluated the significance of many traditional barriers to higher education, including social class, aptitude, ambition, and gender. Child support judgments began to exhibit a wider range of attitudes about who should attend college and to what end.[4]

These perspectives surfaced in reported cases between 1920 (the year of the first published college support order) and 1971 (when many states decreased the age of majority—a change that dramatically lowered the number of child support suits involving college-bound minors).[5] Like other college access cases discussed in this book, these cases constitute a particular subset (most child support cases were unreported or did not include disputes about college expenses) that may share tendencies that could have colored their outcomes.[6] Courts also based some of their rulings on straightforward interpretation of statutes or divorce agreements without delving into broader commentary about higher education. Yet other opinions included lengthy discussions of college access, especially in jurisdictions where the relevant child support laws did not provide clear guidance.[7] And in addition to judicial editorializing, many of these proceedings preserved familial arguments about college that otherwise would have remained largely invisible to historians.

Although these college access cases differ in fundamental ways from the suits against institutions discussed in the preceding chapters, child support litigation provides another means for chronicling the development of perceptions about American higher education. When they adjudicated child support cases, American judges revealed that their attitudes toward college access remained fluid even during the midcentury decades when their deference to academia was most pronounced. Whereas courts almost uniformly defined higher education as a privilege in suits against institutions between 1910 and 1960, they started to regard college as almost indispensible for middle- and upper-class students in the realm of family law during that same era. Judges justified this more expansive approach to child support by citing not only the individual advantages of a degree (in terms of social status and professional training) but also the broader public benefits of mass higher education (in terms of economic growth and engaged citizenship). Especially during the enrollment boom of the 1950s and 1960s, when the realization of universal college access appeared to be just over the horizon, judges stretched the boundaries of child support law because they believed that higher education had become a legitimate state interest. In the process, the expansion of child support reduced a financial barrier that had impeded access to higher education for an increasingly large segment of American students.

Middlebury College v. Chandler: Higher Education as a Luxury

Prior to the 1920s, American judges agreed that college education was a luxury. A Vermont ruling, *Middlebury College v. Chandler*, settled this question for more than eighty years.[8] In 1844, Vermont's high court ruled in favor of an orphaned student who had failed to pay his tuition. The court reasoned that the student was a minor and therefore only able to enter into contracts for "necessary" goods and services. The student's attorney had argued that tuition was not a necessary expense because a college education was "grossly inconsistent with the circumstances" of a boy who had grown up "entirely destitute of means or expectations." The court agreed, adding that "extensive attainments in literature and science" were indulgences of "private enjoyment." The opinion, however, mentioned other students for whom higher education might be considered necessary, such as young men possessing great wealth, high "station in society," or "peculiar indications of genius." The court also indicated that vocational training could be regarded as more necessary than the "adornment" of a classical curriculum. Finally, the ruling suggested that higher education might someday provide indispensible public benefits, especially if "the mass of our citizens" ever attended college.[9]

Despite these caveats, *Middlebury* undermined arguments for the legal necessity of higher education in contract cases for decades to come.[10] At the turn of the century, a New Jersey court extended the logic of *Middlebury* to the realm of divorce law by declaring that noncustodial parents should not be compelled to pay for law school or other unnecessary forms of professional training. The court ruled that higher education was "a special advantage" rather than a necessity and added that the state should generally steer clear of second-guessing paternal choices.[11]

During the early twentieth century, however, several contract cases signaled that state courts remained aware of the potential for extenuating circumstances, as outlined at the end of *Middlebury*. In 1902, the Supreme Court of Rhode Island commented that a father might be responsible for college tuition depending upon a minor's "social position, fortune, prospects, age, circumstances and general situation."[12] The Supreme Judicial Court of Maine ruled that a correspondence course in electrical engineering was unnecessary but felt moved to note, "What might be considered necessaries for one infant, would not be so considered for another whose status is different as to rank, fortune and social position."[13] By 1919, a legal encyclopedia observed that the definition of a "necessary" educational expense for a minor depended upon "the customs of the social circle in which he moves and is likely to move."[14] Although few of these rulings found that college was necessary for the students in question, this pattern would begin to change in the 1920s, when child support cases supplanted contract disputes as the main source of debate over the legal necessity of higher education.

Esteb v. Esteb: Higher Education as a Necessity

The Supreme Court of Washington State heralded this transition when it decided *Esteb v. Esteb*, a case that examined whether or not a divorced father was obligated to defray the college expenses of his estranged daughter. Whereas common law had dictated that parents only needed to provide children with an education consistent with their "station in life," the court concluded that twentieth-century judges should also consider the ideal of social mobility and the demands of modern citizenship when resolving child support cases involving college students.[15] Issued in 1926, *Esteb* prompted other state courts to decide whether college should be viewed as a luxury or a necessity for an increasing number of young people with divorced parents.

The divorce rate had been growing during the two decades preceding *Esteb* and further accelerated in the 1920s, when large numbers of wartime marriages unraveled. By 1928, one out of every six American marriages ended in divorce. This rate leveled off during the Great Depression before continuing a steady increase through the 1970s.[16] Legislatures and courts responded to the rising number of children with divorced parents by placing increasing trust in the power of maternal care. By 1936, alongside a general increase in women's legal authority, wives had gained the right to petition for custody in forty-two states. Meanwhile, judges exhibited a growing enthusiasm for motherhood, perhaps as a result of a long campaign waged by child welfare advocates.[17] Noncustodial fathers, of course, were not always content to defer to maternal judgments, especially when it came to decisions about whether their children merited higher education. These conflicts became so commonplace that a professional journal for high school guidance counselors encouraged proactive outreach to divorced fathers.[18] Needless to say, midcentury courts faced a wave of child support cases that included these disputes over college expenses.

In contrast with their nineteenth-century predecessors, the judges who heard these suits felt a relatively strong obligation to promote the state's interest in remedying the affairs of troubled families. Confident in their authority to overrule paternal decisions, Progressive legislators and judges began to regard the state as a "superparent" responsible for preventing neglect and ensuring school attendance. By the 1930s, state laws across the nation required noncustodial parents to provide for their children.[19] The Superior Court of Pennsylvania, for example, concluded that judges should scrutinize child support proceedings because they were obligated to encourage each child to become "an element of strength, rather than one of weakness, in the social fabric."[20] With *Esteb*, the Washington Supreme Court paved the way for using this rationale to justify child support orders for college students.[21] In the process, *Esteb* outlined questions that would be debated in subsequent child support cases involving students in a range of circumstances.[22]

The case began in 1925, when May Esteb sought an extension of child support for her eighteen-year-old daughter, Carmelita. Having excelled in Latin and Greek, Carmelita graduated early from high school, wished to attend the College of Puget Sound, and dreamed of becoming an English teacher.[23] Initially, her mother's attorney downplayed the expense of Carmelita's college plans, arguing instead that May had begun to suffer from poor health and was unable to support her children.[24] Estranged from his family, Horace Esteb denied a personal solicitation from Carmelita when she turned eighteen and her initial child support order expired. According to Carmelita, her father said she would not "get a damn cent."[25] Horace's attorney argued that his client, a railroad conductor who had been institutionalized because of mental illness, could not afford additional payments. Horace earned $3,000 a year (roughly $37,000 in 2010 dollars) and owned some property. His attorney also cited *Middlebury* and stated that Carmelita's college education was not a legal necessity. The attorney claimed that college was inconsistent with Carmelita's "station in life," since her parents were "common American citizens," neither of whom attended high school or associated with college-educated friends.[26] He argued that the career path of Horace's older daughter, who worked as a stenographer after graduating from high school, proved that Carmelita did not need to attend college.[27] Finally, the attorney questioned Carmelita's aptitude for teaching by alleging that she had a speech impediment and possessed an inflated estimate of her own abilities.[28]

Carmelita responded that she deserved the opportunity to train for the career of her choice. She also suggested that she was unfit for a secretarial position because she had pursued a college preparatory sequence in high school and "wasn't adapted to commercial work." Carmelita reported that her teacher had concluded that she was "too nervous to make a good typist." During cross-examination, Carmelita emphasized that college would prepare her for more rewarding and more lucrative work. Finally, Carmelita stated that her speech difficulties were the result of an obstruction in her nasal passage that could be remedied through surgery. The judge ordered Horace Esteb to continue supporting his daughter but skirted the question of whether she was entitled to a college education. The ruling explained that the extension of child support might or might not be used to defray college expenses.[29]

When the parties reargued their case upon appeal, the Washington Supreme Court provided a more direct endorsement of tuition support for Carmelita and other students in similar circumstances. Written by Judge William D. Askren, the *Esteb* opinion agreed that Carmelita should attend college because she had a "genius" for academics and was "exceptionally well-fitted for her chosen vocation." Judge Askren also stated that students who were denied college degrees would be at a disadvantage in the labor market. More significantly, the ruling sustained the decision of the lower court on "broader ground" that echoed Carmelita's comments about social mobility. *Esteb* proposed that judges should reject precedents that emphasized "the station of the minor in society" (one judge dissented with this aspect of the opinion). Ordering college support for the daughter of a train conductor was a remarkable break with precedent at a time when only 8 percent of college students had fathers who were tradespersons or laborers.[30] And yet Judge Askren could hardly be considered a political radical. Prior to serving on the bench, he was known primarily for prosecuting members of the Industrial Workers of the World. Coincidentally, Askren's own daughter was on the verge of attending college when he wrote the *Esteb* opinion (she would graduate from the University of Washington in 1931).[31]

Instead of radicalism, *Esteb* reflected a realist impulse to interpret the law in light of social change and to consider its relationship with public policy.[32] Judge Askren observed that *Middlebury* was the product of an era when relatively few students attended college. Noting that eighty years had passed since that ruling, *Esteb* urged courts to "take into consideration the progress of society, and the attendant requirements upon the citizens of today." Judge Askren also suggested that courts should not limit their deliberations to the personal and vocational factors that had been debated by the Estebs and their attorneys. Although the relationship between college and citizenship had not been raised during the trial, Judge Askren argued that legislative appropriations for public universities indicated that the state aimed to increase the number of informed and engaged citizens. Finally, the opinion concluded that courts should generally trust maternal judgments when weighing whether a child was suited for college.[33]

Horace Esteb died shortly after the court issued this opinion, but his second wife petitioned for a rehearing on behalf of his estate. The petition accused Judge Askren of ruling that college was beneficial, rather than determining whether it was "regarded as essential by the common opinion of mankind for persons occupying a similar position in society." The attorney representing Horace's estate noted that the proportion of Washington residents who attended college was nowhere near the sort of mass higher education envisioned by the opinion. "To keep pace with progress is desirable," acknowledged the attorney, "but this decision is so far in advance of what is true today, or perhaps ever will be true, that it is radical and revolutionary, rather than progressive." The petition pointed out that Judge Askren had suggested that "almost any child that has the ambition to do so can go to college" regardless of paternal intent or finances.[34] May Esteb's attorney responded by admitting that he had downplayed Carmelita's college plans in his original brief because he never expected the court to provide such an enthusiastic endorsement. Emboldened by the opinion, however, he dismissed *Middlebury* as a relic of "an age when the son of a poor man was but little better than a serf or a slave."[35]

The state supreme court rejected the petition for rehearing and continued to endorse the thrust of *Esteb* in later cases. In one ruling, the court even ordered a noncustodial father to invest funds just in case his young son should decide to attend college at some later date. This opinion explained that even though the father had originally been a laborer (who then started a small trucking business and accumulated some property), all sorts of parents sacrificed in order to pay for higher education.[36] *Esteb* also influenced decisions in other jurisdictions. In 1937, a Washington, DC, court ordered a father to continue paying child support for a daughter who was attending a business college.[37] Five years later, a California court ruled that the children of a divorced police officer could use their own earnings to pay for college rather than having this income counted as contributions toward their mother's expenses.[38]

These opinions signaled the extent to which college had become a common middle-class aspiration during the interwar period, when higher education emerged as the standard route to a wide range of professional and business pursuits. Corporations began to recruit on campus, while colleges offered more vocational courses and established job placement offices to match graduates with employers.[39] In 1938, before the nation recovered from the Great Depression, a survey of thirteen thousand young people found that just 17 percent of college graduates reported dissatisfaction with "dead end" jobs, compared with 44 percent of high school graduates; college graduates also earned a median wage that was 45 percent higher.[40] Whereas college had once been denigrated as four years of arcane lectures and moral dissipation, popular publications began to recommend higher education, even for those who aimed for careers in business or intended to stop working after marriage. According to a guidebook for prospective students, young people who lacked a college degree suffered from a "social stigma," while graduates enjoyed a "magic key to happiness, success and riches."[41] *Scribner's Magazine* observed that "the average American parent" hoped to send his or her children to college because the Great Depression had made education seem like "a weapon to use against adverse economic conditions."[42]

Nevertheless, *Esteb* did not immediately transform child support law.[43] Some judges and scholars questioned the decision because a relatively small number of young people actually attended college.[44] In 1930, an Indiana appeals court stated that higher education remained a luxury and overruled an extension of child support that a lower court had imposed on a wholesale coal dealer. The court doubted that the man would have paid for college even if he had stayed married, adding that it would be reasonable for some parents to believe that their children would develop better character if they supported themselves.[45] Seven years later, a California court overturned a child support order for a nineteen-year-old college student by noting that state law only compelled education until the age of sixteen. Denouncing "the alien philosophy that the child is the creature of the state," the ruling concluded that parents should decide for themselves whether to pay for college.[46]

More commonly, judges who objected to *Esteb* added a number of limiting conditions rather than rejecting its premise altogether. Courts sometimes denied requests for child support for students who had proven that they were capable of earning a living. While *Esteb* had ruled that Carmelita should not have to accept a "low pay job," judges in some other jurisdictions ruled that adult children who were able to secure employment were not entitled to parental support. In one such case, the Supreme Court of Arkansas sided with a father who had arranged for his daughter to get a clerical job after two years of study at a junior college. When the daughter refused the job and pursued a bachelor's degree, the court released the father from his divorce agreement, which had required payments until the child was "employed and self-supporting."[47] Judges who adopted this stance effectively denied all child support for sane, able-bodied college students who had reached the age of majority.[48]

Yet most courts entertained some requests for college support regardless of whether students were employed or employable. In 1931, the Supreme Court of New Hampshire ordered a father to pay for college even though his son had been able to find work during the summer.[49] Thirty years later, the Supreme Court of Mississippi upheld a child support order for a student who testified that she was able bodied but not "trained." The daughter added that she planned to major in commercial art and could not think of "anything" that she could do without a college degree.[50] A Pennsylvania court was unmoved by a father who testified that his daughter had passed an examination qualifying her for a secretarial position at a steel company. While the court ultimately determined that the father could not afford to make additional payments, the ruling echoed *Esteb* by suggesting that they would consider students' *potential* for advancement rather than their ability to merely subsist. One judge added that higher education allowed qualified young people "to contribute to our society to the fullest extent of their abilities."[51] Similar attitudes predisposed many other courts to favor requests for child support on behalf of college students.

During the half century following *Esteb*, judges authorized these orders with increasing frequency, even in the states where courts had initially been most resistant. Courts sided with requests for additional funds or continuation of past support for college students in 60 percent (54/90) of reported cases between 1920 and 1970. Twenty of the cases that rejected support for students did not object on principle; they emphasized a parent's poverty, a lack of evidence regarding the child's aptitude, or the child's age. Therefore, judges affirmed the general principle of child support for college students in 82 percent (74/90) of cases. Some courts would only order support for college students if the noncustodial parent had entered into a voluntary agreement during the divorce or otherwise indicated a previous intent to pay for college.[52] Yet in cases that did not include evidence of any prior intent or agreement, judges still ruled on behalf of students 59 percent (40/68) of the time.[53] In California, for example, an appellate court instructed judges to disregard paternal intentions and consider the "broadest connotation" when determining what level of education was necessary for particular children.[54]

These broad interpretations became more common over time. Judges ordered child support for college students in 45 percent (9/20) of cases between 1920 and 1944, compared with 64 percent (45/70) of cases between 1945 and 1970.[55] As mentioned at the outset of this book, it is an oversimplification to label decisions as going either "for" or "against" students, since judges were not merely expressing sympathy (or lack thereof) for a plaintiff. However, since child support statutes, precedents, and agreements often included vague statements about "education," courts often had to decide whether to err on the side of the student or the noncustodial parent when faced with disputes over college tuition. These interpretations, along with the total number of cases considered, lend support to broad conclusions based upon a tally of wins and losses. Furthermore, it is important to note that two-thirds of the cases that rejected support for college students occurred in just four states (Pennsylvania, New York, New Jersey, and Indiana), and three of these states (Pennsylvania, New Jersey, and Indiana) changed course by the end of the 1960s.[56] Depending upon the circumstances (i.e., wealth, status, aptitude, and interests), courts even ruled that some students were entitled to the additional expense of attending a private rather than public institution.[57]

Mass Higher Education: Class, Aptitude, and Gender

Not only did midcentury courts increasingly favor child support for college students, but they also ordered these payments for students whose class background, high school performance, or gender had traditionally reduced their likelihood of enrollment (none of the reported cases mentioned racial identity).[58] Of course, courts sometimes continued to enforce more restrictive standards for awarding college support. In 1949, for example, a New Jersey judge explained that he evaluated a family's wealth and status in order to decide whether college would have seemed "normal" if the parents had remained married.[59] In 1960, an Ohio trial court ordered an increase in child support for a student after noting that the parents were educated, "top notch" individuals.[60]

However, other courts followed the lead of *Esteb* by regarding social class as a "transient" and relatively insignificant factor in college support cases.[61] In 1945, a Tennessee court came close to disregarding parental status altogether. The court compelled a father to support his daughter while she attended college even though neither the father nor the mother had experienced much in the way of formal education. The ruling concluded that a family's social class no longer factored into these disputes. Ultimately, the court praised the mother (who was working in a cannery) for striving to enable her daughter to "go farther" than she had.[62] A Missouri court adopted a similar stance when compelling payments from a train conductor who had only just returned to work after a period of unemployment.[63]

Needless to say, judges could only justify college support orders when a parent could plausibly afford to pay tuition or related expenses. Yet there were no self-evident boundaries separating parents who could pay from those who could not.[64] In a series of decisions during the mid-1960s, the Superior Court of Pennsylvania could agree only that parents who earned less than $40,000 a year (in 2010 dollars) were unable to afford additional support for children in college. They could not reach unanimous decisions regarding parents who earned between $40,000 and $60,000 a year, such as a postal worker, a machinist, and a beverage distributor.[65] The court acknowledged that "no mathematical rule can be formulated to determine how extensive the hardship upon a father must be before it will excuse him from supporting a child in college."[66] Because of inconsistent evidence in the trial records, it is not possible to measure these determinations systematically across all the cases examined in this chapter. Yet the overall trend suggests that judges became more willing to compel divorced middle-class parents to pay for college.[67]

Courts also became more likely to endorse child support orders for students who had ordinary or even subpar academic records. Certainly, judges were encouraged when a child had earned a high grade point average. A Mississippi judge, for example, noted that any high school student who graduated with "an excellent record" should be entitled to a college education.[68] Yet as early as the 1940s, many courts affirmed child support orders for typical students. The Supreme Court of Oregon rejected the argument of an attorney who claimed that *Esteb* should only influence the cases of students who earned exceptional grades.[69] The court ruled that a student only needed to exhibit "sufficient" aptitude, as evidenced by a high school diploma regardless of grade point average. The court determined that "attitude, character, desire for learning, and well-directed ambition" were as significant as academic ability. "A father who has lost the custody of his child," the court declared, "is asking that a most difficult task be performed if he insists that his child must be subjected to an aptitude test before he can be required to provide funds for further education." Invoking *Esteb*, the opinion also concluded that judges should generally defer to mothers' determination of their children's fitness for college.[70] In 1945, the Supreme Court of Michigan ordered a father to contribute to his daughter's college expenses even though she had been a C student in high school.[71] That same year, a Tennessee court agreed that a mother's assessment of her daughter's potential was sufficient evidence of academic aptitude despite an "average" transcript that included several Ds.[72]

These attitudes about college readiness continued to prevail during the 1960s. In 1963, an Alabama judge suggested that any student who gained admission to a state university had demonstrated enough aptitude to justify the continuation of child support.[73] A Maryland court affirmed a support order for a student even though his high school grades had disqualified him from attending any four-year public institutions in the state.[74] In 1968, a New Jersey court ordered payments for a college-bound son who had ranked in the middle of his high school class. Four years later, the court approved an order for a student even after acknowledging his history of "dubious scholastic ability and lackadaisical determination."[75]

These decisions echoed the prevailing beliefs of liberal policy makers, who looked forward to a new age of mass higher education and emphasized that ordinary students could benefit from college.[76] Most prominently, the Truman administration called for a 50 percent increase in enrollment.[77] The success of students who were subsidized by the GI Bill encouraged this more expansive vision of higher education. Even skeptics of ivory tower erudition, such as Alabama congressman John Rankin, argued that veterans deserved "just as much training as if they were going to Harvard and studying all the sociology and other ologies that might be afforded them." Altogether, veterans outperformed expectations based on their previous academic records, suggesting that an even broader swath of Americans could benefit from higher education.[78] By the 1960s, the United States Department of Labor believed that 97 percent of young people could profit from some form of higher education.[79] This ambition harmonized with public opinion. According to a poll administered in 1965, most Americans saw college as "practically the birthright" of every child.[80]

For most judges, this birthright extended to daughters as well as sons. True, women who pursued higher education in the middle of the twentieth century were often expected to sacrifice their academic goals for the sake of marriage and motherhood. Judges sometimes indicated that these attitudes had predisposed them to deny child support for college-bound daughters. The Superior Court of Pennsylvania ruled that a father did not have to support his daughter while she attended the College of New Rochelle because it was a mere "finishing school" for young women.[81] A decade later, that court rejected a similar suit after a father testified that his daughter was a cheerleader and destined to marry before graduation.[82]

On average, however, courts were somewhat *more* likely to rule in favor of college-bound daughters than college-bound sons. Out of a sample of cases that resulted in clear judgments for one side or another, daughters received payments 76 percent (16/21) of the time, while sons received payments 71 percent (24/34) of the time.[83] The size of this sample is too small to allow for conclusive analysis of change over time, yet it is suggestive that no reported cases denied college support to a daughter between 1953 and 1970.[84] It is also significant that virtually the same numbers of sons (41) and daughters (40) were involved in college support litigation.[85] Evidently, the divorced parents (primarily mothers) who initiated these suits believed that the higher education of young women was as important as the higher education of young men.[86]

Especially in the postwar era, as more married women remained in the paid workforce, these sentiments were also shared by policy makers and judges who had gained an increasing appreciation of the economic and civic contributions of educated women. By 1957, one out of every five women between the ages of eighteen and twenty-one attended college. This trend would continue through the 1960s, alongside the end of the "marriage bar" that had derailed the careers of many educated women. More Americans appreciated how married women's employment facilitated the consumption that characterized middle-class status and fueled American industrial development.[87] Evidence from a number of child support cases reflects these changing views, albeit with varying degrees of deviation from patriarchal attitudes.[88] Although she lost her case, a mother attempted to persuade a New York judge in 1930 that her daughters deserved to gain "financial independence" by going to college rather than continuing to work as restaurant hostesses.[89] In 1965, a dissenting Pennsylvania judge agreed that a daughter was entitled to a higher education that would "enable her to provide for herself in the future."[90]

Courts sometimes emphasized that higher education was necessary for many careers that were traditionally associated with women. Recall that *Esteb* revolved around Carmelita's desire to become a schoolteacher.[91] In 1950, a New York court recognized that teaching, social work, and other common occupations for middle-class women tended to require college degrees. The court affirmed a support order for two students because college "would greatly enhance the usefulness of these two young ladies to the community, to themselves and to any family that they in turn may be called upon to rear."[92] A Mississippi judge approved a college support order after hearing testimony from a school superintendent who suggested that a young woman should study "anything having to do with journalism, social work, the humanities." The Mississippi Supreme Court upheld this decision and endorsed the higher education of women for vocational ends, as well as for the benefit of "society, government, and all human relations."[93] Many other judges emphasized these civic purposes when affirming child support for college students. These civic goals bolstered the cases of young women in particular by justifying college even if judges suspected that daughters might ultimately leave the paid workforce.[94]

Mass Higher Education: Vocational and Civic Rationales

Nevertheless, the association between higher education and vocational objectives was foremost in the minds of most parents during the postwar era. By the 1960s, the *Saturday Evening Post* felt compelled to reassure parents that their children would not be "condemned to the welfare rolls or the lowest level of sweaty-shirt labor" if they did not attend college.[95]

Whereas higher education had once emphasized religious and civic leadership, these purposes receded during the late nineteenth and early twentieth centuries as college emerged as the default route to the middle class.[96]

Thus it is not surprising that the success or failure of some child support petitions hinged upon whether students had articulated clear vocational goals. In 1930, an Indiana court denied a son's right to a "general college education," noting that *Esteb* addressed a child who desired specific occupational training.[97] The Superior Court of Pennsylvania agreed that a daughter was not entitled to her father's support if she pursued a degree in the "social cultures generally."[98] In the midst of the Great Depression, the Supreme Court of Montana compelled a father to pay for his son's degree in electrical engineering after the mother's attorney offered proof of the increased earning capacity of college graduates and pointed out that the boy was not merely pursuing a "general education."[99] Three decades later, a New Jersey court affirmed a child support order while declaring, "Opportunities for earning an adequate livelihood without college, professional or technical training are already very scarce and they are becoming scarcer."[100]

While parents, students, and attorneys almost always focused on vocational training, judges sometimes emphasized the civic contributions of college graduates. Perhaps judges were influenced by their personal experiences with college and their own subsequent career paths, which presumably encouraged them to pay special attention to the nonmaterial dimensions of higher education.[101] Indeed, while the majority of cases focused on financial matters, the decisions that included the most substantial dicta tended to discuss the preparation of citizens. The relationship between higher education and citizenship was one of the distinguishing features of *Esteb* and several other influential decisions. Ironically, praise for the collective civic benefits of higher education seemed more prominent in cases that applied to private family units rather than cases that concerned public colleges and universities themselves.

Starting with *Esteb*, a number of courts concluded that higher education improved the quality of citizenship and, therefore, could be considered a necessary expense for virtually any high school graduate. Most prominently, the Supreme Court of Oregon emphasized this line of reasoning when adjudicating the 1941 child support case of *Jackman v. Short*. In this case, as in many others, the father's attorney argued that his client was only obligated to provide postsecondary education if his child exhibited exceptional fitness for a particular profession that required college training.[102] The court disagreed with this interpretation and noted that "the needs of society and government, as well as the needs of the family, must be taken into consideration." Noting that the daughter had not mentioned whether she planned to pursue a specific career, the court rejected the suggestion that the sole purpose of college was "to train the student so that he can make money." The opinion declared that higher education provided young people with "such knowledge of our government and American institutions that upon reaching majority they will intelligently perform their part in the great social order."[103] Whereas earlier cases had focused primarily on the economic benefits of higher education, *Jackman* started a transition toward an increasing emphasis on cultural and political purposes.[104] As early as 1952, a scholar associated with the Carnegie Foundation for the Advancement of Teaching predicted that divorce courts would soon stop distinguishing between students pursuing vocational training and those seeking a liberal education.[105]

Especially after the Second World War, increasing numbers of political leaders echoed *Jackman*'s connection between higher education and citizenship. Although schooling had always been praised for cultivating more informed citizenship, the challenges of the Cold War seemed to require *higher* education to be fully understood.[106] The Cold War sparked more interest in tracking the depth of public opinion and renewed hopes within academia that increased college enrollment could generate "enlightened public consensus."[107]

When adjudicating child support cases, judges sometimes indicated that the Cold War fueled their enthusiasm for the civic dimensions of higher learning. In 1950, a New York court explained that colleges produced "a finer race of men and women" to defend the nation against "ill-advised agitators."[108] At the end of that decade, an Ohio juvenile court observed, "The conflicting ideologies of the great powers of the world are in a competitive race for the minds of men." Citing the launch of Sputnik, the court urged young people to study the humanities as well as the sciences so that they could understand American political culture as well as the ideologies of other nations.[109] In 1960, the Supreme Court of Mississippi explained its approval of an increase in child support for a college student by arguing that the cultivation of citizenship was "a duty which the parent not only owes to his child, but to the state as well, since the stability of our government must depend upon a well-equipped, a well-trained, and well-educated citizenship."[110] Similarly, the Supreme Court of Indiana ruled that higher education could be considered "a necessity for both this state's citizens and the state itself."[111] These views were consistent with a national education report issued in 1964, which concluded that denying postsecondary training to a young person was akin to saying that he or she was incapable of intelligent citizenship.[112]

Judges who sympathized with these views found encouragement when state legislatures expanded financial aid and increased appropriations for public higher education. Between 1932 and 1957, state spending on higher education rose by 800 percent, as legislatures began providing reliable annual appropriations to public colleges and universities in order to maintain low tuition rates in the midst of surging enrollment.[113] In addition to *Jackman*, rulings in California, Illinois, New York, and Ohio interpreted these appropriations as proof that child support for college students was consistent with a broader public policy of promoting mass higher education.[114]

Regardless of their rationale, courts became more likely to allow college expenses to be included in child support orders during the middle decades of the twentieth century. In contrast, judicial treatment of students who filed suit against institutions remained comparatively static—with the major exception of desegregation suits, courts generally deferred to institutions of higher education in this period. In other words, courts began to vigorously enforce certain private *familial* obligations during an era when public *institutional* obligations were defined in a relatively lenient fashion. Eventually, judicial support for college access reemerged within institutional cases as well, beginning with *Dixon v. Alabama State Board of Education* in the 1960s and the overall proliferation of higher education lawsuits during the 1970s.[115] When viewed alongside the shifts in judicial perceptions of higher education that transpired after *Esteb*, the *Dixon* ruling seems to express a similar sort of enthusiasm for higher education, albeit within a different legal context.

By 1965, one legal scholar believed that this enthusiasm was becoming so powerful that college students might become entitled to financial assistance from their parents regardless of their parents' marital status.[116] This prediction, audacious at the time, would seem even less plausible six years later, when the passage of the Twenty-Sixth Amendment encouraged most states to lower their age of majority from twenty-one to eighteen. During the 1970s, amid growing concerns about a sluggish labor market for college graduates, several state courts began to reject all requests for postmajority tuition support. Some courts ruled that divorced parents had no obligation whatsoever to adult children. Other courts sidestepped this issue by ordering additional support for younger siblings with the tacit understanding that these increases would offset the college expenses of older brothers and sisters. A few legislatures intervened on behalf of these students by authorizing postmajority support for higher education.[117]

These decisions and statutes would affect the educational opportunities of large numbers of American youth. When considering the impact of college access litigation in midcentury America, an argument could be made for ranking the evolution of child support as second only to the campaign against desegregation. In addition to this tangible significance, these cases also serve to highlight the indeterminate legal status of American higher education during its era of rapid postwar growth, when college began to hover somewhere between a right and a privilege for students, and between an obligation and a choice for parents. To be sure, child support rulings did not establish any actual right to higher education. They simply compelled divorced parents to uphold private obligations to their daughters and sons. Yet the cases signaled the development of an increasingly powerful public interest in college access, an interest that some judges even expanded into embryonic arguments for universal higher education. While higher education will never be a necessity comparable to food, shelter, or even elementary education, *Esteb* and its descendants determined that college was necessary to allow many young people to maximize their contribution to the state. In this way, American courts reconciled the limits of the common law tradition with a more expansive modern creed of social mobility.

It is noteworthy that the judges who provided the most substantial arguments in favor of this expansion tended to emphasize students' potential for civic as well as economic contributions to the state. Whereas citizenship no longer seems to serve as a particularly influential rationale for expanding college access during the twenty-first century, assumptions about the civic leadership of graduates encouraged twentieth-century judges to embrace mass higher education.[118] Yet these sentiments stood in stark contrast with the attitudes expressed by students, parents, and their attorneys, who emphasized vocational training and never mentioned civics even after decades of opinions had indicated that judges were receptive to this line of argumentation.[119] Thus, while these cases documented the growth of American higher education, they also prefigured the increasingly distant relationship between the transcendent mission statements of universities and the more prosaic goals of many students and parents. In this sense, judicial enthusiasm for civic training may have reflected the naïveté, as well as the triumph, of American higher education in the postwar era.

Conclusion

In 2013, a student sued Lehigh University for more than a million dollars in damages after receiving a grade of C+ in a counseling practicum course. The presiding judge expressed skepticism toward the suit, remarking that he had "never seen something like this." Lehigh's attorney was keen to reinforce this perception by predicting that a ruling in favor of the student would attract scrutiny to "the first court in the history of jurisprudence to change an academic grade."[1] As indicated by this exchange, conventional notions about the history of academic deference continue to inform contemporary deliberations about the rights of students and the obligations of universities. By portraying legal autonomy as a venerable tradition, this historical narrative fortifies the academy's (understandable) apprehension toward external oversight.

Yet as I have demonstrated, judicial deference toward academia has been less constant than these sorts of remarks would suggest. Although courts tended to defer to colleges and universities, absolute words such as "never" and "first" are inconsistent with the full record of admission, expulsion, and tuition cases. Lehigh's version of legal history, for example, overlooked a turn-of-the-century Nebraska Supreme Court ruling that ordered a medical school to reinstate a student after independent doctors testified that she deserved to pass her final examinations.[2] Especially in the nineteenth century, American courts entertained and sometimes supported college access suits that questioned the decisions of faculty and administrators.

Some of these suits focused on constitutional or statutory language, while others based their complaints on contractual obligations or other common law principles. But regardless of their legal basis, college access cases asked courts to reconsider the fundamental justifications for deference—the premise that judges lacked the expertise to resolve academic conflicts and, more broadly, the presumption that legal autonomy enabled colleges to maximize their contributions to the greater good. Admission suits invited judges to determine whether the public interest was best served by state university policies that erred on the side of accessibility or selectivity.

Expulsion suits occasionally explored whether particular discipline policies violated an institution's moral or civic responsibilities. Some tuition suits disputed whether fees or scholarship policies were consistent with the mission of public higher education.

The only era in which courts steadily refrained from examining these questions (with the major exception of desegregation suits) lasted from 1910 to 1960—a half century in which Americans exhibited an unusual degree of respect for intellectual and administrative expertise. This correlation suggests that academic deference did not emerge primarily out of age-old admiration for the priesthood of higher education but evolved within the cultural and institutional contexts of midcentury America.[3] Deference, in itself, was a conditional and mutable basis for academia's legal privileges. Throughout much of the history of American higher education, faculty and administrators have had to explain their conduct to the courts and the public, rather than simply citing their traditional independence.

The fragility of judicial deference toward higher education has been particularly evident since the 1960s. In all likelihood, it was the seemingly swift degeneration of this concept in the wake of *Dixon v. Alabama State Board of Education* that caused the previous epochs of higher education law to appear almost entirely deferential in comparison. As I describe in chapter 4, *Dixon* was a federal ruling issued in 1961 that characterized college enrollment as a property right worthy of protection by the due process clause of the Fourteenth Amendment. Whereas the Supreme Court of the early twentieth century had viewed enrollment as a privilege granted by academic authorities, *Dixon* considered public higher education to be a right possessed by matriculated students.[4]

Yet as many legal scholars have noted, one must be careful to avoid overstating the extent of the post-*Dixon* revolution. Most courts have continued to defer to universities whenever students challenge assessments of their academic work (such as the grading dispute at Lehigh). Whereas deference to administrators waned after *Dixon*, deference to faculty remains strong in cases related to the core of their scholarly expertise. In cases that pertain to academic performance, courts sometimes question whether the process of evaluation was adequate, but they generally avoid passing judgment on the quality of student work. According to one scholar, students still have "low or nil" odds of prevailing in these sorts of cases unless they can tie their grievances to constitutionally protected rights or prove that colleges exhibited "bad faith" in some blatant fashion.[5]

Nevertheless, the past five decades have witnessed an unmistakable increase in the quantity and scope of college access litigation. In response to the legalization of college and university affairs, higher education emerged as a distinct professional specialization for attorneys during the 1960s.[6] By 1969, a leader in the nascent field suggested that administrators and law school students could profit from an entire seminar dedicated to the rapidly evolving field of college access litigation.[7] Although courts remained reluctant to second-guess academic decisions, the boundaries between academic and nonacademic matters were becoming hazy. Furthermore, the courts increasingly granted constitutional protections to students in cases related to racial discrimination, due process, and free speech.[8] This legalization of student life prompted administrators to establish institutional hearing boards, appeals processes, and other quasi-judicial procedures designed to reduce the frequency of litigation.[9] Yet these efforts failed to stem the tide of lawsuits, in part because legal challenges were attracting funding from political advocacy organizations.[10]

The underlying factors that fueled these developments have been well documented. The campus protests of the 1960s and 1970s had a far-reaching impact on the relationship between students and their institutions. Students spearheaded the emergence of modern rights consciousness, which encouraged challenges to admissions, discipline, and curricular policies. Confrontational administrative responses to these protests, including the involvement of law enforcement agencies, weakened universities' claim to provide quasi-parental supervision. The doctrine of in loco parentis also seemed particularly inappropriate after 1971, when eighteen-year-olds gained the right to vote and became legal adults in most states. Meanwhile, Congress provided new grounds for litigation by passing statutes that targeted discrimination based on race, gender, and disability. While the rising prominence of colleges and universities may have attracted judicial respect from 1910 to 1960, the expansion of American higher education eventually diminished the mystique of the academy and increased its exposure to litigation. With large enrollments, substantial federal research grants, and a dedication to regional economic development, universities found it harder to argue that they should operate beyond the realm of ordinary legal norms. The ideal of autonomy was further eroded by the perceived politicization of academic life, regardless of whether accusations of bias were leveled by antiwar protestors or conservative critics. Finally, the commercialization of higher education, signaled by more proactive marketing and increasing attention to "return on investment," contributed to the perception that colleges were businesses that should be subject to ordinary contractual norms.[11] Rarefied yet commonplace, exclusive yet indispensible, detached yet partisan, American institutions of higher education attracted contradictory labels that have generated inconsistent levels of judicial deference toward expulsion, admissions, and tuition policies.

Some of these conflicting perceptions of the legal authority of universities stem from ongoing analogies to elementary and secondary schools. By the 1960s, the volume of higher education cases reached the point where courts no longer needed to seek guidance from elementary or secondary school rulings.[12] Nevertheless, courts continued to transfer principles between the two spheres, albeit with somewhat more frequent recognition of their distinctiveness. Courts also tended to hold universities accountable to rulings in cases that concerned the less rarefied and rapidly expanding context of the two-year community college.[13] In contrast to the middle of the twentieth century, when lower school case law usually reinforced deference toward higher education, a number of elementary and secondary school rulings weakened collegiate authority during the past half century. In particular, renewed skepticism toward school officials and a growing emphasis on the importance of education prompted courts to examine whether school rules actually promote learning rather than merely examining if those policies are discriminatory or arbitrary. Tethered to this emerging body of case law, colleges and universities have had a somewhat harder time persuading courts to refrain from evaluating their policies.[14]

Admissions cases have provided many of the most prominent examples of this post-1960 uncertainty about challenges to academic authority. Although courts generally viewed admissions policies as manifestations of academic expertise, judges nevertheless exhibited a mixture of deference and scrutiny depending on the type of case. When faced with suits that do not allege racial discrimination, courts continued to refrain from questioning most admissions procedures. In one representative case, a New York court ruled that the judicial branch should generally avoid "interjecting its views within those delicate areas of school administration which relate to the eligibility of applicants."[15] In 1968, an influential district court statement affirmed that state universities should be allowed to set academic standards that were "higher than the average of the population"—a commonplace twentieth-century sentiment that would have troubled many nineteenth-century legislators.[16] In the twenty-first century, courts still decline to invalidate admissions policies unless institutions reject applicants who meet legislated requirements, violate printed statements, or discriminate according to race, sex, disability, or age.[17] Judicial deference, of course, does not tell the whole story of state oversight. During the 1960s and 1970s, the executive and legislative branches of state government intensified their supervision of admissions policies in order to coordinate and stratify public institutions of higher education.[18]

For constitutional and ethical reasons, courts were much less reluctant to intervene when admission policies discriminated based on gender or race.[19] In 1982, the Supreme Court ruled that the Mississippi University for Women did not have a compelling reason to continue excluding men. Fourteen years later, the court applied similar guidelines when it ordered the Virginia Military Institute to admit women.[20] Courts also consistently endorsed the goal of racial equity and occasionally policed lackluster state desegregation plans that were supposed to remedy long-standing bias against African American students.[21] In recent decades, Asian American and Latino students have also been able to pursue some claims against discriminatory admissions policies.[22] However, judicial oversight of desegregation has weakened during the past several decades because of sagging political will and unsuccessful suits against indirect drivers of segregation, such as curricular offerings and entrance requirements, that are more likely to be regarded as protected arenas of academic discretion.[23]

Affirmative action policies have received especially ambivalent treatment by the courts because they combine these two opposing legal impulses—the requirement to inspect potentially discriminatory actions and the instinct to defer to academic authorities.[24] These policies have attracted a great deal of attention, perhaps a disproportionate amount in light of the fact that affirmative action affects small numbers of students at a few selective institutions. Nevertheless, affirmative action suits are now the most common category of admissions case and the most conspicuous focus of disputes about academic deference.[25] In addition to highlighting competing definitions of merit and different ideas about the purpose of higher education, these cases debate whether public universities are entitled to some sort of exemption from the Supreme Court's usual scrutiny of state-sponsored racial classifications.[26] Beginning in 1974, with *DeFunis v. Odegaard*, elite state universities infused their arguments on behalf of affirmative action with invocations of the traditional discretion afforded to academic authorities.[27] Four years later, Justice Lewis Powell's tie-breaking opinion in *Regents of the University of California v. Bakke* stated that a degree of affirmative action was protected by an institution's quasi-constitutional right to academic freedom (loosely based on the right to free speech).[28] Justice Harry Blackmun offered a more pointed argument for academic deference by stating that the courts were "ill-equipped and poorly trained" to evaluate admissions policies. Echoing a phrase from an amicus brief submitted by Ivy League institutions, he urged the court to regard judicial intervention in university affairs as a "rare exception" to the norm.[29]

More recently, the court deferred to the relatively subjective race-conscious admissions procedure employed by the University of Michigan Law School because it fell within the protective sphere of academic freedom. Meanwhile, the court rejected the point system employed by the university's undergraduate admissions office because it amounted to an automatic approach that did not involve the expert judgment of university officials on a case-by-case basis.[30] In 2013, the court's ruling in *Fisher v. University of Texas* continued to acknowledge the doctrine of academic deference, though the majority opinion granted considerably less discretion to university officials.[31] In a sense, this conflict has become the inverse of the first wave of desegregation suits, in which state universities asked courts to defer to their special expertise, while civil rights lawyers argued that administrators must base admissions decisions solely on high school performance.[32] For the time being, the court has attempted to resolve the rival ideals of deference and nondiscrimination by analyzing admissions processes (to discern if race is considered holistically or mechanistically) while refraining from questioning the substance of decisions to admit or reject particular applicants.

The past fifty years of expulsion case law has generated similar distinctions between process and substance. By redefining enrollment as a property right, *Dixon* heralded a reintensification of judicial oversight of due process in cases that challenged disciplinary expulsions. A wave of subsequent suits reinforced the presumption that state universities could not expel students without first providing some semblance of disciplinary proceeding.[33] To be sure, the traditional doctrine of in loco parentis remained influential, and some campuses were slow to respond to *Dixon*'s instructions (and all private institutions remained technically exempt from the precedent).[34] Yet by the 1970s, courts emphasized students' contractual and constitutional rights (especially the protections afforded by the First and Fourteenth Amendments) more often than they referred to older models of quasi-parental supervision.[35]

Even private institutions have amended their own internal regulations in order to conform to the basic legal norms that govern discipline at state colleges and universities. Although court oversight of private schools has been less intense, judges usually expect these institutions to provide students with at least rudimentary hearings and fact-finding procedures in order to demonstrate that expulsions were neither arbitrary nor biased.[36] At the very least, courts continue to require private colleges and universities to abide by the statements published in their catalogs, though this "implied contract" is usually interpreted in a manner that favors institutions rather than students. Some courts, however, have considered the university-student relationship to be a contract of "adhesion" (a contract between highly unequal partners that should be interpreted in favor of the weaker party).[37]

Yet as noted above, judges still defer more readily to expulsions based on academic performance, as opposed to disciplinary violations. Students who are dismissed because of poor academic performance remain unlikely to prevail in court as long as a college's guidelines are publicized and administered without malice.[38] In 1978, the Supreme Court reaffirmed this stance in *University of Missouri v. Horowitz* by upholding the expulsion of a medical student who had received a weak evaluation of her clinical performance. While stating that the school had provided ample procedural due process prior to expulsion, Justice William Rehnquist noted that institutions of higher education faced "less stringent" requirements when dismissing a student on academic grounds. Seven years later, while ruling against a student who challenged his expulsion from the University of Michigan Medical School, the court repeated that judges "should show great respect for the faculty's professional judgment."[39] At times, however, the distinction between academic and disciplinary expulsion can seem blurry. Dissenting from *Horowitz*, Justice Thurgood Marshall noted that the line between these categories could be especially unclear in professional programs with clinical components.[40] Similarly, cases of plagiarism and cheating may require relatively stringent due process because they include disciplinary as well as academic dimensions and threaten to tarnish the reputations of the accused.[41]

Compared to admissions and expulsion cases, tuition suits occupy a less prominent and more stable location with respect to judicial deference toward higher education since 1960.[42] Courts have considered a variety of tuition issues, including contractual claims about whether students meet the terms of a scholarship and due process claims about the revocation of aid.[43] Yet most of the core legal questions about tuition have remained settled since the 1910s. Courts continue to defer to university decisions regarding tuition and fees as long as these policies do not directly clash with state statutes. For instance, public universities in states where tuition is not set by the legislature have enjoyed the authority to institute annual rate increases since the 1970s.[44] Judicial support for miscellaneous student fees also remains strong despite a number of legal challenges.[45] In turn, legislators and other policy makers have reduced the likelihood of litigation by clarifying earlier jurisdictional disputes and exercising greater control over tuition policies. More broadly, the dearth of reported tuition cases may reflect the extent to which higher education has become defined as a commodity. While consumerism has encouraged student suits over reimbursement policies and faulty "products," this framework also suggests that schools should be able to charge what the market will bear.[46] To be sure, courts have done nothing to encourage tuition increases (which result from a combination of higher costs and relatively low public funding), but neither have they looked favorably on suits that attempted to stem the tide.

In light of these increasing tuition costs, it is probably fortunate that American courts no longer entertain the nineteenth-century suits that challenged need-based scholarships. Yet even though courts have stopped questioning whether scholarships serve a "public purpose" worthy of state funding, the county scholarship programs that were the target of these suits have become vulnerable to changes in state priorities.[47] Especially since the 1990s, need-based aid for state university students has competed with merit-based programs designed to increase the academic profile of entering classes.[48] Whereas need-based aid remains on firm legal footing, courts have issued injunctions against scholarship programs that discriminate against students based on race or gender. In 1989, for example, a federal court ruled that New York State could not award scholarships based entirely on standardized test scores that showed bias against women.[49] Meanwhile, conservatives have challenged scholarship programs that are intended to increase the enrollment of students of color.[50]

Yet the primary legal clash over tuition and scholarship policies in recent years has focused on qualifications for in-state tuition benefits. Since the 1960s, courts have subjected the details of these residency requirements to increased scrutiny. Although states continue to have the authority to charge higher tuition to nonresidents, judges sometimes question whether certain definitions of residency violate the federal right to equal protection.[51] The most heated aspect of this debate has centered on the residency status of undocumented immigrants. In *Plyler v. Doe*, the Supreme Court struck down a Texas law that permitted districts to charge or exclude undocumented students from elementary and secondary schools. Legislatures and courts are currently determining whether this ruling will apply to institutions of higher education. In the meantime, some states have erected barriers to in-state tuition, while others have allowed undocumented students to establish residency. Undocumented students and their advocates continue to lobby for passage of a federal Development, Relief, and Education for Alien Minors Act that would facilitate eligibility for in-state tuition at public colleges and universities.[52]

Much has been written about the extent to which students are taking out loans, even when they qualify for these subsidized in-state tuition rates.[53] Much less well known is the fact that American courts once protected students against education-related debt. As noted in the preceding chapter, common law once dictated that minors could not enter into financial contracts except for food, shelter, or other "necessary" expenses. Yet when college no longer seemed to be a luxury item, the rationale for preventing institutions from pursuing unpaid tuition charges began to fade. By the 1960s, legislatures facilitated the proliferation of student debt by authorizing minors to take out college loans.[54] Recently, accreditors and lawmakers have begun to express concern about the extent of this debt, especially among students who attend for-profit institutions of higher education.[55]

As courts and legislatures dismantled the earlier restraints that once may have impeded universities from passing costs along to students, they simultaneously smoothed the way for students who requested financial support from noncustodial parents. In a sense, the legal system discouraged student claims against public institutions of higher education, while authorizing increased responsibility for tuition within the private realm of the family.[56] Many courts have continued to regard the economic and civic functions of higher education as vital enough to justify considerable oversight of the financial support provided by divorced parents.[57] A noteworthy exception to this trend occurred during the 1990s, when Pennsylvania's high court ruled that including college tuition in child support orders amounted to an equal protection violation because the practice distinguished between students with married parents and students with divorced parents.[58] However, other jurisdictions have rejected this argument and maintained that the classification is reasonable because the children of divorced parents are more vulnerable to financial neglect.[59] This justification has protected postmajority child support for college students in many states, despite the fact that judges and legislators have not reached consensus about the significance of variables such as social class and academic aptitude. In the twenty-first century, courts still wrestle with subjective interpretations of the extent to which payments should be determined by a child's "standard of living" or "station in life" prior to their parents' divorce.[60] Since the 1960s and 1970s, the stakes associated with these cases have been lowered slightly because of the introduction of systematic federal financial aid. Yet familial contributions remain crucial, and despite fairly sympathetic treatment from the courts, students with divorced parents tend to shoulder a greater financial burden.[61]

The precise influence of admission, expulsion, tuition, and child support litigation is difficult to isolate from other variables that have shaped college access. Yet some concluding remarks about the impact of these cases is warranted, even if this book has focused primarily on documenting the evolution of academic deference and its relationship to broader perceptions of higher education. Admissions cases, of course, yielded clear results for the students who were directly involved (though students often embarked on other paths before the final resolution of their cases). However, the relatively hands-off posture of nondesegregation admissions judgments over the last one hundred years has offered little substantive guidance for policy makers or administrators. At most, these rulings have worked in subtle ways to enshrine selective policies at a small number of flagship state universities. Desegregation suits generated dramatic civil rights triumphs that reverberated across the nation, and yet they exerted underwhelming influence on the total attendance of students of color at historically white flagship universities. Similarly, affirmative action rulings have reinforced (at least for the time being) the authority of institutions to seek diverse student bodies, but they have direct consequences only for students at a small number of highly selective schools. Modern tuition cases have generally protected institutional prerogatives and done little to restrain the rising price of college. Compared to these categories of college access litigation, expulsion rulings have exerted perhaps the most widespread influence by facilitating the development of a nationwide norm for disciplinary procedures.

This brisk summary of the effect of college access litigation is consistent with the findings of legal scholars who examine the murky relationship between the courts and social change. The legal process often fosters accommodation, cooptation, or redirection in lieu of dramatic changes to the status quo. Although litigation can galvanize social movements, legal victories themselves tend to have relatively moderate results in the long run.[62] The goal of college access may also be an especially ill-suited objective for sustained legal activism because the identity of the "student" is temporary and amorphous. In particular, students have not been able to organize consistent efforts, either as lobbyists or litigants, to promote favorable tuition or loan policies.[63] When responding to student-initiated suits, American courts have also conformed to their overall tendency of favoring demands for increased regulation more than demands for social provision. Judges have been fairly sympathetic to calls for greater procedural due process yet predisposed against attempts to preserve low-cost higher education.[64]

Yet whereas litigation has had limited concrete impact on college access, the ideal of academic deference has radiated considerable symbolic power. Part of the identity of faculty and administrators, and long established as the canonical historical backdrop for surveys of higher education law, the interpretative prism of deference is often used to array judicial decisions along a spectrum from early autonomy to more recent oversight. This framework tempts us to yearn for an era when courts were supposed to grant broad discretion to college authorities.

However, the historiographical emphasis on academic deference obscures the complex and long-standing tension between institutional independence and social prominence. Decisions that upheld academic autonomy tended to characterize enrollment as a special privilege, whereas less deferential decisions tended to characterize enrollment as a vital right. Some courts communicated a reverential view of higher education, while others justified intervention by defining enrollment as a businesslike transaction. Regardless, the concept of academic deference has done little to resolve, and may even have exacerbated, the fundamental love-hate relationship between American higher education and its ever-increasing profile. Simply put, academics want to be understood as crucial to society and yet wish to be left alone.[65] One of the paradoxes of the American academy is that it has become at once too important and too pedestrian to operate all that far outside the bounds of ordinary legal scrutiny. And so the supposed golden age of academic deference remains compelling (minus its acceptance of many forms of discrimination) because it serves to delegitimize a proliferation of judicial oversight that has become costly in terms of resources, relationships, and respect.

Yet despite the substantial evolution of higher education law since the 1960s, it would be inaccurate to assume that courts had been disengaged before that decade or, for that matter, very strongly predisposed toward intervention afterward. As this book has illustrated, the commonalities between these eras are as striking as their contrasts. The contours of academic deference, like the law in general, have *always* depended heavily on social, institutional, and political contexts. The legal privileges granted to American colleges and universities have typically relied on the extent to which they appear to operate in service of the public interest, however defined.[66] It is also important to recognize that judicial intervention has often emphasized, and sometimes shaped, this public mission.[67]

A disproportionate focus on deference can distract faculty and administrators from the task of demonstrating how we marshal our authority in support of these missions. Of course, public service has long been a staple of the actual and rhetorical fabric of higher education.[68] Yet a slow shift from an emphasis on leadership and republican virtue to an emphasis on professional training and individual success has been under way since the second half of the nineteenth century. By the 1970s, relatively little remained of American higher education's original focus on service to church, state, and community.[69] In the twenty-first century, college students rank civic purposes dead last on their list of priorities.[70] As a result, it seems to be an open question whether colleges and universities remain public-minded enough to counter the arguments in favor of greater legal oversight. If we wish to continue enacting an ambitious and independent vision for American higher education, advocates for academic deference should assertively promote the public services performed by staff, faculty, students, and alumni.

Appendix A

College Access Litigation, 1860–1960

This table lists reported cases related to admission, expulsion, or tuition at colleges and professional schools. Only the ultimate decision is listed for each case. The table excludes suits by PhD candidates, suits by students at correspondence or commercial schools, and grade-challenge suits that did not lead to expulsion. Some cases that are discussed in the book are omitted from this table because they did not involve a student suing an institution.

Key

Outcome	Ruling for institution or student
Status	Public or private institution
Ex(a)	Academic expulsion
Ex(d)	Disciplinary expulsion
Ex	Unstated or overlapping grounds for expulsion
*	Desegregation case
#	Normal school, community college, or military institute

Case	Outcome	Status	Type
Illinois Female College v. Cooper, 25 Ill. 133 (1861)	Student	Private	Admission
Pratt v. Wheaton College, 40 Ill. 186 (1866)	Institution	Private	Ex(d)
Foltz v. Hoge, 54 Cal. 28 (1879)	Student	Public	Admission
State ex rel. Priest v. Univ. of Wis., 54 Wis. 159 (1882)	Institution	Public	Tuition
State ex rel. Stallard v. White, 82 Ind. 278 (1882)	Student	Public	Admission
Comm. ex rel. Hill v. McCauley, 2 Pa. Co. Ct. 459 (1887)	Student	Private	Ex(d)
#State ex rel. Clark v. Osborne, 32 Mo. App. 536 (1888)	Student	Public	Ex(d)
North v. University of Illinois, 137 Ill. 296 (1891)	Institution	Public	Ex(d)
Cecil v. Bellevue College, 14 N.Y.S. 490 (1891)	Student	Private	Ex(d)
People v. NY Medical College, 20 N.Y.S. 379 (1892)	Institution	Private	Ex(a)
O'Sullivan v. NY Law School, 22 N.Y.S. 663 (1893)	Institution	Private	Ex(d)
State ex rel. Little v. Univ. of Kansas, 55 Kan. 389 (1895)	Student	Public	Tuition
Niedermeyer v. Univ. of Missouri, 61 Mo. App. 654 (1895)	Student	Public	Tuition
#Jackson v. Majors, 57 Neb. 183 (1898)	Student	Public	Ex(a)
#Brown v. Board of Education, 8 Ohio Dec. 378 (1899)	Student	Public	Ex(a)
Niles v. Orange, 63 N.J.L. 528 (1899)	Institution	Private	Ex(a)
Koblitz v. Western Reserve Univ., 21 Ohio Cir. Ct. 144 (1901)	Institution	Private	Ex(d)

(*continued*)

Case	Outcome	Status	Type
Kaplan v. Kuhn, 11 Ohio Dec. 321 (1901)	Student	Public	Tuition
#Miller v. Dailey, 136 Cal. 212 (1902)	Student	Public	Ex(a)
Steinhauer v. Arkins, 18 Colo. App. 49 (1902)	Institution	Public	Ex(a)
Goldstein v. New York University, 78 N.Y.S. 739 (1902)	Institution	Private	Ex(d)
Addy v. W. PA Medical College, 11 Pa. D. 687 (1902)	Institution	Private	Ex(a)
Baltimore University v. Colton, 98 Md. 623 (1904)	Student	Private	Ex
Gannon v. Georgetown Univ., 28 App. D.C. 87 (1906)	Institution	Private	Ex(d)
Burg v. Milwaukee Medical College, 128 Wis. 7 (1906)	Institution	Private	Ex(a)
Gleason v. University of Minnesota, 104 Minn. 359 (1908)	Student	Public	Ex
Nelson v. Lincoln Medical College, 81 Neb. 533 (1908)	Student	Private	Ex(a)
*Booker v. GR Medical College, 156 Mich. 95 (1909)	Institution	Private	Ex
New Orleans v. Tulane University, 123 La. 550 (1909)	Student	Private	Tuition
Connell v. Gray, 33 Okla. 591 (1912)	Student	Public	Tuition
Williams v. Wheeler, 23 Cal. App. 619 (1913)	Institution	Public	Admission
Tate v. North Pacific College, 70 Or. 160 (1914)	Institution	Private	Ex(a)
#Kentucky Military Inst. v. Bramblet, 158 Ky. 205 (1914)	Institution	Private	Ex(d)
Waugh v. University of Mississippi, 237 U.S. 589 (1915)	Institution	Public	Admission
Litchman v. Shannon, 90 Wash. 186 (1916)	Institution	Public	Tuition
Pacella v. Bennett, 205 Ill. App. 324 (1917)	Institution	Private	Ex(a)
Barker v. Crum, 177 Ky. 637 (1917)	Institution	Public	Tuition
Samson v. Columbia University, 167 N.Y.S. 202 (1917)	Institution	Private	Ex(d)
#Kayser v. Board of Education, 273 Mo. 643 (1918)	Institution	Public	Admission
Goldenkoff v. Albany Law School, 191 N.Y.S. 349 (1921)	Institution	Public	Ex(d)
Bryan v. Regents of UC, 188 Cal. 559 (1922)	Institution	Public	Tuition
Barker v. Bryn Mawr College, 278 Pa. 121 (1923)	Institution	Private	Ex(d)
#Tanton v. McKenney, 226 Mich. 245 (1924)	Institution	Private	Ex(d)
Woods v. Simpson, 146 Md. 547 (1924)	Institution	Public	Ex(d)
Wallace v. Regents of UC, 75 Cal. App. 274 (1925)	Institution	Public	Admission
Stetson University v. Hunt, 88 Fla. 510 (1925)	Institution	Private	Ex(d)
Ingersoll v. Clapp, 81 Mont. 200 (1927)	Institution	Public	Ex(d)
Anthony v. Syracuse University, 231 N.Y.S. 435 (1928)	Institution	Private	Ex(d)
West v. Board of Trustees, 41 Ohio App. 367 (1931)	Institution	Public	Ex(a)
White v. Portia Law School, 274 Mass. 162 (1931)	Institution	Private	Ex(d)
Foley v. Benedict, 122 Tex. 193 (1932)	Institution	Public	Ex(a)
#State ex rel. Dodd v. Tison, 175 La. 235 (1932)	Institution	Public	Ex
#Teachers College v. Morris, 165 Miss. 758 (1932)	Institution	Public	Tuition
University of Maryland v. Coale, 165 Md. 224 (1933)	Institution	Public	Ex(d)
Rheam v. University of Oklahoma, 161 Okla. 268 (1933)	Institution	Public	Tuition
*State ex rel. Weaver v. Ohio State, 126 Ohio 290 (1933)	Institution	Public	Admission
State ex rel. Veeder v. Board of Ed., 97 Mont. 121 (1934)	Institution	Public	Tuition

Case	Outcome	Status	Type
State of Georgia v. Univ. of Georgia, 179 Ga. 210 (1934)	Institution	Public	Tuition
People v. Lory, 94 Colo. 595 (1934)	Institution	Public	Ex(a)
Hamilton v. Regents of UC, 293 U.S. 245 (1934)	Institution	Public	Ex(d)
*Pearson v. Murray, 169 Md. 478 (1936)	Student	Public	Admission
Mestice v. Partch, 119 N.J.L. 212 (1937)	Institution	Private	Admission
SMU v. Evans, 131 Tex. 333 (1938)	Institution	Private	Ex
*Missouri ex rel. Gaines v. Canada, 305 U.S. 337 (1938)	Student	Public	Admission
Rainey v. Malone, 141 S.W.2d 713 (1940)	Institution	Public	Tuition
Sherman v. Hyman, 180 Tenn. 99 (1942)	Institution	Public	Ex(d)
*Michael v. Witham, 179 Tenn. 250 (1942)	Institution	Public	Admission
#Lynch v. Commissioner of Ed., 317 Mass. 73 (1944)	Institution	Public	Tuition
Tinkoff v. Northwestern Univ., 333 Ill. App. 224 (1947)	Institution	Private	Admission
*Wrighten v. Univ. of S. Carolina, 72 F. Supp. 948 (1947)	Student	Public	Admission
*Sipuel v. University of Oklahoma, 332 U.S. 631 (1948)	Student	Public	Admission
*Johnson v. Univ. of Kentucky, 83 F. Supp. 707 (1949)	Student	Public	Admission
*McLaurin v. OK State Regents, 339 U.S. 637 (1950)	Student	Public	Admission
*Sweatt v. Painter, 339 U.S. 629 (1950)	Student	Public	Admission
*Wilson v. LSU, 92 F. Supp. 986 (1950)	Student	Public	Admission
*Parker v. University of Delaware, 31 Del. Ch. 381 (1950)	Student	Public	Admission
*#State ex rel. Toliver v. Board, 360 Mo. 671 (1950)	Institution	Public	Admission
*McCready v. Byrd, 195 Md. 131 (1950)	Student	Public	Admission
*McKissick v. Carmichael, 187 F.2d 949 (1951)	Student	Public	Admission
*Gray v. University of Tennessee, 97 F. Supp. 463 (1951)	Student	Public	Admission
Holcomb v. Armstrong, 39 Wn. 2d 860 (1952)	Institution	Public	Admission
*#Wichita Falls Jr. College v. Battle, 204 F.2d 632 (1953)	Student	Public	Admission
Halaby v. Board of Directors, 162 Ohio St. 290 (1954)	Student	Public	Tuition
Coffelt v. Nicholson, 224 Ark. 176 (1954)	Institution	Public	Ex
*Constantine v. SLA Institute, 120 F. Supp. 417 (1954)	Student	Public	Admission
*Frasier v. UNC, 134 F. Supp. 589 (1955)	Student	Public	Admission
*Lucy v. Adams, 350 U.S. 1 (1955)	Student	Public	Admission
Bluett v. University of Illinois, 10 Ill. App. 2d 207 (1956)	Institution	Public	Ex(d)
*LSU v. Tureaud, 228 F.2d 895 (1956)	Student	Public	Admission
*Hawkins v. Board of Control, 350 U.S. 413 (1956)	Student	Public	Admission
*Booker v. Tennessee Board of Ed., 240 F.2d 689 (1957)	Student	Public	Admission
*Ward v. University of Georgia, 191 F. Supp. 491 (1957)	Institution	Public	Admission
Dehaan v. Brandeis University, 150 F. Supp. 626 (1957)	Institution	Private	Ex(d)
Robinson v. University of Miami, 100 So. 2d 442 (1958)	Institution	Public	Ex(d)
Hanauer v. Elkins, 217 Md. 213 (1958)	Institution	Public	Ex(d)
Heaton v. Bristol, 317 S.W.2d 86 (1958)	Institution	Public	Admission

(continued)

Case	Outcome	Status	Type
Steier v. NY Education Commissioner, 271 F.2d 13 (1959)	Institution	Public	Ex
*LSU v. Ludley, 252 F.2d 372 (1958)	Student	Public	Admission
*Hunt v. Arnold, 172 F. Supp. 847 (1959)	Student	Public	Admission
Newman v. Graham, 82 Idaho 92 (1960)	Student	Public	Tuition
Allred v. Heaton, 336 S.W.2d 251 (1960)	Institution	Public	Admission

Appendix B

Common School Citations in College Admissions and Expulsion Cases, 1860–1960

The first table lists the total citations and the number of K–12 cases cited in the majority opinions of reported higher education desegregation cases. The second table lists the total citations and the number of K–12 cases cited in the majority opinions of other reported (nondesegregation) college admissions and expulsion cases. Citations of K–12 cases that addressed matters other than admissions or expulsion are omitted.

Key

* Student victory

Desegregation Case	Citations	K–12 Citations
Booker v. Grand Rapids Med. College, 156 Mich. 95 (1909)	3	0
State ex rel. Weaver v. Ohio State Univ., 126 Ohio St. 290 (1933)	7	6
*Pearson v. Murray, 169 Md. 478 (1936)	28	15
*Gaines v. Canada, 305 U.S. 337 (1938)	10	2
Michael v. Witham, 179 Tenn. 250 (1942)	5	1
*Wrighten v. University of South Carolina, 72 F. Supp. 948 (1947)	8	2
*Sipuel v. University of Oklahoma, 332 U.S. 631 (1948)	1	0
*Johnson v. University of Kentucky, 83 F. Supp. 707 (1949)	2	0
*McLaurin v. Oklahoma State Regents, 339 U.S. 637 (1950)	3	0
*Sweatt v. Painter, 339 U.S. 629 (1950)	6	0
*Wilson v. Louisiana State University, 92 F. Supp. 986 (1950)	4	0
*Parker v. University of Delaware, 31 Del. Ch. 381 (1950)	9	0
State ex rel. Toliver v. Board of Education, 360 Mo. 671 (1950)	17	6
*McCready v. Byrd, 195 Md. 131 (1950)	4	0
*McKissick v. Carmichael, 187 F.2d 949 (1951)	2	0
*Gray v. University of Tennessee, 97 F. Supp. 463 (1951)	12	1
*Wichita Falls Junior College v. Battle, 204 F.2d 632 (1953)	11	2
*Constantine v. SLA Institute, 120 F. Supp. 417 (1954)	11	3
*Lucy v. Adams, 350 U.S. 1 (1955)	3	0
*Frasier v. University of North Carolina, 134 F. Supp. 589 (1955)	7	1
*Louisiana State University v. Tureaud, 228 F.2d 895 (1956)	0	0
*Booker v. Tennessee Board of Education, 240 F.2d 689 (1957)	12	3
Ward v. University of Georgia, 191 F. Supp. 491 (1957)	13	0
*Hawkins v. Board of Control, 350 U.S. 413 (1956)	4	1
*Louisiana State University v. Ludley, 252 F.2d 372 (1958)	7	2
*Hunt v. Arnold, 172 F. Supp. 847 (1959)	12	6

Admission or Expulsion Case	Citations	K–12 Citations
Pratt v. Wheaton College, 40 Ill. 186 (1866)	0	0
*Foltz v. Hoge, 54 Cal. 28 (1879)	0	0
*State ex rel. Stallard v. White, 82 Ind. 278 (1882)	22	17
*Comm ex rel. Hill v. McCauley, 2 Pa. Co. Ct. 459 (1887)	6	5
*State ex rel. Clark v. Osborne, 32 Mo. App. 536 (1888)	1	1
North v. University of Illinois, 137 Ill. 296 (1891)	10	2
*Cecil v. Bellevue College, 14 N.Y.S. 490 (1891)	0	0
People v. New York Medical College, 20 N.Y.S. 379 (1892)	0	0
O'Sullivan v. New York Law School, 22 N.Y.S. 663 (1893)	2	0
*Jackson v. Majors, 57 Neb. 183 (1898)	18	4
*Brown v. Board of Education, 8 Ohio Dec. 378 (1899)	3	2
Niles v. Orange, 63 N.J.L. 528 (1899)	1	0
Koblitz v. Western Reserve University, 21 Ohio C.C. 144 (1901)	4	2
*Miller v. Dailey, 136 Cal. 212 (1902)	6	2
Steinhauer v. Arkins, 18 Colo. App. 49 (1902)	1	0
Goldstein v. New York University, 78 N.Y.S. 739 (1902)	2	0
*Baltimore University v. Colton, 98 Md. 623 (1904)	1	0
Gannon v. Georgetown University, 28 App. D.C. 87 (1906)	4	0
Burg v. Milwaukee Medical College, 128 Wis. 7 (1906)	56	2
*Gleason v. University of Minnesota, 104 Minn. 359 (1908)	2	0
*Nelson v. Lincoln Medical College, 81 Neb. 533 (1908)	13	5
Williams v. Wheeler, 23 Cal. App. 619 (1913)	3	3
Tate v. North Pacific College, 70 Or. 160 (1914)	3	0
Kentucky Military Institute v. Bramblet, 158 Ky. 205 (1914)	1	0
Waugh v. University of Mississippi, 237 U.S. 589 (1915)	0	0
Samson v. Columbia University, 167 N.Y.S. 202 (1917)	1	0
Kayser v. Board of Education, 273 Mo. 643 (1918)	1	1
Goldenkoff v. Albany Law School, 191 N.Y.S. 349 (1921)	3	0
Barker v. Bryn Mawr College, 278 Pa. 121 (1923)	0	0
Tanton v. McKenney, 226 Mich. 245 (1924)	13	13
Woods v. Simpson, 146 Md. 547 (1924)	5	0
Wallace v. Regents of UC, 75 Cal. App. 274 (1925)	7	3
Stetson University v. Hunt, 88 Fla. 510 (1925)	22	15
Ingersoll v. Clapp, 81 Mont. 200 (1927)	13	2
Anthony v. Syracuse University, 231 N.Y.S. 435 (1928)	8	0
West v. Board of Trustees, 41 Ohio App. 367 (1931)	0	0
White v. Portia Law School, 274 Mass. 162 (1931)	0	0
Foley v. Benedict, 122 Tex. 193 (1932)	14	3
State ex rel. Dodd v. Tison, 175 La. 235 (1932)	5	4

Admission or Expulsion Case	Citations	K–12 Citations
University of Maryland v. Coale, 165 Md. 224 (1933)	3	0
People v. Lory, 94 Colo. 595 (1934)	1	0
Hamilton v. Regents of UC, 293 U.S. 245 (1934)	36	2
Mestice v. Partch, 119 N.J.L. 212 (1937)	2	0
Southern Methodist University v. Evans, 131 Tex. 333 (1938)	2	0
Sherman v. Hyman, 180 Tenn. 99 (1942)	7	3
Tinkoff v. Northwestern University, 333 Ill. App. 224 (1947)	13	0
Holcomb v. Armstrong, 39 Wn. 2d 860 (1952)	6	2
Coffelt v. Nicholson, 224 Ark. 176 (1954)	2	0
Bluett v. University of Illinois, 10 Ill. App. 2d 207 (1956)	7	3
Dehaan v. Brandeis University, 150 F. Supp. 626 (1957)	8	5
Robinson v. University of Miami, 100 So. 2d 442 (1958)	8	0
Hanauer v. Elkins, 217 Md. 213 (1958)	11	3
Heaton v. Bristol, 317 S.W.2d 86 (1958)	43	0
Steier v. NY Education Commissioner, 271 F.2d 13 (1959)	18	0
Allred v. Heaton, 336 S.W.2d 251 (1960)	0	0

Appendix C

Child Support Cases Involving College Expenses, 1920–70

This table omits cases that were exclusively concerned with the difference between paying for public or private higher education, cases that hinged on the disability of a child, and cases that ended without a clear resolution (i.e., cases remanded to lower court for fact finding or cases that provided support to one sibling but not another).

Key

Support	ruling continued or expanded support for a college student
No support	ruling did not order non-custodial parent to continue or increase support
No (age)	ruling did not order a continuation or expansion of support because child reached age of majority
No ($)	ruling did not order a continuation or expansion of support because parent could not afford additional payments
Yes	ruling states that noncustodial parent agreed to pay for college during divorce proceedings or previously expressed this intent
No	the ruling did not mention a prior agreement or other parental intent to pay for college

Case	Outcome	Gender	Intent
Dunham v. Dunham, 189 Iowa 802 (1920)	Support	Both	Yes
Tribe v. Tribe, 59 Utah 112 (1921)	Support	Male	No
Esteb v. Esteb, 138 Wash. 174 (1926)	Support	Female	No
Wynn v. Wynn, 6 Ohio L. Abs. 450 (1928)	No support	Male	Yes
Halsted v. Halsted, 239 N.Y.S. 422 (1930)	No (age)	Female	No
Morris v. Morris, 92 Ind. App. 65 (1930)	No support	Male	No
Underwood v. Underwood, 162 Wash. 204 (1931)	Support	Male	No
Payette v Payette, 85 N.H. 297 (1931)	Support	Male	No
Gillen v. Gillen, 102 Pa. Super 136 (1931)	No (age)	Male	No
Campbell v. Campbell, 20 Ohio L. Abs. 605 (1935)	No support	Male	No
Refer v. Refer, 102 Mont. 121 (1936)	Support	Male	No
Feek v. Feek, 187 Wash. 573 (1936)	Support	Male	No
Bloedorn v. Bloedorn, 67 App. D.C. 214 (1937)	No (age)	Female	No
Boens v. Bennett, 20 Cal. App. 2d 477 (1937)	No support	Male	No
Jackman v. Short, 165 Or. 626 (1941)	Support	Female	No
Binney v. Binney, 146 Pa. Super. 374 (1941)	No support	Male	Yes
Howton v. Howton, 51 Cal. App. 2d 323 (1942)	Support	Both	No

Case	Outcome	Gender	Intent
Rufner v. Rufner, 131 N.J. Eq. 193 (1942)	No ($)	Female	Yes
Hale v. Hale, 55 Cal. App. 2d 879 (1942)	No ($)	Male	Yes
Worthington v. Worthington, 207 Ark. 185 (1944)	No support	Female	No
Titus v. Titus, 311 Mich. 434 (1945)	Support	Female	No
Atchley v. Atchley, 29 Tenn. App. 124 (1945)	Support	Female	No
Hachet v. Hachet, 117 Ind. App. 294 (1947)	No support	Female	No
Hart v. Hart, 239 Iowa 142 (1948)	Support	Male	No
Cohen v. Cohen, 82 N.Y.S.2d 513 (1948)	Support	Male	No
Straver v. Straver, 26 N.J. Misc. 218 (1948)	Support	Female	No
Rawley v. Rawley, 94 Cal. App. 2d 562 (1949)	No ($)	Female	No
Golay v. Golay, 35 Wn. .2d 122 (1949)	No ($)	Female	No
Werner v. Werner, 7 N.J. Super. 229 (1950)	No support	Female	No
Herbert v. Herbert, 98 N.Y.S.2d 846 (1950)	Support	Female	No
Rogers v. Rogers, 335 Mich. 207 (1952)	Support	Both	No
Green v. Green, 111 N.Y.S.2d 72 (1952)	No support	Male	No
Jenkins v. Jenkins, 257 S.W.2d 250 (1953)	Support	Both	Yes
Samson v. Schoen, 121 N.Y.S.2d 489 (1953)	No support	Female	No
Mapes v. Mapes, 336 Mich. 137 (1953)	Support	Male	No
Brackob v. Brackob, 265 Wis. 513 (1953)	Support	Both	No
Jonitz v. Jonitz, 25 N.J. Super. 544 (1953)	No support	Male	No
Sirianni v. Sirianni, 127 N.Y.S.2d 387 (1953)	Support	Male	Yes
Commonwealth v. Wingert, 173 Pa. Super. 613 (1953)	No support	Female	No
Clark v. Graves, 282 S.W.2d 146 (1955)	Support	Male	No
Sloan v. Sloan, 145 N.Y.S.2d 797 (1955)	No (age)	Female	No
Johnson v. Johnson, 346 Mich. 418 (1956)	Support	Female	Yes
Peck v. Peck, 272 Wis. 466 (1956)	No ($)	Male	Yes
Grossman v. Grossman, 188 Pa. Super. 236 (1958)	Support	Both	Yes
Robrock v. Robrock, 167 Ohio St. 479 (1958)	Support	Female	Yes
Calogeras v. Calogeras, 10 Ohio Op. 2d 441 (1959)	Support	Male	No
Maitzen v. Maitzen, 24 Ill. App. 2d 32 (1959)	Support	Female	No
Haag v. Haag, 240 Ind. 291 (1959)	No support	Male	No
Mitchell v. Mitchell, 81 Ohio L. Abs. 88 (1960)	Support	?	No
Pass v. Pass, 238 Miss. 449 (1960)	Support	Female	No
Carey v. Carey, 132 Ind. App. 30 (1961)	Support	Female	Yes
Allison v. Allison, 188 Kan. 593 (1961)	Support	Female	No
Commonwealth v. Martin, 196 Pa. Super. 355 (1961)	Support	Female	Yes
Howell v. Howell, 198 Pa. Super. 396 (1962)	Support	Female	Yes
O'Berry v. O'Berry, 36 Ill. App. 2d 163 (1962)	Support	Female	No
Smith v. Smith, 227 Md. 355 (1962)	Support	Male	No

(continued)

Case	Outcome	Gender	Intent
Ulmer v. Sommerville, 200 Pa. Super. 640 (1963)	No ($)	Female	No
Clark v. Clark, 191 Kan. 95 (1963)	No (age)	Male	Yes
Straub v. Straub, 213 Cal. App. 2d. 792 (1963)	Support	Male	No
Commonwealth v. Camp, 201 Pa. Super. 484 (1963)	Support	Male	Yes
Weingast v. Weingast, 255 N.Y.S.2d 341 (1964)	Support	Male	Yes
Decker v. Decker, 204 Pa. Super. 156 (1964)	Support	Male	Yes
Rice v. Rice, 206 Pa. Super. 393 (1965)	No ($)	Female	No
Hoffman v. Hoffman, 210 A.2d 549 (1965)	No ($)	Male	No
Sportsman v. Sportsman, 409 S.W.2d 787 (1966)	Support	Male	No
Gerk v. Gerk, 259 Iowa 293 (1966)	Support	Male	No
Mowrer v. Mowrer, 3 Mich. App. 516 (1966)	Support	Male	No
Schearer v. Schearer, 208 Pa. Super. 196 (1966)	No ($)	Female	No
Brown v. Weidner, 208 Pa. Super. 114 (1966)	No ($)	Female	Yes
Wagner v. Wagner, 273 N.Y.S.2d 572 (1966)	No support	Both	No
Weber v. Weber, 274 N.Y.S.2d 791 (1966)	Support	Male	Yes
Dicker v. Dicker, 283 N.Y.S.2d 941 (1967)	No support	Male	No
Young v. Young, 413 S.W.2d 887 (1967)	No (age)	Female	No
Herzmark v. Herzmark, 199 Kan. 48 (1967)	Support	Female	No
Davis v. Davis, 8 Mich. App. 104 (1967)	Support	Female	Yes
Nebel v. Nebel, 99 N.J. Super. 256 (1968)	Support	Male	No
Dorman v. Dorman, 251 Ind. 272 (1968)	Support	Female	No
Hoover v. Voigtman, 103 N.J. Super. 535 (1968)	Support	Male	No
Yannacone v. Yannacone, 214 Pa. Super. 244 (1969)	No ($)	Female	No
Beasley v. Beasley, 159 N.W.2d 449 (1968)	Support	Male	No
Sylvester v. Sylvester, 21 Ohio App. 2d 58 (1969)	No (age)	?	No
Johnson v. Johnson, 1 Wn. App. 527 (1969)	Support	Male	No
Beberfall v. Beberfall, 44 Wis. 2d 540 (1969)	Support	Female	No
Sandler v. Sandler, 165 N.W.2d 799 (1969)	Support	Male	No
Anderson v. Anderson, 437 S.W.2d 704 (1969)	Support	Female	No
Turner v. Turner, 441 S.W.2d 105 (1969)	Support	Female	No
Bates v. Bates, 310 N.Y.S.2d 26 (1970)	No support	Male	Yes
Miller v. Miller, 459 S.W.2d 81 (1970)	No support	?	No
Spence v. Spence, 266 A.2d 29 (1970)	No (age)	Female	No
Rhoderick v. Rhoderick, 257 Md. 354 (1970)	Support	Male	No

Notes

Introduction

1. *Grutter v. Bollinger*, 539 U.S. 306 at 328 (2003); *Fisher v. University of Texas*, 133 S. Ct. 2411 (2013).

2. *Dartmouth* determined that a corporate charter insulated the college against legislative interference. *Dartmouth College v. Woodward*, 17 U.S. 518 (1819). Also see Richard Hofstadter and Walter P. Metzger, *The Development of Academic Freedom in the United States* (New York: Columbia University Press, 1955), 6; Edward N. Stoner and J. Michael Showalter, "Judicial Deference to Educational Judgment," *Journal of College and University Law* 30 (2004): 583–617.

3. J. Peter Byrne, "Academic Freedom: A 'Special Concern of the First Amendment,'" *Yale Law Journal* 99 (1989), 251–340; Comment, "Private Government on the Campus: Judicial Review of University Expulsions," *Yale Law Journal* 72 (1963): 1362–1410.

4. Donald L. Reidhaar, "Assault on the Citadel: Reflections on a Quarter Century of Change in the Relationships between Students and the University," *Journal of College and University Law* 12 (1985): 345; William W. Van Alstyne, "A Suggested Seminar in Student Rights," *Journal of Legal Education* 21 (1969): 548; William A. Kaplin and Barbara A. Lee, *The Law of Higher Education: A Comprehensive Guide to Legal Implications of Administrative Decision Making*, 5th ed., vol. 1 (San Francisco: Jossey-Bass, 2013), 9. Also see Judith Areen and Peter F. Lake, *Higher Education and the Law*, 2nd ed. (St. Paul, MN: Foundation, 2014), 757; Amy Gajda, *The Trials of Academe: The New Era of Campus Litigation* (Cambridge, MA: Harvard University Press, 2009), 3–4; Robert D. Bickel and Peter F. Lake, *The Rights and Responsibilities of the Modern University: Who Assumes the Risks of College Life?* (Durham, NC: Carolina Academic, 1999), 7; Michael J. Natali, "Judicial Deference and University Academic Policy Modifications: When Should Courts Intervene on Behalf of Injured Students?," *Indiana Law Review* 37 (2003–2004): 508.

5. Westlaw's (westlaw.com) "Students" subtopic of its "College" category lists more than 2,000 state and federal cases prior to 2010, only 187 of which occurred before 1970. Whereas college enrollment grew from 175,000 to 3.6 million between 1900 and 1960, the incidence of reported student suits remained between 8 and 16 cases per decade. In contrast, 162 cases were reported during the 1970s, a total that far outpaced that decade's enrollment growth. For enrollment statistics, see Thomas D. Snyder, *120 Years of American Education: A Statistical Portrait* (Washington, DC: National Center for Education Statistics, 1993), 64–66; Susan Aud et al., *The Condition of Education: 2011* (Washington, DC: National Center for Education Statistics, 2011), 34. These findings are consistent with a case study of Iowa. Lelia B. Helms, "Patterns of Litigation in Postsecondary Education: A Case Law Study," *Journal of College and University Law* 14 (1987): 99–119. Litigation has increased in many domains of American society since 1970. Lawrence M.

Friedman, *American Law in the 20th Century* (New Haven, CT: Yale University Press, 2002), 8.

6. *Dixon v. Alabama State Board of Education*, 294 F.2d 150 (1961); Gajda, *The Trials of Academe*, 4; Bickel and Lake, *The Rights and Responsibilities of the Modern University*, 7; Thomas A. Schweitzer, "'Academic Challenge' Cases: Should Judicial Review Extend to Academic Evaluations of Students?," *American University Law Review* 41 (1991–92): 295; Terrence Leas, "Higher Education, the Courts, and the Doctrine of Academic Deference," *Journal of Law and Education* 20 (1991): 135–36; John S. Brubacher, "The Impact of the Courts on Higher Education," *Journal of Law and Education* 2 (1973): 267–82.

7. For a representative employment case, see *Head v. University*, 86 U.S. 526 (1873). Regarding personal injury, see M. M. Chambers, "The Tort Liability of Colleges and Universities," *Educational Law and Administration* 2 (1933): 4–14; Bickel and Lake, *The Rights and Responsibilities of the Modern University*, 30. Regarding taxes and property, see Edward Elliot and M. M. Chambers, *The Colleges and the Courts: Judicial Decisions Regarding Institutions of Higher Education in the United States* (New York: Carnegie Foundation for the Advancement of Teaching, 1936). Courts also sometimes defended universities against legislative incursions. Gajda, *The Trials of Academe*, 32–33; David Laird Jr., *The Regents of the University of Michigan and the Legislature of the State, 1920–1950* (Ann Arbor: University of Michigan Press, 1972), 56–57.

8. Students won sixteen out of twenty-nine admissions, expulsion, and tuition suits between 1860 and 1910. See appendix A. For the sake of brevity, I refer to these suits as "college access" litigation, though this term evokes somewhat different meanings for scholars of contemporary higher education, who tend to associate "access" with a broader array of inequities related to the K–16 pipeline. See, for example, the National College Access Network, accessed November 13, 2013, http://www.collegeaccess.org/.

9. Students won twenty-four out of seventy-three college access suits between 1910 and 1960. See appendix A. All three nondesegregation victories were tuition suits; students did not win a nondesegregation admission or expulsion suit in this era.

10. Students won 40 out of 102 suits between 1860 and 1960. See appendix A. One can only speculate as to why no college access cases were reported prior to the 1860s. Part of the explanation, of course, is simply that American society was not as litigious in this era. It is also possible that college students had little motive to sue at a time when entrance standards were relatively lax, the status distinctions between schools were relatively minor, and the economic value of a degree was relatively insignificant. Or, since most antebellum colleges were closely associated with local boosters and religious denominations, perhaps conflicts were resolved in other venues besides the courts. John Kirkpatrick, *Academic Organization and Control* (Yellow Springs, OH: Antioch, 1931), 179. Also see Colin B. Burke, *American Collegiate Populations: A Test of the Traditional View* (New York: New York University Press, 1982).

11. Students won nineteen out of seventy-five nondesegregation suits between 1860 and 1910. See appendix A.

12. See, for example, Michael J. Klarman, *From Jim Crow to Civil Rights: The Supreme Court and the Struggle for Racial Equality* (New York: Oxford University Press, 2004); Gerald N. Rosenberg, *The Hollow Hope: Can Courts Bring About Social Change?* (Chicago: University of Chicago Press, 1991); Aryeh Neier, *Only Judgment: The Limits of Litigation in Social*

Change (Middletown, CT: Wesleyan University Press, 1982); Stuart A. Scheingold, *The Politics of Rights: Lawyers, Public Policy, and Political Change* (New Haven, CT: Yale University Press, 1974). Regarding higher education in particular, see George R. LaNoue and Barbara A. Lee, *Academics in Court: The Consequences of Faculty Discrimination Litigation* (Ann Arbor: University of Michigan Press, 1987), 231. It is also important to recognize that the odds of entering and completing college may be determined at least as much by social class and early educational experiences as by institutional policies. Richard Kazis, Joel Vargas, and Nancy Hoffman, eds., *Double the Numbers: Increasing Postsecondary Credentials for Underrepresented Youth* (Cambridge, MA: Harvard Education Press, 2004).

13. The book also discusses a handful of unreported cases and a few relevant cases (such as the scholarship suits discussed in chapter 5) that did not involve students suing institutions. In addition, chapter 6 analyzes ninety child support cases (these cases are examined up until 1971, rather than 1960, for reasons discussed at the start of that chapter). Most cases were identified through LexisNexis searches and law review articles.

14. As popular election of judges became the norm during the nineteenth century, most courts became literally politicized. Lawrence M. Friedman, *A History of American Law*, 3rd ed. (New York: Simon and Schuster, 2005), 279–88, 342, 503, 553. For a classic analysis of the extent to which jurisprudence tends to reflect social and institutional currents, see Morton Horwitz, *The Transformation of American Law, 1870–1960: The Crisis of Legal Orthodoxy* (New York: Oxford University Press, 1992).

15. G. Edward White, "The Appellate Opinion as Historical Source Material," *Journal of Interdisciplinary History* 1 (1971): 491–509; Friedman, *A History of American Law*, 298–99; Richard Arum, *Judging School Discipline: The Crisis of Moral Authority* (Cambridge, MA: Harvard University Press, 2003), 51, 289n34.

16. *Waugh v. University of Mississippi*, 237 U.S. 589 (1915); *Hamilton v. University of California*, 293 U.S. 245 (1934). Regarding the Supreme Court and higher education, see Michael A. Olivas, *Suing Alma Mater: Higher Education and the Courts* (Baltimore: Johns Hopkins University Press, 2013).

17. George Priest, "Selective Characteristics of Litigation," *Journal of Legal Studies* 9 (1980): 399–421; George Priest and Benjamin Klein, "The Selection of Disputes for Litigation," *Journal of Legal Studies* 13 (1984): 1–55. In order to gauge whether a large number of unreported cases might exist beyond the scope of state and federal reporters, I searched for unreported suits against the University of Massachusetts and nearby private colleges. The archives did not contain any college access cases between 1860 and 1960. Hampshire County Superior Court Records, Civil Volumes, Massachusetts Supreme Judicial Court Archives. Research assistance provided by Victor John, Wheaton College class of 2015.

18. Gerard A. Fowler, "The Legal Relationship between the American College Student and the College: An Historical Perspective and the Renewal of a Proposal," *Journal of Law and Education* 13 (1984): 401–16; Gregory E. Michael, "The Unitary Theory: A Proposal for a Stable Student-School Legal Relationship," *Journal of Law and Education* 1 (1972): 411–34; Victoria J. Dodd, "The Non-contractual Nature of the Student-University Contractual Relationship," *University of Kansas Law Review* 33 (1985): 701–31; Bickel and Lake, *The Rights and Responsibilities of the Modern University*, 36.

19. Robert M. O'Neil, "Judicial Deference to Academic Decisions: An Outmoded Concept?," *Journal of College and University Law* 36 (2010): 746; Michael A. Olivas and Kathleen McCartan Denison, "Legalization in the Academy: Higher Education and the Supreme Court," *Journal of College and University Law* 11 (1984): 2.

20. Richard Arum has argued that tallying student wins and losses in appellate courts demonstrates the "court climate" of various eras and provides some indication of whether judges leaned toward students or school authorities. Arum, *Judging School Discipline*, 46–48, 280n13, 288n29.

21. Bickel and Lake, *The Rights and Responsibilities of the Modern University*, 30–31. Also see Note, "Common Law Rights for Private University Students," *Yale Law Journal* 84 (1974): 120–50; William Cohen, "The Private-Public Legal Aspects of Institutions of Higher Education," *Denver Law Journal* 45 (1968): 643–48.

22. Gajda, *The Trials of Academe*, 25, 39; Byrne, "Academic Freedom," 323; Harry T. Edwards and Virginia Davis Nordin, *Higher Education and the Law* (Cambridge, MA: Institute for Educational Management, 1979), 4, 14, 17; Comment, "Private Government on the Campus," 1367. An early scholar of the subject concluded that higher education law was infrequently studied because its "peculiar" nature was incompatible with the standard categories of legal analysis. Kirkpatrick, *Academic Organization and Control*, xiii.

23. Regarding the current emphasis on academic (as opposed to institutional) deference, see Robert M. Hendrickson, Jason E. Lane, James T. Harris, and Richard H. Dorman, *Academic Leadership and Governance of Higher Education: A Guide for Trustees, Leaders, and Aspiring Leaders of Two- and Four-Year Institutions* (Sterling, VA: Stylus, 2013), 144–46.

24. Julie A. Reuben, *The Making of the Modern University: Intellectual Transformation and the Marginalization of Morality* (Chicago: University of Chicago Press, 1996). Regarding the emergence of professional administration, see Charles W. Eliot, *University Administration* (New York: Houghton Mifflin, 1908).

25. Burke, *American Collegiate Populations*, 215, 240; Roger Geiger, "The Rise and Fall of Useful Knowledge: Higher Education for Science, Agriculture and the Mechanic Arts, 1850–1875," *History of Higher Education Annual* 18 (1998): 47–66; Lyman A. Glenny and Thomas K. Dalglish, *Public Universities, State Agencies, and the Law: Constitutional Autonomy in Decline* (Berkeley: University of California Center for Research and Development in Higher Education, 1973), 13; Marc A. VanOverbeke, *The Standardization of American Schooling: Linking Secondary and Higher Education, 1870–1910* (New York: Palgrave Macmillan, 2008). The courts have wrestled with the proper definition of a "college" in a number of cases. Olivas, *Suing Alma Mater*, 9.

26. Scott M. Gelber, *The University and the People: Envisioning American Higher Education in an Era of Populist Protest* (Madison: University of Wisconsin Press, 2011). Student litigants were more successful west of the Mississippi River, where they won eight out of nine cases before 1910. In contrast, students won just seven out of eighteen eastern cases in this period. These regional tendencies may reflect the populistic leanings of some western judges as well as the greater prominence and obligations of public universities in western states. See appendix A.

27. Peter Karsten, *Heart versus Head: Judge-Made Law in Nineteenth-Century America* (Chapel Hill: University of North Carolina Press, 1997), 2–7, 204, 245. Rulings that pro-

moted college access may have also been encouraged by the common law tradition of regulating institutions in the name of the public welfare. William J. Novak, *The People's Welfare: Law and Regulation in Nineteenth-Century America* (Chapel Hill: University of North Carolina, 1996).

28. For comparison and contrast of university regulation and economic regulation, see Nathan Glazer, "Regulating Business and the Universities: One Problem or Two?," *Public Interest* 56 (1979): 46.

29. Regarding this justification of common law, see Kunal Parker, *Common Law, History, and Democracy in America, 1790–1900: Legal Thought before Modernism* (New York: Cambridge University Press, 2011), 206.

30. Byrne, "Academic Freedom," 324. Also see Kaplin and Lee, *The Law of Higher Education*, vol. 1, 10; Edwards and Nordin, *Higher Education and the Law*, 14.

31. See, for example, *General Laws of the State of Texas, Passed at the Regular Session of the 17th Legislature* (Galveston: State Printer, 1881), 81.

32. Public institutions were the target of 71 percent (72/102) of college access suits between 1860 and 1960. See appendix A. Also see Robert A. Lowry, "An Analysis of Court Cases Concerning the Authority of Colleges and Universities to Establish Policies Pertaining to the Admission, Dismissal, Control and Graduation of Students" (PhD diss., University of Pittsburgh, 1970), 203–4. Normal schools belong in this analysis of higher education because they overlapped with colleges in terms of their purpose, curriculum, and students during the nineteenth century. The briefs and opinions of early college lawsuits routinely cited precedents involving normal schools, which were sometimes defined as the legal equivalent of high schools and sometimes defined as colleges. Christine A. Ogren, *The American State Normal School: An Instrument of Great Good* (New York: Palgrave Macmillan, 2005); Jurgen Herbst, *And Sadly Teach: Teacher Education and Professionalization in American Culture* (Madison: University of Wisconsin Press, 1989). In recent decades, community college cases are typically seen as applicable to four-year colleges. Olivas, *Suing Alma Mater*, 18; Robert C. Cloud, ed., *Legal Issues in the Community College* (San Francisco: Jossey-Bass, 2004). Community colleges rarely appear in college access suits before 1960, in part because they did not enroll a large percentage of college students up until that decade. The lack of early community colleges suits may have also resulted from their open-access policies and the lack of financial and social capital among community college students. Steven Brint and Jerome Karabel, *The Diverted Dream: Community Colleges and the Promise of Educational Opportunity in America, 1900–1985* (New York: Oxford University Press, 1985), 26, 66, 71–73, 180. Normal schools and community colleges were the target of 12 suits (5 of which were won by students) out of the 102 suits that are the focus of this book.

33. Students won ten out of thirteen suits against public colleges before 1910. See appendix A.

34. Before the Civil War, state legislatures routinely allocated funds to private institutions. Some public institutions initially resembled private classical colleges, while some private institutions mirrored the typical public emphases of access and practicality. Laurence R. Veysey, *The Emergence of the American University* (Chicago: University of Chicago Press, 1965), 112–13; John S. Whitehead, *The Separation of College and State: Columbia, Dartmouth, Harvard, and Yale, 1776–1876* (New Haven, CT: Yale University Press, 1973).

35. John Aubrey Douglass, *The Conditions for Admission: Access, Equity, and the Social Contract of Public Universities* (Palo Alto, CA: Stanford University Press, 2007), 13–20.

36. *The General Statutes of the State of Kansas* (Lawrence: State Printers, 1868), 75.

37. Amy Dru Stanley, *From Bondage to Contract: Wage Labor, Marriage, and the Market in the Age of Slave Emancipation* (New York: Cambridge University Press, 1998).

38. Michael A. Olivas, "Reflections on Professorial Academic Freedom: Second Thoughts on the 'Third Essential Freedom,'" *Stanford Law Review* 45 (1993): 1835–58; Matthew W. Finkin, "On 'Institutional' Academic Freedom," *Texas Law Review* 61 (1983): 817–57.

39. University of Wisconsin president John Bascom recalled that only one regent during his tenure exhibited much familiarity with the substance of higher education. Merle Curti and Vernon Carstensen, *University of Wisconsin: A History, 1848–1925*, vol. 1 (Madison: University of Wisconsin Press, 1949), 255. Also see Clyde W. Barrow, *Universities and the Capitalist State: Corporate Liberalism and the Reconstruction of American Higher Education, 1894–1928* (Madison: University of Wisconsin Press, 1990). Viewing these cases as indications of a lack of deference is consistent with *Dartmouth*, which focused on corporate law and had relatively little to say in defense of scholarly autonomy. John Whitehead, "How to Think about the Dartmouth College Case," *History of Education Quarterly* 26 (1986): 333–49.

40. Roger L. Geiger, *To Advance Knowledge: The Growth of American Research Universities, 1900–1940* (New York: Oxford University Press, 1986), 41–43, 108, 123; Reuben, *The Making of the Modern University*, 244; Hofstadter and Metzger, *The Development of Academic Freedom in the United States*, 468–506. Faculty still remained vulnerable, especially during wartime. Carol S. Gruber, *Mars and Minerva: World War I and the Uses of the Higher Learning in America* (Baton Rouge: Louisiana State University Press, 1975); Ellen Schrecker, *No Ivory Tower: McCarthyism and the Universities* (New York: Oxford University Press, 1986). Regarding liberal arts colleges, see W. Bruce Leslie, *Gentlemen and Scholars: College and Community in the "Age of the University," 1865–1917* (University Park: Pennsylvania State University Press, 1992), 231, 235–36. See chapters 2 and 5 for examples of statutes that expanded university authority over admissions and tuition.

41. William J. Novak, "The Legal Origins of the Modern American State," in Austin Sarat, Bryant Garth, and Robert A. Kagan, eds., *Looking Back at Law's Century* (Ithaca, NY: Cornell University Press, 2002), 265–68; Brian Balogh, *A Government Out of Sight: The Mystery of National Authority in Nineteenth-Century America* (New York: Cambridge University Press, 2009), 325–26. The legal traditions that undergirded many early prostudent rulings lost influence during the twentieth century, when common law competed for influence with increasing numbers of statutes and administrative agencies. Parker, *Common Law, History, and Democracy in America*, 3–4.

42. Courts had tended to defer to government officials since the growth of administrative units in the late nineteenth century, and they became even more deferential during the first decades of the twentieth century. Along with respect for administrative expertise, the potentially overwhelming regulatory burden for legislatures and courts discouraged close oversight of these agencies. Jerry L. Mashaw, *Due Process in the Administrative State* (New Haven, CT: Yale University Press, 1985), 21l; Horwitz, *The Transformation of American Law*, 4, 207, 223.

43. John Dickinson, *Administrative Justice and the Supremacy of Law in the United States* (New York: Russell and Russell, 1927), 11, 42n13; Alexander M. Bickel and Benno C. Schmidt Jr., *The Judiciary and Responsible Government, 1910–1921*, part I (New York: Macmillan, 1984), 664; William C. Chase, *The American Law School and the Rise of Administrative Government* (Madison: University of Wisconsin Press, 1982); Mashaw, *Due Process in the Administrative State*, 25; Novak, "The Legal Origins of the Modern American State," 270–71. Also see Daniel P. Carpenter, *The Forging of Bureaucratic Autonomy: Reputations, Networks, and Policy Innovation in Executive Agencies, 1862–1928* (Princeton, NJ: Princeton University Press, 2001). Formal legal training went from an exception to a rule by 1910. Friedman, *American Law in the Twentieth Century*, 35–38.

44. O'Neil, "Judicial Deference to Academic Decisions," 734.

45. Dickinson, *Administrative Justice*, 61–72; Friedman, *A History of American Law*, 341–42.

46. Stephen Skowronek, *Building a New American State: The Expansion of National Administrative Capacities, 1877–1920* (New York: Cambridge University Press, 1982), 42; Frederick Rudolph, *The American College and University: A History* (New York: Knopf, 1962), 364–65. The close relationship between faculty and state officials in Wisconsin served as an example for reformers across the nation. Charles McCarthy, *The Wisconsin Idea* (New York: Macmillan, 1912).

47. When scholars think about legal questions related to the administrative expertise of state agencies, they tend to focus on agencies that regulate the private sector (such as environmental protection) rather than agencies that provide public services (such as schools). Glenny and Dalglish, *Public Universities, State Agencies, and the Law*, 42–44.

48. M. M. Chambers, "The Position of the University Governing Board in the Total Scheme of the State Government," *Proceedings of the Association of Governing Boards of State Universities* (1931), 73; Edward Elliott, "The Board of Control," in R. A. Kent, ed., *Higher Education in America* (Boston: Ginn, 1930), 611; Roy R. Ray, "Powers and Authorities of the Governing Boards of State Colleges and Universities," *Kentucky Law Journal* 17 (1928): 17–18; Edwards and Nordin, *Higher Education and the Law*, 80.

49. Arthur J. Klein, "Survey of Land-Grant Colleges and Universities," *United States Office of Education Bulletin*, vol. 2 (Washington, DC: Government Printing Office, 1930), 36; Glenny and Dalglish, *Public Universities, State Agencies, and the Law*, 14–41, 146–47.

50. Glenny and Dalglish, *Public Universities, State Agencies, and the Law*, 45.

51. Horwitz, *The Transformation of American Law*, 233.

52. Bickel and Lake, *The Rights and Responsibilities of the Modern University*, 18.

53. Gajda, *The Trials of Academe*, 16.

Chapter 1. Common Schools

1. *State ex rel. Stallard v. White*, 82 Ind. 278, 283–84 (1882).

2. Project, "Education and the Law: State Interests and Individual Rights," *University of Michigan Law Review* 74 (1976): 1455; David Tyack, Thomas James, and Aaron Benavot, *Law and the Shaping of Public Education, 1785–1954* (Madison: University of Wisconsin Press, 1987), 108.

3. J. E. Allen, "The Legal Rights of School Authorities Regarding Admission and Expulsion of Pupils," *Peabody Journal of Education* 2 (1925): 175; Benjamin Justice, *The War*

That Wasn't: Religious Conflict and Compromise in the Common Schools of New York State, 1865–1900 (Albany: State University of New York Press, 2005).

4. Richard Arum, *Judging School Discipline: The Crisis of Moral Authority* (Cambridge, MA: Harvard University Press, 2003), 17–18, 82.

5. Tyack, James, and Benavot, *Law and the Shaping of Public Education*, 66–68, 130.

6. Tyack, James, and Benavot, *Law and the Shaping of Public Education*, 70, 117.

7. Michael Farris and Bradley P. Jacob, "Public Schools' Pyrrhic Victories over Parental Rights," *Perspectives on Law and the Public Interest* 3 (1998): 123–44.

8. Tracy L. Steffes, *School, Society, and State: A New Education to Govern Modern America, 1890–1940* (Chicago: University of Chicago Press, 2012), 122; Newton Edwards, *The Courts and the Public Schools: The Legal Basis of School Organization and Administration* (Chicago: University of Chicago Press, 1933), 480.

9. In general, compulsory attendance laws were loosely applied until the early twentieth century, when concerns over child labor, immigration, and urbanization prompted states to develop more robust enforcement mechanisms. Stephen Provasnik, "Judicial Activism and the Origins of Parental Choice: The Court's Role in the Institutionalization of Compulsory Education in the United States, 1891–1925," *History of Education Quarterly* 46 (2006): 318–20; Ethan L. Hutt, "Formalism over Function: Compulsion, Courts, and the Rise of Educational Formalism in America, 1870–1930," *Teachers College Record* 114 (2012): 1–27; Steffes, *School, Society, and State*, 87, 120–23.

10. Carl F. Kaestle, *Pillars of the Republic: Common Schools and American Society, 1760–1860* (New York: Hill and Wang, 1983).

11. William G. Buss, "Procedural Due Process for School Discipline: Probing the Constitutional Outline," *University of Pennsylvania Law Review* 119 (1971): 570; David B. Tyack, *The One Best System: A History of American Urban Education* (Cambridge, MA: Harvard University Press, 1974), 19; Steffes, *School, Society, and State*, 49–51, 123.

12. Stephen R. Goldstein, "Reflections on Developing Trends in the Law of Student Rights," *University of Pennsylvania Law Review* 118 (1970): 612–13.

13. Tyack, James, and Benavot, *Law and the Shaping of Public Education*, 64–66; Terrence Leas, "Evolution of the Doctrine of Academic Deference in American Jurisprudence" (PhD diss., Florida State University, 1989), 104.

14. Harvey Cortlandt Voorhees, *The Law of the Public School System of the United States* (Boston: Little, Brown, 1916), 179.

15. Irwin Taylor, *Public School Law of the United States* (Topeka: Crane, 1892), 171–92, 197–200, 347; Allen, "The Legal Rights of School Authorities," 175–89; Provasnik, "Judicial Activism and the Origins of Parental Choice," 323–24.

16. John Aubrey Douglass, *The Conditions for Admission: Access, Equity, and the Social Contract of Public Universities* (Palo Alto, CA: Stanford University Press, 2007); Harold Wechsler, *The Qualified Student: A History of Selective College Admission in America* (New York: John Wiley and Sons, 1977).

17. *Proceedings and Addresses of the National Educational Association* (1889), 374–75; Joseph L. Henderson, *Admission to College by Certificate* (New York: Teachers College, 1912), 24.

18. Comment, "Private Government on the Campus: Judicial Review of University Expulsions," *Yale Law Journal* 72 (1963): 1380.

19. See appendix B. Common school cases constituted 50 percent (36/72) of the total citations in prostudent college expulsion rulings during this era, compared to 25 percent (6/24) of the citations in procollege opinions. This calculation omits *Burg v. Milwaukee Medical College*, 128 Wis. 7 (1906), an outlier that cited 56 cases (only two of which concerned common schools). If *Burg* is included in the tally of procollege rulings, the results are 10 percent (rather than 25 percent), making the contrast even more substantial.

20. Appellant's Brief (hereafter *Stallard* brief), filed May 4, 1882, *State ex rel. Stallard v. White*, case no. 9986, Indiana Supreme Court records and briefs, Indiana State Archives, 11; Closing Argument of the Faculty to the Tippecanoe Circuit Court (undated) (hereafter Purdue Closing Argument), *State ex rel. Stallard v. White*, case no. 9986, Indiana Supreme Court records and briefs, Indiana State Archives, 10, 14; Appellees' Petition for Rehearing (hereafter Purdue Petition for Rehearing), filed August 10, 1882, *State ex rel. Stallard v. White*, case no. 9986, Indiana Supreme Court records and briefs, Indiana State Archives, 16–18.

21. Kaestle, *Pillars of the Republic*, 67–68.

22. Frederic H. Chase, *Lemuel Shaw: Chief Justice of the Supreme Judicial Court of Massachusetts, 1830–1860* (Boston: Houghton Mifflin, 1918), 73.

23. *Spear v. Cumming*, 40 Mass. 224 (1839).

24. *Henry Hodgkins v. Inhabitants of Rockport*, 105 Mass. 475 (1870).

25. *State ex rel. Burpee v. Burton*, 45 Wis. 150, 157, 158 (1878).

26. *Dritt v. Snodgrass*, Supreme Court of Missouri, 66 Mo. 286, 293 (1877).

27. Textbook cited in Kaestle, *Pillars of the Republic*, 93. It is important to note, however, that Benjamin Justice has demonstrated that many religious conflicts were resolved through compromises that offered some protection for minority rights. Justice, *The War That Wasn't*.

28. Daniel F. Reilly, *The School Controversy, 1891–1893* (Washington, DC: Catholic University Press, 1943), 106; Donald Boles, *The Two Swords: Commentaries and Cases in Religion and Education* (Ames: Iowa State University Press, 1967), 67, 84; Ward M. McAfee, *Religion, Race, and Reconstruction: The Public School in the Politics of the 1870s* (Albany: State University of New York Press, 1998), 27–41; Tyack, James, and Benavot, *Law and the Shaping of Public Education*, 155, 162–64. See, for example, *Donahoe v. Richards*, 38 Me. 379 (1854); *Spiller vs. Inhabitants of Woburn*, 94 Mass. 127 (1866).

29. Purdue Closing Argument, 10, 14; Purdue Petition for Rehearing, 16–18.

30. *Sherman v. Inhabitants of Charlestown*, 62 Mass. 160, 162, 163 (1851).

31. Appellants' Abstract of Record, filed December 1870, *Burdick v. Babcock*, Iowa Supreme Court records and briefs, Iowa State Law Library, 4, 13, 17, 22.

32. Appellees' Argument, April 1871, *Burdick v. Babcock*, Iowa Supreme Court records and briefs, Iowa State Law Library, 6, 9–10; *Burdick v. Babcock*, 31 Iowa 562 (1871). Truancy was a common complaint among nineteenth-century education leaders. Kaestle, *Pillars of the Republic*, 111.

33. *Burdick*, 31 Iowa at 570–71.

34. Purdue Petition for Rehearing, 16–18. In one case, the Supreme Court of Missouri rejected the argument that common schools were required "to throw open and leave open the doors of the school" and mocked the perception that pupils could be "at liberty to go a fishing during school hours." *King v. Jefferson City School Board*, 71 Mo. 628,

629, 630 (1880). The petition also cited *Russell v. Lynnfield*, 116 Mass. 365 (1874); *Sewell v. Board of Education*, 29 Ohio St. 89, 91 (1876), and *State v. Minzer*, 50 Iowa 145 (1878).

35. *Stallard* brief, 9.

36. *Nourse v. Meriam*, 62 Mass. 11 (1851).

37. *Morrow v. Wood*, 35 Wis. 59 (1874); *Waukesha Freeman*, September 17, 1874, 1; Amended Complaint, *Morrow v. Wood* (January Term 1874), Wisconsin Supreme Court records and briefs, Wisconsin State Law Library.

38. Bill of Exceptions, *Morrow v. Wood* (January Term 1874), Wisconsin Supreme Court records and briefs, Wisconsin State Law Library, 19.

39. Appellant's Brief, *Morrow v. Wood* (January Term 1874), Wisconsin Supreme Court records and briefs, Wisconsin State Law Library, 11–12.

40. *Morrow*, 35 Wis. at 66.

41. *Stallard*, 82 Ind. at 285.

42. William M. Rockel, "School Teacher-Rights and Liabilities in Relation to His Pupil," *Central Law Journal* 25 (1887): 339–44.

43. *Rulison v. Post*, 79 Ill. 567 (1875); Bill of Exceptions from the Circuit Court of Winnebago County, *Rulison v. Post* (October Term 1873), General Record 8113, Clerk of the Circuit Court, Rockford, Illinois.

44. *Rulison*, 79 Ill. at 570, 571. Regarding discipline in nineteenth-century common schools, see Kaestle, *Pillars of the Republic*, 160.

45. *Chicago Daily Tribune*, September 25, 1876, 4.

46. *Trustees v. Van Allen*, 87 Ill. 303 (1877).

47. Petition for Mandamus, filed October 7, 1874, *Van Allen v. Trustees*, case no. S-51562, Superior Court of Cook County records and briefs, Office of the Clerk of the Circuit Court of Cook County; *Chicago Tribune*, September 24, 1874, 3, and July 22, 1872, 4.

48. *Trustees*, 87 Ill. at 306, 307.

49. John Joseph Flinn, *The Handbook of Chicago Biography* (Chicago: Standard Guide, 1893), 365–66.

50. *State v. Osborne*, 24 Mo. App. 309 (1887); *State v. Osborne*, 32 Mo. App. 536 (1888).

51. *Commonwealth ex rel. Hill v. McCauley*, 2 Pa. Co. Ct. 459 (1887).

52. *State ex rel. Andrews v. Webber*, 108 Ind. 31 (1886).

53. *New York Times*, October 28, 1935, 19.

54. Appellant's Brief, filed January 4, 1886, *State ex rel. Andrew v. Webber*, case no. 12753, Indiana Supreme Court records and briefs, Indiana State Archives, 14; Appellant's Additional Brief, filed February 26, 1886, *State ex rel. Andrew v. Webber*, case no. 12753, Indiana Supreme Court records and briefs, Indiana State Archives, 4.

55. Appellee's Brief, filed February 23, 1886, *State ex rel. Andrew v. Webber*, case no. 12753, Indiana Supreme Court records and briefs, Indiana State Archives, 6–7.

56. *Andrews*, 108 Ind. at 35. The son, Abram Piatt Andrews Jr., became a professor of economics at Harvard University before serving six terms as a congressional representative for Massachusetts. *Biographical Dictionary of the United States Congress*, accessed September 26, 2013, http://bioguide.congress.gov/scripts/biodisplay.pl?index=A000240.

57. *Hill*, 2 Pa. Co. Ct. at 461.

58. *Perkins v. West Des Moines*, 56 Iowa 476 (1881). The Nebraska case was *Jackson v. State ex rel. Majors*, 57 Neb. 183 (1898).

59. Argument for Appellant, *Perkins v. West Des Moines*, 1881, Iowa Supreme Court records and briefs, Iowa State Law Library, 3–5.

60. *Perkins*, 56 Iowa at 479. This was a common conclusion. Edwards, *The Courts and the Public Schools*, 532–33.

61. The ruling is especially striking because the father merely said that grammar was unnecessary because he never studied it. *State ex rel. Sheibley v. School District No. 1*, 31 Neb. 552, 554 (1891). *Sheibley* was also cited in *Nelson v. Lincoln Medical College*, 81 Neb. 533 (1908).

62. *Brown v. Board of Education*, 8 Ohio Dec. 378 (1899). The common school cases were *Roe v. Denning*, 21 Ohio St. 666 (1871), and *Board of Education v. Minor*, 23 Ohio St. 211 (1872).

63. Tyack, James, and Benavot, *Law and the Shaping of Public Education*, 123; Tyack, *The One Best System*, 127, 141; David Tyack and Elisabeth Hansot, *Managers of Virtue: Public School Leadership in America, 1820–1980* (New York: Basic Books, 1982), 98, 108; Steffes, *School, Society, and State*, 17, 120, 145–48; Edwards, *The Courts and the Public Schools*, 500, 526.

64. Paul R. Mort, *The Law and Public Education* (Chicago: Foundation, 1941), 16.

65. Provasnik, "Judicial Activism and the Origins of Parental Choice," 337; M. R. Sumption, "The Control of Pupil Conduct by the School," *Law and Contemporary Problems* 20 (1955): 90; Edwards, *The Courts and the Public Schools*, 1; Steffes, *School, Society, and State*, 89.

66. In the antebellum era, a "graded" school system meant that a district had primary, grammar, and high schools rather than a single school for all children. After the Civil War, "graded" gradually began to assume its current meaning of different classes for each age group within a single school. Kaestle, *Pillars of the Republic*, 132; Tyack, *The One Best System*, 45.

67. Appellee's Brief, filed February 23, 1886, *State ex rel. Andrew v. Webber*, case no. 12753, Indiana Supreme Court records and briefs, Indiana State Archives, 9; *State ex rel. Andrews v. Webber*, 108 Ind. 31 (1886). Also see *Bourne v. Board of Trustees*, 35 Neb. 1 (1892).

68. *Barnard v. Inhabitants of Shelburne*, 216 Mass. 19, 21 (1913).

69. *Meyer v. Nebraska*, 262 U.S. 390 (1923); *Pierce v. Society of Sisters*, 268 U.S. 510 (1925). Also see Goldstein, "Reflections on Developing Trends in the Law of Student Rights," 612–13; Provasnik, "Judicial Activism and the Origins of Parental Choice," 342–46.

70. *Hamilton v. Regents of the University of California*, 293 U.S. 245 (1934).

71. C. H. Katenkamp, "The Law in School Discipline," *Phi Delta Kappan* 21 (1938): 147, 150; Steffes, *School, Society, and State*, 150–51.

72. *West Virginia State Board of Education v. Barnette*, 319 U.S. 624 (1943). This decision was likely influenced by the court's desire to distance itself from German and Italian fascism. Stephen R. Goldstein, "Reflections on Developing Trends in the Law of Student Rights," *University of Pennsylvania Law Review* 118 (1970), 613–14; Farris and Jacob, "Public Schools' Pyrrhic Victories over Parental Rights," 123–44.

73. From 1910 to 1960, 39 percent (13/33) of college exclusion opinions included at least one common school citation, and 23 percent (61/265) of the total citations in these opinions were common school cases. The corresponding figures for 1860 to 1910 are 48 percent (10/21) and 44 percent (42/96). The proportion of procollege opinions that

included common school citations remained similar (at roughly a third) from 1860 to 1910 and from 1910 to 1960. See appendix B. The relationship between lower and higher education law remained fluid well into the twentieth century. Note the inconsistent chapter titles in *The First Yearbook of School Law* (Washington, DC: M. M. Chambers, 1933), *The Third Yearbook of School Law* (Washington, DC: M. M. Chambers, 1935), and *The Fourth Yearbook of School Law* (Washington, DC: M. M. Chambers, 1936).

74. *Waugh v. University of Mississippi*, 237 U.S. 589 (1915).

75. *Hobbs v. Germany*, 94 Miss. 469, 479 (1909). Statement of Case and Brief on Behalf of Appellee, filed June 19, 1913, *University of Mississippi v. Waugh*, case no. 16700, Mississippi Supreme Court records and briefs, Mississippi Department of Archives and History; Brief of A. F. Fox, Attorney for Appellee, filed June 16, 1913, *University of Mississippi v. Waugh*, case no. 16700, Mississippi Supreme Court records and briefs, Mississippi Department of Archives and History.

76. *University of Mississippi v. Waugh*, 105 Miss. 223 (1913); *Waugh v. University of Mississippi*, 237 U.S. 589 (1915).

77. *Tanton v. McKenney*, 226 Mich. 245 (1924).

78. *Foley v. Benedict*, 122 Tex. 193 (1932). The school cases were *Wilson v. Board*, 233 Ill. 464 (1908); *Zucht v. San Antonio*, 170 S.W. 840 (1914); *Pugsley v. Sellmeyer*, 158 Ark. 247 (1923). Courts consistently upheld vaccination requirements. Steffes, *School, Society, and State*, 137.

79. See appendix B. *Dehaan v. Brandeis University*, 150 F. Supp. 626, 628 (1957).

80. Kaestle, *Pillars of the Republic*, 104, 151, 166; Tyack, James, and Benavot, *Law and the Shaping of Public Education*, 20–42, 73, 81, 85, 142.

81. Voorhees, *The Law of the Public School System of the United States*, 183; Lee O. Garber, "Legal Requirements for Admission to Public Schools," *Law and Contemporary Problems* 20 (1955): 37.

82. *State ex rel. Bowe v. Board of Education of Fond Du Lac*, 63 Wis. 234, 235 (1885).

83. *State ex rel. Priest v. Regents of University of Wisconsin*, 54 Wis. 159 (1882); *State ex rel. Little v. Regents of University of Kansas*, 55 Kan. 389 (1895).

84. *State ex rel. Garth v. Switzler*, 143 Mo. 287 (1898); *Sewickley School District v. Osborne School District*, 19 Pa. Co. Ct. 257 (1897). The university's unsuccessful defense called attention to cases that allowed high schools to receive public appropriations even though they enrolled relatively few students. Argument of Frederick N. Judson, filed December 10, 1897, *State ex rel. Wilfley v. Rassiey* and *State ex rel. Garth v. Switzler* (combined), Missouri Supreme Court records and briefs, Missouri State Archives, 18. State high courts heard challenges to high school funding nine times during the 1870s and 1880s and generally upheld the practice. B. J. Burrell and R. H. Eckelberry, "The High-School Question before the Courts in the Post-Civil-War Period," *School Review* 42 (1934): 255–65; J. L. Pickard, "The High School: Its Necessity and Right to Exist as a Part of the True System of Public Education," *Education* 3 (1882): 162.

85. *Barker v. Crum*, 177 Ky. 637 (1917). The common school case was *Dawson v. Lee*, 83 Ky. 49 (1884). In vain, the university cited cases that endorsed special state support for the education of orphans, blind children, and the "feeble-minded." Petition by Appellees for Rehearing, filed February 7, 1918, *Barker v. Crum*, case no. 46049, Kentucky Court of

Appeals records and briefs, Kentucky Department for Libraries and Archives, Public Records Division, iii, 54.

86. *Rheam v. University of Oklahoma*, 161 Okla. 268 (1933); *Bryant v. Whisenant*, 167 Ala. 325 (1910).

87. *State ex rel. Veeder v. State Board of Education*, 97 Mont. 121 (1934). The Georgia case was *Linton v. Lucy Cobb Institute*, 117 Ga. 678 (1903). It was also cited in a similar case that authorized fees at the University of Georgia. *State of Georgia v. University of Georgia*, 179 Ga. 210 (1934). Regarding the influence of *Bryant*, also see Edwards, *The Courts and the Public Schools*, 506.

88. J. Morgan Kousser, *Dead End: The Development of Nineteenth-Century Litigation on Racial Discrimination in Schools* (New York: Oxford University Press, 1986); Davison M. Douglas, *Jim Crow Moves North: The Battle over Northern School Segregation, 1865–1954* (New York: Cambridge University Press, 2005), 62–122.

89. Tyack, James, and Benavot, *Law and the Shaping of Public Education*, 152; J. Morgan Kousser, "'The Onward March of Right Principles': State Legislative Actions on Racial Discrimination in Schools in Nineteenth-Century America," *Historical Methods: A Journal of Quantitative and Interdisciplinary History* 35 (2002): 5, 182; Andrew Kull, *The Color-Blind Constitution* (Cambridge, MA: Harvard University Press, 1994). The most racially liberal decision was issued by a Kansas court that wished for all children to "mingle together and learn to know each other." *Board of Education v. Tinnon*, 26 Kan. 1, 30, 32 (1881).

90. See appendix B.

91. *State ex rel. Weaver v. OSU*, 126 Ohio St. 290 (1933).

92. Appellee's Brief, *Pearson v. Murray*, case no. 53 (October Term 1935), Maryland Court of Appeals records and briefs, Maryland State Archives; *Pearson v. Murray*, 169 Md. 478 (1936).

93. *Cumming v. Richmond*, 175 U.S. 528 (1899); *Gong Lum v. Rice*, 275 U.S. 78 (1927); *State ex rel. Gaines v. Canada*, 342 Mo. 121 (1938).

94. For example, see *Wrighten v. University of South Carolina*, 72 F. Supp. 948 (1947).

95. *Cumming* accepted the district's argument that it would be inefficient to divert funds from the crowded common schools that served the vast majority of black students. The case against this policy was probably weakened when attorneys changed course during the trial and began to argue for closure of the white high school. *Cumming*, 175 U.S. at 545; Alexander M. Bickel and Benno C. Schmidt Jr., *The Judiciary and Responsible Government, 1910–1921*, part II (New York: Macmillan, 1984), 758–59.

96. *Gong Lum*, 275 U.S. at 85.

97. Perhaps these analogies should come as no surprise. Slavery has been used as a metaphor throughout many of the nation's legal conflicts. Barbara Young Welke, *Law and the Borders of Belonging in the Long Nineteenth Century United States* (New York: Cambridge University Press, 2010); Amy Dru Stanley, *From Bondage to Contract: Wage Labor, Marriage, and the Market in the Age of Slave Emancipation* (New York: Cambridge University Press, 1998).

98. *Foltz v. Hoge*, 54 Cal. 28 (1879); Respondent's Points and Authorities, filed August 4, 1879, *Foltz v. Hoge*, case no. 6581, California Supreme Court records and briefs, California

State Archives, 5. The Michigan case was *People v. Board of Education of Detroit*, 18 Mich. 400 (1869).

99. Appellant's Points and Authorities, filed August 7, 1879, *Foltz v. Hoge*, case no. 6581, California Supreme Court records and briefs, California State Archives, 2, 7.

100. In 1863, the California legislature officially sanctioned what had been an informal tradition of segregation by banning "Negroes, Mongolians, and Indians" from attending public schools. The statute was revised the following year to require the construction of separate schools whenever ten or more students of color lived in a district. Ultimately, *Ward* required towns to educate African American students regardless of how few children resided in a district but otherwise validated the state's segregation statute. *Ward v. Flood*, 48 Cal. 36 (1874); Charles Wollenberg, *All Deliberate Speed: Segregation and Exclusion in California Schools, 1855–1975* (Berkeley: University of California Press, 1976), 10–16.

101. In addition to the faulty parallel between *Ward* and *Foltz*, the argument for segregation itself had become weaker since San Francisco, Oakland, and Sacramento integrated their schools in the interim. Wollenberg, *All Deliberate Speed*, 10–16, 24–26.

102. The normal school case, discussed in chapter 4, was *Miller v. Dailey*, 136 Cal. 212 (1902). The first case ruled that San Francisco's school board could not exclude an eight-year-old lifelong resident of the city. *Tape v. Hurley*, 66 Cal. 473, 474 (1885). The other case targeted a district that had violated the terms of *Ward* by failing to make any arrangements for black students. *Wysinger v. Crookshank*, 82 Cal. 588 (1890).

103. *Commonwealth ex rel. Hill v. McCauley*, 2 Pa. Co. Ct. 459 (1887). One case ruled that a state segregation law violated the constitutional guarantee of equal protection of the law. *Commonwealth ex rel. Allen v. Davis*, 10 W.N.C. 156 (1881). The other ordered a district to abide by the desegregation statute that was passed in response to the first decision. *Kaine v. Commonwealth ex rel. Manaway*, 101 Pa. 490 (1882).

104. *Roberts v. City of Boston*, 5 Cush. 198 (1849).

105. A Massachusetts law authorized parents to sue for damages in these circumstances in the 1840s. Kousser, "The Onward March of Right Principles," 182.

106. Kaestle, *Pillars of the Republic*, 177; Hilary Moss, *Schooling Citizens: The African American Struggle for Education in Antebellum America* (Chicago: University of Chicago Press, 2009), 164–67, 173–78; Douglas, *Jim Crow Moves North*, 52–53.

107. Moss, *Schooling Citizens*, 179–81.

108. *Roberts*, 5 Cush. at 208, 209. Also see Kull, *The Color-Blind Constitution*, 28–28, 41–43, 95–95; Leonard W. Levy, *The Law of the Commonwealth and Chief Justice Shaw* (Cambridge, MA: Harvard University Press, 1957), 109–17.

109. *Stallard* brief; *State ex rel. Stallard v. White*, 82 Ind. 278 (1882).

110. *State v. Duffy*, 7 Nev. 342 (1872). The brief also cited an Indiana ruling that reiterated that black children were entitled to public schooling. *Cory v. Carter*, 48 Ind. 327 (1874). Yet this opinion also ruled that Indiana's constitution did not apply to black students because they were not considered citizens when that document was ratified. Also see Douglas, *Jim Crow Moves North*, 73–74.

111. *Chase v. Stephenson*, 71 Ill. 383 (1874). Also see Robert L. McCaul, *The Black Struggle for Public Schooling in Nineteenth-Century Illinois* (Carbondale: Southern Illinois University Press, 1987), 114–36; *Inter Ocean* (Chicago), December 14, 1874, 5.

112. *Chase*, 71 Ill. at 385.

113. *Stallard* brief, 7–8.

114. Purdue Closing Argument, 10. This interpretation clashed with the origins of the amendment, which was designed to protect the civil rights of African Americans, as well religious minorities, women, and white northerners residing in southern states after the Civil War. William E. Nelson, *The Fourteenth Amendment: From Political Principle to Judicial Doctrine* (Cambridge, MA: Harvard University Press, 1988), 163–79.

115. *Stallard*, 82 Ind. 278.

116. Purdue Petition for Rehearing, 17.

117. Attorneys for the University of Mississippi also cited three other segregation cases besides *Roberts*: *Reynolds v. Board of Education*, 66 Kan. 672 (1903); *Martin v. Board of Education*, 42 W. Va. 514 (1896); *Lehew v. Brummel*, 103 Mo. 546 (1890). Appellant's Brief, filed May 16, 1913, *University of Mississippi v. Waugh*, case no. 16700, Mississippi Supreme Court records and briefs, Mississippi Department of Archives and History, 13.

118. Statement of Case and Brief on Behalf of Appellee, filed June 19, 1913, *University of Mississippi v. Waugh*, case no. 16700, Mississippi Supreme Court records and briefs, Mississippi Department of Archives and History; Brief of A. F. Fox, Attorney for Appellee, filed June 16, 1913, *University of Mississippi v. Waugh*, Mississippi Supreme Court records and briefs, Mississippi Department of Archives and History. The cases included *People ex rel. King v. Gallagher*, 93 N.Y. 438 (1883); *McFarland v. Goins*, 96 Miss. 67 (1909); *Tape v. Hurley*, 66 Cal. 473 (1885).

119. Brief and Argument, *Waugh v. Board of Trustees of University of Mississippi*, case no. 692 (October Term 1913), United States Supreme Court, 30.

120. School segregation law regularly intersected with transportation rulings. Kull, *The Color-Blind Constitution*, 96.

121. *Hamilton v. Regents of the University of California*, 293 U.S. 245, 262 (1934). This observation was included in the court's ruling in order to explain why the lower school rulings of *Meyer* and *Pierce* did not apply to the higher education case at hand.

Chapter 2. Admissions

1. State and federal reporters published six college admissions rulings before 1936, the year of the first reported NAACP desegregation case. See appendix A.

2. The lack of secondary schooling available to African Americans in the South meant that historically black colleges maintained flexible admissions standards well into the twentieth century. Arthur J. Klein, "Survey of Land-Grant Colleges and Universities," *United States Office of Education Bulletin*, vol. 2 (Washington, DC: Government Printing Office, 1930), 893–94; Charles H. Thompson, "Introduction: The Problem of Negro Higher Education," *Journal of Negro Education* 2 (1933): 260–64; Henry N. Drewry and Humphrey Doermann, *Stand and Prosper: Private Black Colleges and Their Students* (Princeton, NJ: Princeton University Press, 2001), 46, 51, 75.

3. Although colleges and universities increased the quantity and depth of required subjects in accordance with the growth of high school enrollment, secondary school principals successfully lobbied for greater flexibility alongside these rising standards. Marc A. VanOverbeke, *The Standardization of American Schooling: Linking Secondary and Higher Education, 1870–1910* (New York: Palgrave Macmillan, 2008), 102–3, 120–23;

Edwin C. Broome, *A Historical and Critical Discussion of College Admission Requirements* (Princeton, NJ: College Entrance Examination Board, 1963), 82; W. J. Chase and C. H. Thurber, "Tabular Statement of Entrance Requirements to Representative Colleges and Universities of the United States," *School Review* 4 (1896): 341–412; Roger L. Geiger, "The Era of Multipurpose Colleges in American Higher Education," *The American College in the Nineteenth Century* (Nashville: Vanderbilt University Press, 2000), 128, 149.

4. John Aubrey Douglass, *The Conditions for Admission: Access, Equity, and the Social Contract of Public Universities* (Palo Alto, CA: Stanford University Press, 2007); Harold Wechsler, *The Qualified Student: A History of Selective College Admission in America* (New York: John Wiley and Sons, 1977); John Thelin, *A History of American Higher Education* (Baltimore: Johns Hopkins University Press, 2004), 171–74.

5. Wechsler, *The Qualified Student*, 24, 121–22. In 1922, with high school curricula persistently out of sync with college expectations, roughly three-quarters of institutions permitted conditional admissions. Harry Charles McKown, *The Trend of College Entrance Requirements, 1913–1922* (Washington, DC: Government Printing Office, 1925), 127–28.

6. *Proceedings and Addresses of the National Educational Association* (1889), 374–75; Joseph L. Henderson, *Admission to College by Certificate* (New York: Teachers College, 1912), 24.

7. Lester William Bartlett, *State Control of Private Incorporated Institutions of Higher Education* (New York: Teachers College, 1926), 73.

8. M. M. Chambers, "Constitutional Provisions Regarding State Universities," *Educational Law and Administration* 2 (1933): 38; Douglass, *The Conditions for Admission*, 13–17. Unusually, Arizona also obligated its territorial university to make "suitable provisions for the accommodation and education" of deaf, mute, and blind students. This mandate may have been the work of reformers who argued that blind students required higher education because they were not likely to be hired to perform physical labor. *Session Laws of the 16th Legislative Assembly of the Territory of Arizona* (n.p., 1891), 119; Charles Ben Minner, "The Question of Higher Education for the Blind," *Pedagogical Seminary and Journal of Genetic Psychology* 31 (1924): 363–64.

9. William A. Link, *A Hard Country and a Lonely Place: Schooling, Society, and Reform in Rural Virginia, 1870–1920* (Chapel Hill: University of North Carolina Press, 1986), 6, 53–54; Paul Theobald, *Call School: Rural Education in the Midwest to 1918* (Carbondale: Southern Illinois University Press, 1995), 119; James L. Leloudis, *Schooling the New South: Pedagogy, Self, and Society in North Carolina, 1880–1920* (Chapel Hill: University of North Carolina Press, 1996), 10–13.

10. Scott M. Gelber, *The University and the People: Envisioning American Higher Education in an Era of Populist Protest* (Madison: University of Wisconsin Press, 2011), 77.

11. Douglass, *The Conditions for Admission*, 17–18.

12. *The Statutes of California Passed at the 17th Session of the Legislature* (Sacramento: State Printers, 1868), 254.

13. *Laws of Missouri Passed at the Adjourned Session of the 26th General Assembly* (Jefferson City: State Printers, 1872), 168. Also see *The State of Ohio: General and Local Acts Passed and Joint Resolutions Passed by the 59th General Assembly* (Columbus: State Printers, 1870), 21.

14. *Laws of the State of New York passed at the 88th Session of the Legislature* (Albany: William Gould, 1865), 1192.

15. Gelber, *The University and the People*, 68–71; Henderson, *Admission to College by Certificate*, 73, 82–83; VanOverbeke, *The Standardization of American Schooling*, 64–65; Wechsler, *The Qualified Student*, 6, 11, 21; Michael Dennis, *Lessons in Progress: State Universities and Progressivism in the New South, 1880–1920* (Urbana: University of Illinois Press, 2001), 4, 76, 92–93; James E. Pollard, *History of The Ohio State University: The Story of Its First Seventy-Five Years, 1873–1948* (Columbus: Ohio State University Press, 1952), 37–39; Winton U. Solberg, *The University of Illinois, 1867–1894: An Intellectual and Cultural History* (Urbana: University of Illinois Press, 1968), 232, 269.

16. Harry Kersey Jr., *John Milton Gregory and the University of Illinois* (Urbana: University of Illinois Press, 1968), 71–75, 106, 124.

17. *Acts of the General Assembly of the Commonwealth of Kentucky* (Frankfort: State Printer, 1893), 906–7. A similar law constrained Michigan State Agricultural College (now Michigan State University) until 1909. Madison Kuhn, *Michigan State: The First Hundred Years* (East Lansing: Michigan State University Press, 1955), 238.

18. *General Laws of the State of Texas, Passed at the Regular Session of the 17th Legislature* (Galveston: State Printer, 1881), 91. The act designating the University of North Carolina a land grant institution specified that applicants to its A&M programs should be admitted without the same standards required of applicants to the regular college course. *Public Laws of the State of North Carolina Passed by the General Assembly Passed at the Session of 1866–67* (Raleigh: State Printers, 1867), 6.

19. *The General Statutes of the State of Kansas* (Lawrence: State Printers, 1868), 76.

20. *The Revised Laws of Indiana, Adopted and Enacted by the General Assembly at Their 8th Session, to Which are Prefixed the Constitution of the State of Indiana* (Corydon: Carpenter and Douglass, 1824), 48. Also see McKown, *The Trend of College Entrance Requirements*, 36–37.

21. *The State of Ohio: General and Local Acts Passed and Joint Resolutions Passed by the 59th General Assembly* (Columbus: State Printers, 1870), 21.

22. Alabama, Arkansas, Colorado, Mississippi, North Carolina, and South Carolina were among the states whose constitutions mandated free education for students through the age of twenty-one. David C. Harrington, *Education of Minors—What Are "Necessaries"?* (Scranton, PA: n.p., n.d.), 30–42.

23. Henderson, *Admission to College by Certificate*, 135–36.

24. Universities that adopted this system still allowed students who had not attended accredited schools or taken approved college preparatory curriculum to enter by passing the traditional series of examinations. George Edwin MacLean, "Present Standards of Higher Education in the United States," *United States Bureau of Education Bulletin*, no. 4 (Washington, DC: Government Printing Office, 1913), 40–41; Wechsler, *The Qualified Student*, 17, 24, 40; Henderson, *Admission to College by Certificate*, 76. On mechanical admissions in general, see Douglass, *Conditions for Admission*, 58.

25. *Foltz v. Hoge*, 54 Cal. 28 (1879).

26. Barbara Solomon, *In the Company of Educated Women: A History of Women and Higher Education in America* (New Haven, CT: Yale University Press, 1985), 53; Frederick Rudolph, *The American College and University: A History* (New York: Knopf, 1962), 314–15;

Thomas D. Snyder, ed., *120 Years of American Education: A Statistical Portrait* (Washington, DC: National Center for Education Statistics, 1993), 75–76. Also see Andrea G. Radke-Moss, *Bright Epoch: Women and Coeducation in the American West* (Lincoln: University of Nebraska Press, 2008).

27. Lynn D. Gordon, *Gender and Higher Education in the Progressive Era* (New Haven, CT: Yale University Press, 1990); Ruth Bordin, *Women at Michigan: The "Dangerous Experiment," 1870s to the Present* (Ann Arbor: University of Michigan Press, 1999).

28. See, for example, *Session Laws of the State of Washington Enacted by the First State Legislature* (Olympia: State Printer, 1890), 395.

29. Douglass, *The Conditions for Admission*, 21–25. Also see John A. Douglass, *The California Idea and American Higher Education: 1850 to the 1960 Master Plan* (Palo Alto, CA: Stanford University Press, 2000).

30. *Statutes of California Passed at the 22nd Session of the Legislature* (Sacramento: State Printer, 1878), 533; Thomas G. Barnes, *Hastings College of the Law: The First Century* (San Francisco: Hastings College of the Law Press, 1978).

31. Transcript on Appeal (hereafter *Foltz* transcript), filed April 22, 1879, *Foltz v. Hoge*, case no. 6581, California Supreme Court records and briefs, California State Archives, 7–10; Clara S. Foltz, "Struggles and Triumphs of a Woman Lawyer," *New American Woman*, November 1915, 10–11, 15–16; *San Francisco Chronicle*, March 6, 1879, 3; Mortimer D. Schwartz, Susan L. Brandt, and Patience Milrod, "Clara Foltz: Pioneer in the Law," *Hastings Law Journal* 27 (1976): 545–64.

32. *San Francisco Chronicle*, January 30, 1879, 3; Barbara A. Babcock, "Clara Shortridge Foltz: 'First Woman,'" *Valparaiso University Law Review* 28 (1994): 1231–85.

33. Yet a decade later, public law schools in states such Connecticut, Colorado, and Indiana continued to discriminate. Joan Hoff, *Law, Gender, and Injustice: A Legal History of U.S. Women* (New York: New York University Press, 1991), 151–64.

34. *San Francisco Chronicle*, January 30, 1879, 3; Babcock, "Clara Shortridge Foltz," 1231–85; Karen Berger Morello, *The Invisible Bar: The Woman Lawyer in America, 1638 to the Present* (New York: Random House, 1986), 57–58.

35. *Foltz* transcript; Foltz, "Struggles and Triumphs of a Woman Lawyer," 10–11, 15–16. Making matters worse, the United States Supreme Court ruled that women were not constitutionally entitled to practice law. *Bradwell v. Illinois*, 83 U.S. 130 (1873).

36. *Foltz* transcript, 12.

37. Clara Foltz to Laura Gordon, May 6, 1879, Laura Gordon Papers, box 1, Bancroft Library, University of California, Berkeley. Judge Hastings reported that he did not want to appeal the decision but was overruled by the board of directors. As dean, he had initially decided to admit Foltz and Gordon before the board of directors voted to ban women (three days into the spring semester). *San Francisco Chronicle*, March 6, 1879, 3.

38. Respondent's Points and Authorities, filed August 4, 1879, *Foltz v. Hoge*, case no. 6581, California Supreme Court records and briefs, California State Archives, 5.

39. *Foltz* transcript, 7–10.

40. Appellant's Points and Authorities (hereafter Hastings brief), filed August 7, 1879, *Foltz v. Hoge*, case no. 6581, California Supreme Court records and briefs, California State Archives, 4–5, 9. The *Dartmouth* case is discussed in the introduction.

41. Hastings brief, 3, 7–9.

42. Hastings brief, 6–7.

43. *Foltz*, 54 Cal. at 32; *Constitution of the State of California* (Sacramento: State Printer, 1880), 34.

44. *Foltz*, 54 Cal. at 34.

45. *Foltz*, 54 Cal. at 33.

46. *State ex rel. Stallard v. White*, 82 Ind. 278 (1882).

47. Nicholas L. Syrett, *The Company He Keeps: A History of White College Fraternities* (Chapel Hill: University of North Carolina Press, 2009), 122–31; James McCosh, "Discipline in American Colleges," *North American Review* 126 (1878): 41–42; *Journal of Proceedings and Addresses of the National Educational Association* (1890), 707–11; H. Lloyd Church, "College Fraternities and the Law," *Law Notes* 19 (1915): 166.

48. Robert W. Topping, *A Century and Beyond: The History of Purdue University* (West Lafayette, IN: Purdue University Press, 1988), 97.

49. H. A. Huston, "The Fraternity Controversy at Purdue, Including Some Facts Not in the Records," typescript (1943), Collection of Sigma Chi Fraternity Court Case Materials, 1881–2000, folder 3, Archives and Special Collections, Purdue University Libraries; Purdue University Board of Trustees minutes, December 9, 1881, accessed May 19, 2011, http://earchives.lib.purdue.edu/u?/bot,20273; Topping, *A Century and Beyond*, 85–86, 109.

50. For example, he eliminated instruction in Latin and German. *Seventh Annual Report of Purdue University* (Indianapolis: State Printers, 1882), 29–30; Topping, *A Century and Beyond*, 88–89, 99–100, 107–8.

51. Howard Gillman, *The Constitution Besieged: The Rise and Demise of the Lochner Era Police Powers Jurisprudence* (Durham, NC: Duke University Press, 1993), 72–73.

52. *Seventh Annual Report of Purdue University*, 28; "Closing Argument for the Faculty" before the Tippecanoe Circuit Court (undated), *State ex rel. Stallard v. White*, case no. 9986, Indiana Supreme Court records and briefs, Indiana State Archives.

53. Tippecanoe Circuit Court opinion (undated), *State ex rel. Stallard v. White*, case no. 9986, Indiana Supreme Court records and briefs, Indiana State Archives, 2.

54. *Seventh Annual Report of Purdue University*, 43. During the course of these trials, Purdue administrators expelled five students who continued to participate in fraternity activities. Topping, *A Century and Beyond*, 109.

55. Similarly, the brief referred to the "judgment of the trustees, aided by the experience of a faculty, largely composed of college-bred men." Brief on Behalf of the Trustees of Purdue University, filed August 10, 1882, *State ex rel. Stallard v. White*, case no. 9986, Indiana Supreme Court records and briefs, Indiana State Archives.

56. *Stallard*, 82 Ind. at 284. The same court that protected student rights so enthusiastically in *Stallard* expressed much more deference to local school boards that determined how to educate African American students in districts where the black population was not dense enough to facilitate the operation of segregated schools. *Cory v. Carter*, 48 Ind. 327 (1874).

57. William Estus McVey, "Standards for the Accreditation of Secondary Schools" (PhD diss., University of Chicago, 1942), 29; Henderson, *Admission to College by Certificate*, 89.

58. Appellant's Brief, filed May 4, 1882, *State ex rel. Stallard v. White*, case no. 9986, Indiana Supreme Court records and briefs, Indiana State Archives. The equal protection

argument was not emphasized in the opinion, but it figured more prominently in the decision to overrule Purdue's petition for rehearing. The court stated that the fraternity policy constituted "discrimination against a class of inhabitants of the state." Answer to the Petition for Rehearing (hereafter *Stallard* Answer to Rehearing Petition), filed August 10, 1882, *State ex rel. Stallard v. White*, case no. 9986, Indiana Supreme Court records and briefs, Indiana State Archives.

59. *Stallard*, 82 Ind. at 280, 284.

60. *Stallard*, 82 Ind. at 285, 287, 284. In his dissenting opinion, Judge Woods responded that more rigorous admission standards could be justified by the fact that many students did not possess "the high standard of culture and manhood which will enable him to appreciate, and will insure his respect for that implied obligation which arises from the mere fact of admission to the college." *Stallard*, 82 Ind. at 289.

61. In 1876, the court became the subject of a partisan "Upholstery War" when Republicans criticized the extent of renovations to the judicial chambers. Although Judge Niblack belonged to a fraternal society (Sons of the American Revolution), this membership does not necessarily explain his ruling, because the dissenting Judge Woods also belonged to a fraternity. Amy Gajda, *The Trials of Academe: The New Era of Campus Litigation* (Cambridge, MA: Harvard University Press, 2009), 271–72n55; Rebecca A. Shepherd et al., eds., *Biographical Directory of the Indiana General Assembly*, vol. 1 (Indianapolis: Indiana Historical Bureau, 1980), 292; Leander J. Monks, *Courts and Lawyers of Indiana*, vol. 1 (Indianapolis: Federal Publishing, 1916), 264–65; *Biographical Directory of the United States Congress*, accessed April 8, 2011, http://bioguide.congress.gov/scripts/biodisplay.pl?index=N000083; John McAuley Palmer, *The Bench and the Bar of Illinois: Historical and Reminiscent*, vol. 1 (Chicago: Lewis, 1899); John A. Garraty and Mark C. Carnes, eds., *American National Biography*, vol. 23 (New York: Oxford University Press, 1999), 816; Jacob P. Dunn, *Indiana and Indianans: A History of Aboriginal and Territorial Indiana and the Century of Statehood*, vol. 5 (New York: American Historical Society, 1919), 1939–40.

62. Topping, *A Century and Beyond*, 23–24, 92–94, 107, 117. Regarding this tension in other states, see Gelber, *The University and the People*, 30–31, 65–77.

63. *Stallard* Answer to Rehearing Petition.

64. Huston, "The Fraternity Controversy at Purdue"; Topping, *A Century and Beyond*, 109.

65. Gajda, *The Trials of Academe*, 271–72n55.

66. *Stallard*, 82 Ind. at 288. Purdue's lawyers repeated this point in an unsuccessful petition for rehearing. Appellees' Petition for Rehearing, filed August 10, 1882, *State ex rel. Stallard v. White*, case no. 9986, Indiana Supreme Court records and briefs, Indiana State Archives.

67. *Williams v. Wheeler*, 23 Cal. App. 619 (1913). The court also ruled in favor of the university in a similar case twelve years later. *Wallace v. Regents of the University of California*, 75 Cal. App. 274 (1925).

68. *University of Mississippi v. Waugh*, 105 Miss. 623 (1913); Original Bill, filed May 17, 1913, case no. 4263, *Waugh v. University of Mississippi*, Chancery Court of Lafayette County, Mississippi Department of Archives and History, 6; *New Orleans Daily Picayune*, May 2, 1913, 7.

69. *Biloxi Daily Herald*, February 22, 1912, 1.

70. Statement of Case, filed June 19, 1913, *University of Mississippi v. Waugh*, case no. 16700, Mississippi Supreme Court, Mississippi Department of Archives and History, 2.

71. Gillman, *The Constitution Besieged*, 4–5.

72. Lawrence M. Friedman, "Freedom of Contract and Occupational Licensing, 1890–1910: A Legal and Social Study," *California Law Review* 53 (1965): 487–534; Bartlett, *State Control of Private Incorporated Institutions*, 7. For example, when the Illinois legislature empowered the state department of education to establish standards for professional degrees, the statute explicitly authorized admission requirements for institutions that trained doctors, dentists, nurses, pharmacists, architects, engineers, and horseshoers. *Laws of the State of Illinois Enacted by the 50th General Assembly at the Regular Biennial Session* (Springfield: State Printers, 1917), 32–34.

73. Appellant's Brief, May 16, 1913, *University of Mississippi v. Waugh*, case no. 16700, Mississippi Supreme Court, Mississippi Department of Archives and History, 11–12. Also see Reply Brief of Appellants (undated), *University of Mississippi v. Waugh*, case no. 16700, Mississippi Supreme Court, Mississippi Department of Archives and History, 6–7. Ralston began his career as a supporter of Henry George but became better known for representing Fred Korematsu later in his career. See the front matter of Jackson H. Ralston, *Confronting the Land Question* (Bayside, NY: Scientific Taxation, 1945).

74. *Waugh*, 105 Miss. at 633.

75. Burkitt had previously campaigned to redirect college appropriations toward common schools. John K. Bettersworth, *People's University: The Centennial History of Mississippi State* (Jackson: University Press of Mississippi, 1980), 95–103; *Chickasaw Messenger*, January 6, 1887, 1, August 25, 1887, 6, March 15, 1888, 1, and April 12, 1888, 1; *Progressive Farmer*, August 4, 1887, 4. Also see Lilibel Hurshel Henry Broadway, "Frank Burkitt: The Man in the Wool Hat" (MS thesis, Mississippi State University, 1948), 1–8, 18, 36, 44, 48.

76. David G. Sansing, *Making Haste Slowly: The Troubled History of Higher Education in Mississippi* (Jackson: University Press of Mississippi, 1990), 77–81; David G. Sansing, *The University of Mississippi: A Sesquicentennial History* (Jackson: University Press of Mississippi, 1999), 177–85; *New Orleans Daily Picayune*, February 20, 1912, 15.

77. Appellant's Brief, May 16, 1913, *University of Mississippi v. Waugh*, case no. 16700, Mississippi Supreme Court, Mississippi Department of Archives and History, 11–12.

78. *Waugh*, 105 Miss. at 633.

79. *Waugh v. University of Mississippi*, 237 U.S. 589 (1915).

80. *Waugh*, 237 U.S. at 595, 596, 597. The court also upheld the ruling because Waugh's lawyers had based their appeal in part on the weak argument that UM's enforcement of the fraternity statute unconstitutionally distinguished between current and future students. Brief and Argument, *Waugh v. University of Mississippi*, United States Supreme Court case no. 692 (October Term, 1913), 33, 38. Also see Transcript of Record, filed August 28, 1913, *Waugh v. University of Mississippi*, United States Supreme Court case no. 255 (October Term, 1914). Justice Holmes argued elsewhere that courts should apply a loose standard of rationality because some degree of classification was inevitable (except for cases involving racial discrimination or other particularly vicious forms of bigotry).

Alexander M. Bickel and Benno C. Schmidt Jr., *The Judiciary and Responsible Government, 1910–1921*, part I (New York: Macmillan, 1984), 640.

81. Bickel and Schmidt Jr., *The Judiciary and Responsible Government*, 639.

82. *Waugh* has been cited in seventy-five appellate opinions, including the final ruling of the *Scopes* trial, which cited the case to support the state's authority to regulate public services. *Scopes v. State*, 154 Tenn. 105 (1927). Justice Black also cited *Waugh* as an example of why school boards ought to have broad authority over student conduct. *Tinker v. Des Moines*, 393 U.S. 503 (1969).

83. William W. Van Alstyne, "The Demise of the Right-Privilege Distinction in Constitutional Law," *Harvard Law Review* 81 (1968): 1439–64; Roy Lucas, "The Right to Higher Education," *Journal of Higher Education* 41 (1970): 55–64. The right-privilege distinction placed university lawyers in the awkward position of arguing that higher education was too eminent to be subjected to ordinary judicial oversight, yet not vital enough to be defined as a property right.

84. See appendix A.

85. Wechsler, *The Qualified Student*, 168.

86. Most lawmakers also sided with school superintendents who wanted universities to count vocational courses as valid college preparatory credits. *The State of Ohio: Legislative Acts Passed and Joint Resolutions Adopted by the 80th General Assembly* (Springfield: State Printers, 1914), 125; Merle Curti and Vernon Carstensen, *University of Wisconsin: A History, 1848–1925* (Madison: University of Wisconsin Press, 1949), 244–48; Wechsler, *The Qualified Student*, 19, 23, 56–58, 242–44; Henderson, *Admission to College by Certificate*, 80–81, 93, 136–37. Also see Edward C. Eliot and M. M. Chambers, *Charters and Basic Laws of Selected American Universities and Colleges* (New York: Carnegie Foundation for the Advancement of Teaching, 1934), 253. Not all colleges were eager to implement firm admission standards. In 1928, the North Central Association (an accreditation agency) reported that many of its members violated its requirements with respect to entrance standards. In 1934, the association replaced its fifteen-unit requirement with a more flexible standard. George Zook and M. E. Haggerty, *Principles of Accrediting Higher Institutions* (Chicago: University of Chicago Press, 1936), 10–15, 53, 56, 119, 136.

87. R. L. Duffus, *Democracy Enters the College: A Study of the Rise and Decline of the Academic Lockstep* (New York: Scribners, 1936), 178.

88. Alexander G. Roberts, "A Program of Admission to and Elimination from a Tax-Supported State Institution," *School and Society* 18 (1923): 457; J. B. Johnston, "Selection of Students," in R. A. Kent, ed., *Higher Education in America* (Boston: Ginn, 1930), 417–18; Duffus, *Democracy Enters the College*, 89; Millard E. Gladfelter, "Status and Trends of College-Entrance Requirements," *School Review* 45 (1937): 742–43; McKown, *The Trend of College Entrance Requirements*, 106–10; Wechsler, *The Qualified Student*, 45, 58, 238–47; David O. Levine, *The American College and the Culture of Aspiration, 1915–1940* (Ithaca, NY: Cornell University Press, 1986), 165–66; Roger L. Geiger, *To Advance Knowledge: The Growth of American Research Universities, 1900–1940* (New York: Oxford University Press, 1986), 129; Klein, "Survey of Land-Grant Colleges and Universities," 25–27.

89. The conversion of normal (teachers') colleges into regional state colleges was a common occurrence during the 1920s and 1930s. Community college enrollment expanded rapidly in the 1950s and 1960s and had a particularly significant relationship

with the growing selectivity of flagship state universities. Steven Brint and Jerome Karabel, *The Diverted Dream: Community Colleges and the Promise of Educational Opportunity in America, 1900–1985* (New York: Oxford University Press, 1985), 90. Harvard emphasized the new "scientific" approach to admissions during the 1920s by producing a 104-page report on its enrollment titled "Statistical Report of the Statisticians." The report was intended to respond to allegations of anti-Semitism. Jerome Karabel, *The Chosen: The Hidden History of Admission and Exclusion at Harvard, Yale, and Princeton* (New York: Houghton Mifflin Harcourt, 2006), 95.

90. *Acts and Joint Resolutions of the General Assembly of the State of South Carolina: Regular Session of 1940* (n.p., 1940), 2028–29.

91. *Kayser v. Board of Education*, 273 Mo. 643, 653 (1918).

92. *Mestice v. Partch*, 119 N.J.L. 212, 214 (1937). The student had been rejected from a graduate program because he did not have an undergraduate degree from an accredited institution.

93. The university had offered a deferred acceptance to a young student but then rejected him after he filed suit for immediate admission. *Tinkoff v. Northwestern University*, 333 Ill. App. 224, 230 (1947).

94. *State ex rel. Holcomb v. Armstrong*, 39 Wash. 2d 860 (1952).

95. Discrimination against Jewish applicants had become commonplace at selective institutions in the 1920s and 1930s despite the fact that institutional charters or state statutes required most colleges to operate in a "nonsectarian" manner. In order to publicize the issue, the American Jewish Congress asked the New York Tax Commission to revoke Columbia University's exemption because state law forbade nonprofit educational corporations from discriminating based on race or religion. However, a state court interpreted the law in a narrow fashion and concluded that the tax commission was not authorized to investigate discrimination and revoke exemptions. *Goldstein v. Mills*, 57 N.Y.S.2d 810 (1945); Wechsler, *The Qualified Student*, 194–96, 204; Martha Biondi, *To Stand and Fight: The Struggle for Civil Rights in Postwar New York City* (Cambridge, MA: Harvard University Press, 2003), 106–10.

96. "Chapter 726: An Act to Secure Fair Educational Practices," August 22, 1949, Papers of the Boston Jewish Community Relations Council (hereafter BJCRC), box 97, folder 3, American Jewish Historical Society, Boston.

97. In fairness to the state office, it could be difficult to disentangle potential discrimination from other possible explanations for a student's rejection. One administrator dismissed a grievance initiated by a student because his college reported that he wrote disturbing letters to the dean of women and female students. Informal case no. 20, May 21, 1952, American Jewish Congress Papers (I-77) (hereafter AJC), box 86, folder 2, American Jewish Historical Society, New York City.

98. Colgate University rejected 40 percent of Jewish applicants but just 10 percent of Christian applicants. Report of the Investigation on a Petition Filed against Colgate University, September 29, 1955, AJC, box 86, folder 2; Will Maslow to Mr. Toubin, November 18, 1955, AJC, box 86, folder 2.

99. Joseph B. Robison to Gerald Berlin, June 14, 1954, and Howard Squadron to Will Maslow, June 28, 1954, AJC, box 86, folder 2; State House Hearing before the Committee on Education, March 25, 1947, BJCRC, box 97, folder 3; "State Holds Schools Requiring

Photos Defy Fair Ed Law" and *Harvard Crimson* clipping, January 10, 1958, BJCRC, box 97, folder 5; Memorandum Regarding the Bulletin of Policies and Interpretation of the Fair Educational Practices Law, November 5, 1951, BJCRC, box 97, folder 4; Franklin P. Hawkes to Massachusetts Board of Education, November 6, 1951, BJCRC, box 97, folder 4.

100. *Heaton v. Bristol*, 317 S.W.2d 86 (1958).

101. Another student was subjected to hazing after he formed the Aggie Association for the Advancement of Coeducation. Henry C. Dethloff, *A Centennial History of Texas A&M University*, vol. 2 (College Station: Texas A&M University Press, 1975), 558–60.

102. Madiha Rizvi, "Paving the Way," *Battalin*, November 12, 2008, accessed February 9, 2012, www.thebatt.com/news/paving-the-way-1.1184473.

103. Excerpts of unreported lower court opinion are contained in the appellate decision. *Heaton*, 317 S.W.2d at 90, 91 (1958).

104. *Heaton*, 317 S.W.2d at 100, 94, 95. The court rejected a similar coeducation suit two years later. *Allred v. Heaton*, 336 S.W.2d 251 (1960). The United States Supreme Court denied two requests to review *Heaton*. *Bristol v. Heaton*, 359 U.S. 230 (1959); *Bristol v. Heaton*, 359 U.S. 999 (1959). In 1963, Texas A&M moved toward coeducation by allowing women to attend graduate programs. Wives or daughters of students, staff, or faculty could also enroll, along with women pursuing programs that were unavailable at other state schools. The university became fully coeducational in 1971. Dethloff, *A Centennial History of Texas A&M University*, 568–70.

105. A former law professor, Justice Frankfurter observed that the vitality of higher education depended upon the "exclusion of governmental intervention in the intellectual life of a university." *Sweezy v. New Hampshire*, 354 U.S. 234 (1957).

106. *Lesser v. Board of Education of City of New York*, 239 N.Y.S.2d 776 (1963).

107. See, for example, William A. Kaplin and Barbara A. Lee, *The Law of Higher Education: A Comprehensive Guide to Legal Implications of Administrative Decision Making*, 4th ed., vol. 1 (San Francisco: Jossey-Bass, 2006), 752–54.

Chapter 3. Desegregation

1. *Brown v. Board of Education of Topeka*, 347 U.S. 483 (1954); *Frasier v. University of North Carolina*, 134 F. Supp. 589 (1955). One year later, the Supreme Court noted the differences between universities and elementary schools but nevertheless reaffirmed its stance against segregated higher education. *Florida ex rel. Hawkins v. Board of Control*, 350 U.S. 413 (1956). Also see William A. Kaplin and Barbara A. Lee, *The Law of Higher Education: A Comprehensive Guide to Legal Implications of Administrative Decision Making*, 5th ed., vol. 1 (San Francisco: Jossey-Bass, 2013), 883.

2. *Frasier*, 134 F. Supp. at 593.

3. Scott Baker, "Desegregation, Minimum Competency Testing, and the Origins of Accountability: North Carolina and the Nation," *History of Education Quarterly* 55 (2015): 41.

4. For two exceptions that situate desegregation cases within discussions about judicial deference toward higher education, see Robert M. Hendrickson, Jason E. Lane, James T. Harris, and Richard H. Dorman, *Academic Leadership and Governance of Higher Education: A Guide for Trustees, Leaders, and Aspiring Leaders of Two- and Four-Year Institu-*

tions (Sterling, VA: Stylus, 2013), 140; Amy Gajda, *The Trials of Academe: The New Era of Campus Litigation* (Cambridge, MA: Harvard University Press, 2009), 52–53.

5. *Missouri ex rel. Gaines v. Canada*, 305 U.S. 337 (1938); *Sweatt v. Painter*, 339 U.S. 629 (1950).

6. See, in particular, Richard Kluger, *Simple Justice: The History of Brown v. Board of Education and Black America's Struggle for Equality* (New York: Knopf, [1976] 2004); Mark Tushnet, *The NAACP's Legal Strategy against Segregated Education, 1925–1950* (Chapel Hill: University of North Carolina Press, 1987); Michael J. Klarman, *From Jim Crow to Civil Rights: The Supreme Court and the Struggle for Racial Equality* (New York: Oxford University Press, 2004).

7. *Berea College v. Kentucky*, 211 U.S. 45 (1908). This case does not appear in appendixes A or B because it involved a conflict between the college and the state, rather than between a student and a college. The college had been founded by abolitionists and championed racial equality. Elisabeth S. Peck, *Berea's First Century, 1855–1955* (Lexington: University of Kentucky Press, 1955), 1–3, 50.

8. *Booker v. Grand Rapids Medical College*, 156 Mich. 95 (1909).

9. John Aubrey Douglass, *The Conditions for Admission: Access, Equity, and the Social Contract of Public Universities* (Palo Alto, CA: Stanford University Press, 2007), 49. See, for example, *The Laws of the State of Kansas Passed at the 10th Session of the Legislature* (Topeka: State Printers, 1870), 23. Prompted by the Second Morrill Act of 1890, which mandated the allocation of federal funds to black students in either integrated or segregated settings, the remaining northern and western states officially desegregated their land grant colleges. See, for example, *The State of Ohio: General and Local Acts Passed and Joint Resolutions Passed by the 69th General Assembly* (Columbus: State Printers, 1891), 519–22.

10. Affidavit for Certiorari, filed December 3, 1908, *Booker v. Grand Rapids Medical College*, case no. 23193, Michigan Supreme Court records and briefs, Archives of Michigan (hereafter *Booker* case files); Testimony in the Circuit Court for the County of Kent, October 26, 1908, *Booker* case files; Randal Maurice Jelks, *African Americans in the Furniture City: The Struggle for Civil Rights* (Champaign: University of Illinois Press, 2006), 65–67.

11. Brief for Relators, *Booker* case files. The brief also cited an antebellum case that had held a college accountable to a strict interpretation of its corporate charter. *People v. Trustees of Geneva College*, 5 Wen. 211 (1830).

12. "Closing Argument for the Faculty" before the Tippecanoe Circuit Court (undated), *State ex rel. Stallard v. White*, case no. 9986, Indiana Supreme Court records and briefs, Indiana State Archives; *State ex rel. Stallard v. White*, 82 Ind. 278 (1882). Many white Indianans, especially within the Democratic Party, opposed integration and the public education of African Americans. Davison M. Douglas, *Jim Crow Moves North: The Battle over Northern School Segregation, 1865–1954* (New York: Cambridge University Press, 2005), 73–74.

13. Brief for Relators, *Booker* case files; *Jackson v. Majors*, 57 Neb. 183 (1898); *Gleason v. University of Minnesota*, 104 Minn. 359 (1908); *Commonwealth ex rel. Hill v. McCauley*, 2 Pa. Co. Ct. 459 (1887). These cases are discussed in chapter 4.

14. The expulsion cases favorable to Booker were *Cecil v. Bellevue Hospital Medical College*, 14 N.Y.S. 490 (1891); *Baltimore University v. Colton*, 8 Md. 623 (1904). These cases are discussed in chapter 4.

15. *Eleventh Annual Prospectus of the Grand Rapids Veterinary College* (1908), 17.

16. Affidavit for Certiorari, *Booker* case files.

17. *Booker*, 156 Mich. at 99. One precedent held that writs of mandamus were inapplicable to private colleges. *Burg v. Milwaukee Medical College*, 128 Wis. 7 (1906).

18. Oliver A. Harker, "The Use of Mandamus to Compel Educational Institutions to Confer Degrees," *Yale Law Journal* 20 (1911): 341–52; Isaac A. Pennypacker, "Mandamus to Restore Academic Privileges," *Virginia Law Review* 12 (1926): 645–52. As discussed in chapter 4, judges disagreed about whether these writs could apply to private colleges.

19. Douglas, *Jim Crow Moves North*, 186–87; Genna Rae McNeil, *Groundwork: Charles Hamilton Houston and the Struggle for Civil Rights* (Philadelphia: University of Pennsylvania Press, 1983).

20. *Plessy v. Ferguson*, 163 U.S. 537 (1896).

21. Tushnet, *The NAACP's Legal Strategy against Segregated Education*, 118–19; Kluger, *Simple Justice*, 36, 186.

22. *Pearson v. Murray*, 169 Md. 478 (1936). This case is sometimes styled *University v. Murray.*

23. T. Marshall to C. H. Houston, August 21, 1935, Papers of the NAACP, part 3 (hereafter NAACP Papers), group 1, box D-93, University of Maryland folder (July–August, 1935).

24. Appellee's Brief (hereafter *Murray* brief), *Pearson v. Murray*, case no. 53 (October Term 1935), Maryland Court of Appeals records and briefs, Maryland State Archives, 17.

25. As dean of Howard University Law School, Houston orchestrated an increase in academic standards for enrollment and graduation. Tushnet, *The NAACP's Legal Strategy against Segregated Education*, 35–37; Kluger, *Simple Justice*, 186–88.

26. Kluger, *Simple Justice*, 188–89.

27. Baltimore City Court Stenographer's Record, case no. 53 (October Term 1935), Maryland Court of Appeals records and briefs, Maryland State Archives, C 174-2; *Baltimore Afro-American*, June 22, 1935, 7; Mark V. Tushnet, *Making Civil Rights Law: Thurgood Marshall and the Supreme Court, 1936–1961* (New York: Oxford University Press, 1994), 11, 14–15. Judge O'Dunne held liberal views on race relations and had a previous relationship with Thurgood Marshall. Kenneth W. Mack, *Representing the Race: The Creation of the Civil Rights Lawyer* (Cambridge, MA: Harvard University Press, 2012), 123.

28. *Murray* brief, 12, 15–16, 19–25; Thurgood Marshall, "An Evaluation of Recent Efforts to Achieve Racial Integration in Education through Resort to the Courts," *Journal of Negro Education* 21 (1952): 316–27; Petition to Advance, *Pearson v. Murray*, Maryland Court of Appeals, NAACP Papers, group 1, Box D-93, University of Maryland folder (September 3–30, 1935).

29. Walter White to C. H. Houston, March 20, 1933, NAACP Papers, group 1, box D-96, University of North Carolina folder (April–December 1933); Gilbert Ware, "Hocutt: Genesis of Brown," *Journal of Negro Education* 52 (1983): 227–33; Jerry Gershenhorn, "*Hocutt v. Wilson* and Race Relations in Durham, North Carolina, during the 1930s," *North Carolina Historical Review* 78 (2001): 275–308; Kluger, *Simple Justice*, 157–58; Tushnet, *The NAACP's Legal Strategy against Segregated Education*, 52–53.

30. *Thomas R. Hocutt v. Thomas J. Wilson Jr.*, March 28, 1933, Minute Docket, Superior Court of North Carolina, Durham County, vol. 25, North Carolina State Archives, 36–37.

UNC's attorneys argued that the university was not the proper target of Hocutt's suit because constitutional and statutory provisions stripped it of the power to admit black students. They argued that only the State of North Carolina could integrate the university. "Memorandum of Authorities for Defendants: *Hocutt v. Wilson* and the University of North Carolina," NAACP Papers, group 1, box D-96, University of North Carolina Briefs folder (1933), 5.

31. Untitled, undated, handwritten note, NAACP Papers, group 1, box D-93, University of Maryland folder (October–November 1935).

32. C. H. Houston to Walter Goldston, August 27, 1936, NAACP Papers, group 1, box D-96, University of North Carolina folder (1934–37).

33. Appellant's Points and Authorities, filed August 7, 1879, *Foltz v. Hoge*, case no. 6581, California Supreme Court records and briefs, California State Archives, 2, 7; *Foltz v. Hoge*, 54 Cal. 28 (1879). Regarding the racial climate in California, see Charles Wollenberg, *All Deliberate Speed: Segregation and Exclusion in California Schools, 1855–1975* (Berkeley: University of California Press, 1976), 13–14, 29–42.

34. Transcript of the shorthand report of the proceedings (hereafter *Murray* proceedings), November 5, 1935, *Pearson v. Murray*, Maryland Court of Appeals (October Term 1935), NAACP Papers, group 1, box D-94, University of Maryland Briefs folder (1935–36), 26–28.

35. *Murray* brief, 14–15. Marshall's preliminary draft included a section on "Admission" that summarized *Stallard* but did not mention the case by name. The name of the case was added to the final draft. "Statement of the Nature of the Case" marked "Houston and Marshall's first draft," October 25–26, 1935, NAACP Papers, group 1, box D-93, University of Maryland folder (October–November 1935); Statement of the Nature of the Case marked "Marshall Preliminary Draft of Brief," October 2, 1935, NAACP Papers, group 1, box D-94, University of Maryland Briefs folder (1935–36).

36. *Connell v. Gray*, 33 Okla. 591 (1912); Brief of the Defendant in Error, filed September 17, 1912, *Connell v. Gray*, case no. 4342, Oklahoma Supreme Court records and briefs, Oklahoma Department of Libraries. This case is discussed in chapter 5.

37. *Murray* brief, 14–16.

38. *Murray* proceedings, 36.

39. *Murray* brief, 16; Petition to Advance, *Pearson v. Murray*, Maryland Court of Appeals, NAACP Papers, group 1, box D-93, University of Maryland folder (September 3–30, 1935).

40. *Murray* proceedings, 19–20.

41. *Murray* brief, 11; *Murray* proceedings, 31–32.

42. *Murray* proceedings, 26–28.

43. C. H. Houston to Isadore Polier, July 3, 1935, NAACP Papers, group 1, box D-93, University of Maryland folder (June 2–30, 1935).

44. *Murray* brief, 18; *Murray* proceedings, 29.

45. Peter Wallenstein, "Black Southerners and Nonblack Universities, 1935–1965," in Peter Wallenstein, ed., *Higher Education and the Civil Rights Movement: White Supremacy, Black Southerners, and College Campuses* (Gainesville: University Press of Florida, 2008), 27; Kluger, *Simple Justice*, 194.

46. *Pearson*, 169 Md. 478. The ruling cited *Foltz*, but only as an example of an ostensibly private institution (Hastings College of the Law) that was deemed public and ordered to abide by all relevant laws. Regarding Judge Bond, see Mack, *Representing the Race*, 123.

47. Charles Hamilton Houston, "Educational Inequalities Must Go!," *Crisis* 42 (1935): 316. Emphasis in the original.

48. *Redmond v. Hyman* (hereafter *Redmond* opinion), April 16, 1937, Chancery Court of Shelby County, case no. 41690, University of Tennessee Office of the President Records (AR.0006), University of Tennessee, Knoxville, Special Collections.

49. Bobby L. Lovett, *The Civil Rights Movement in Tennessee: A Narrative History* (Knoxville: University of Tennessee Press, 2005), 3–4.

50. Confidential Office Memorandum, August 27, 1936, NAACP Papers, group 1, box D-96, University of Tennessee folder (August 1936); A Statement Regarding the Mandamus Suit by a Negro Citizen for Admission to the School of Pharmacy of the University of Tennessee, undated, NAACP Papers, group 1, box D-96, University of Tennessee folder (January–March 1937).

51. Excerpts of the Minutes of the Board of Trustees, NAACP Papers, group 1, box D-96, University of Tennessee folder (1935).

52. The dean of UT's pharmacy school would later reveal that the school never reached capacity—every qualified applicant was accepted. Deposition of Dean O. W. Hyman, August 17, 1936, NAACP Papers, group 1, box D-97, University of Tennessee Briefs folder, 16, 22; *Redmond v. Hyman* Petition for Mandamus, April 27, 1936, NAACP Papers, group 1, box D-97, University of Tennessee Briefs folder, 6; Memorandum of Cases Cited in Argument by Counsel for Plaintiff, undated, NAACP Papers, group 1, box D-97, University of Tennessee Briefs folder, 2.

53. James Hoskins to William Redmond, March 7, 1936, NAACP Papers, group 1, box D-96, University of Tennessee folder (January–March, 1936); Answer of the Chancery Court of Shelby County, May 11, 1936, NAACP Papers, group 1, box D-97, University of Tennessee Briefs folder, 7.

54. *Redmond* opinion, 14.

55. Tushnet, *The NAACP's Legal Strategy against Segregated Education*, 54.

56. *State ex rel. Gaines v. Canada*, 342 Mo. 121 (1938).

57. Kluger, *Simple Justice*, 201; Kevin M. Kruse, "Personal Rights, Public Wrongs: The *Gaines* Case and the Beginning of the End of Segregation," *Journal of Supreme Court History* 22 (1997): 113–30.

58. Respondents' Return to the Alternative Writ of Mandamus, April 1936, NAACP Papers, group 2, box L-41, *Gaines v. Canada* Briefs folder (1936).

59. Appellant's Statement, Brief, and Argument, May 1937, NAACP Papers, group 2, box L-42, *Gaines v. Canada* folder (1937–1940).

60. Petition for Certiorari (hereafter *Gaines* petition), October 1937, NAACP Papers, group 2, box L-42, *Gaines v. Canada* folder (1937–1940).

61. *Gaines*, 342 Mo. at 126.

62. David G. Sansing, *The University of Mississippi: A Sesquicentennial History* (Jackson: University Press of Mississippi, 1999), 177–79.

63. Statement of Case and Brief on Behalf of Appellee, filed June 19, 1913, *University of Mississippi v. Waugh*, case 16700, Mississippi Supreme Court records and briefs, Missis-

sippi Department of Archives and History, 13, 15, 18–19, 21; Supplemental Brief of Behalf of Appellee, filed June 28, 1913, *University of Mississippi v. Waugh*, case no. 16700, Mississippi Supreme Court records and briefs, Mississippi Department of Archives and History, 4–5, 8; *Plessy v. Ferguson*, 163 U.S. 537 (1896).

64. Appellant's Brief, filed May 16, 1913, *University of Mississippi v. Waugh*, case no. 16700, Mississippi Supreme Court records and briefs, Mississippi Department of Archives and History, 13; Reply Brief of Appellants (n.d.), *University of Mississippi v. Waugh*, case no. 16700, Mississippi Supreme Court records and briefs, Mississippi Department of Archives and History, 9–10.

65. *Gaines* petition, 21; *Gleason v. University of Minnesota*, 104 Minn. 359 (1908).

66. *Gaines* petition, 23.

67. *Missouri ex rel. Bluford v. Canada*, 348 Mo. 298 (1942).

68. Various statutes called for the segregation of public schools, the establishment of Lincoln University, and the creation of scholarships to support African American students seeking professional education out of state. *Gaines*, 305 U.S. 337.

69. Tushnet, *The NAACP's Legal Strategy against Segregated Education*, 73–74.

70. Ada Lois Sipuel Fisher, *A Matter of Black and White: The Autobiography of Ada Lois Sipuel Fisher* (Norman: University of Oklahoma Press, 1996), 84, 92. The Supreme Court later ruled that the state must provide Sipuel with an equivalent legal education. *Sipuel v. University of Oklahoma*, 332 U.S. 631 (1948).

71. Meeting in Governor Browning's Office, June 5, 1950, University of Tennessee Office of the President Records (AR.0006), University of Tennessee, Knoxville, Special Collections, 3–5.

72. Kluger, *Simple Justice*, 259–61. Some students supported Sweatt's enrollment. The student body president was cheered at a rally after announcing that students should not mistreat black classmates. Oral history of Oscar H. Mauzy, April 26, 1996, Rare Books and Special Collections, Tarlton Law Library, University of Texas at Austin, accessed June 13, 2012, www.houseofrussell.com/legalhistory/sweatt/index.htm.

73. Brief of Respondents in Opposition to Petition for Writ of Certiorari, filed May 19, 1949, *Sweatt v. Painter*, United States Supreme Court case no. 44 (October Term 1948), 34–35; Brief for Respondents, filed March, 27, 1950, *Sweatt v. Painter*, United States Supreme Court case no. 44 (October Term 1949), 39.

74. Brief for Appellees, filed October 8, 1934, *Hamilton v. Regents of the University of California*, United States Supreme Court; Brief of Appellants, filed October 10, 1934, *Hamilton v. Regents of the University of California*, United States Supreme Court; *Hamilton v. Regents of the University of California*, 293 U.S. 245 (1934).

75. *Sweatt v. Painter*, 339 U.S. 629 (1950).

76. Wallenstein, "Black Southerners and Nonblack Universities," 21, 34, 45.

77. Michael G. Wade, "Four Who Would: *Constantine v. Southwestern Louisiana Institute* (1954) and the Desegregation of Louisiana's State Colleges," in Wallenstein, *Higher Education and the Civil Rights Movement*, 60–91.

78. Petition for a Writ of Certiorari to the U.S. Court of Appeals, filed June 19, 1958, *Board of Supervisors of Louisiana State University v. Ludley*, United States Court of Appeals (5th Circuit), case no. 16854, 10; *Board of Supervisors of Louisiana State University v. Ludley*, 252 F.2d 372 (1958); *Board of Supervisors of Louisiana State University v. Ludley*, 358 U.S. 819 (1958).

79. *Dixon v. Alabama State Board of Education*, 186 F. Supp. 945, 950 (1960); *Dixon v. Alabama State Board of Education*, 294 F.2d 150 (1961).

80. *U.S. v. Barnett*, 330 F.2d 369 (1963).

81. See appendix A.

82. Michael A. Olivas, *Suing Alma Mater: Higher Education and the Courts* (Baltimore: Johns Hopkins University Press, 2013), 74.

Chapter 4. Expulsion

1. See appendix A. It should be noted that this appendix includes only reported cases. For the sake of brevity, this chapter uses "expulsion" to encompass all disciplinary sanctions (including suspension) that require students to leave campus.

2. Ed Stevens, "Due Process and Higher Education: A Systematic Approach to Fair Decision Making," *ASHE-ERIC Higher Education Report* 27 (1999): 13–14.

3. *Dixon v. Alabama State Board of Education*, 294 F.2d 150 (1961).

4. *Hamilton v. University of California*, 293 U.S. 245 (1934); *Hanauer v. Elkins*, 217 Md. 213 (1958); *Steier v. New York Education Commissioner*, 271 F.2d 13 (1959).

5. Comment, "Private Government on the Campus—Judicial Review of University Expulsions," *Yale Law Journal* 72 (1963): 1366–77.

6. Most schools did not create substantial numbers of administrative positions until the twentieth century. Charles W. Eliot, *University Administration* (New York: Houghton Mifflin, 1908).

7. See appendix A. Students won four out of nine academic cases and three out of nine disciplinary cases between 1860 and 1910. There were twenty-one expulsion cases in this period, but three cases do not fall neatly into either category.

8. David M. Rabban, "Judicial Review of the University-Student Relationship: Expulsion and Governance," *Stanford Law Review* 1 (1973): 96; Thomas A. Schweitzer, "'Academic Challenge' Cases: Should Judicial Review Extend to Academic Evaluations of Students?," *American University Law Review* 41 (1992): 295. Also see Elizabeth Grossi and Terry Edwards, "Student Misconduct: Historical Trends in Legislative and Judicial Decision-Making in American Universities," *Journal of College and University Law* 23 (1997): 829–52.

9. Students won nine out of twenty-one expulsion cases between 1860 and 1910. Students won five out of seven suits against public colleges and four out of fourteen suits against private colleges. See appendix A.

10. See, for example, Edmund S. Morgan, ed., *The Diary of Michael Wigglesworth, 1653–1657: The Conscience of a Puritan* (New York: Harper and Row, 1965).

11. Joseph R. DeMartini, "Student Culture as a Change Agent in American Higher Education: An Illustration from the Nineteenth Century," *Journal of Social History* 9 (1976): 528; Colin B. Burke, *American Collegiate Populations: A Test of the Traditional View* (New York: New York University Press, 1982), 230; Helen Lefkowitz Horowitz, *Campus Life: Undergraduate Culture from the End of the Eighteenth Century to the Present* (New York: Knopf, 1987), 35; Helen Lefkowitz Horowitz, *Alma Mater: Design and Experience in Women's Colleges from Their Nineteenth-Century Beginnings to the 1930s* (New York: Knopf, 1984), 148.

12. Frederick Rudolph, *The American College and University: A History* (New York: Knopf, 1962), 103–7.

13. Charles F. Thwing, "Personal Morals and College Government," *North American Review* 166 (1898): 306; Horowitz, *Campus Life*, 42; Rudolph, *The American College and University*, 165, 345–48; Julie A. Reuben, *The Making of the Modern University: Intellectual Transformation and the Marginalization of Morality* (Chicago: University of Chicago Press, 1996); W. Bruce Leslie, *Gentlemen and Scholars: College and Community in the "Age of the University," 1865–1917* (University Park: Pennsylvania State University Press, 1992), 99–103, 112.

14. *Session Laws of the State of Washington Enacted by the First State Legislature* (Olympia: State Printer, 1890), 264.

15. *Local and Private Acts of the State of Kentucky* (Frankfort: State Printer, 1866), 17.

16. *Special Laws of the 12th Legislature of the State of Texas, First Session* (Austin: State Printer, 1871), 207.

17. Ohio made hazing a crime punishable by six months in jail (for students) and a $100 fine (for complicit faculty and administrators). North Carolina made hazing a misdemeanor offense and ordered the expulsion of all violators. *The State of Ohio: General and Local Acts Passed and Joint Resolutions Passed by the 77th General Assembly* (Springfield: State Printers, 1906), 124; *Public Laws and Resolutions of the State of North Carolina Passed by the General Assembly at the Session of 1913* (Raleigh: State Printers, 1913), 264–65. Also see *The Statutes of California and Amendments to the Codes Passed at the 37th Session of the Legislature* (San Francisco: Bancroft-Whitney, 1907), 888.

18. In 1933, courts seemed to be equally divided regarding whether or not writs of mandamus could apply to private colleges. David A. Lane Jr., "Student and Collegiate Contracts," *Journal of Higher Education* 4 (1933): 79.

19. *Pratt v. Wheaton College*, 40 Ill. 186 (1866).

20. Paul M. Bechtel, *Wheaton College: A Heritage Remembered, 1860–1984* (Wheaton, IL: H. Shaw, 1984), 24–25, 35–37.

21. James Philemon Stoddard to Jonathan Blanchard, October 3, 1865, Jonathan Blanchard Papers, box 5, folder 12, Wheaton College Archives and Special Collections, Wheaton, IL.

22. *Pratt*, 40 Ill. at 186–88.

23. William W. Van Alstyne, "The Tentative Emergence of Student Power in the United States," *American Journal of Comparative Law* 17 (1969): 403–17; Comment, "Private Government on the Campus," 1368; Robert D. Bickel and Peter F. Lake, *The Rights and Responsibilities of the Modern University: Who Assumes the Risks of College Life?* (Durham, NC: Carolina Academic, 1999), 29.

24. See, for example, Amy Gajda, *The Trials of Academe: The New Era of Campus Litigation* (Cambridge, MA: Harvard University Press, 2009), 37.

25. *North v. University of Illinois*, 137 Ill. 296 (1891); *O'Sullivan v. New York Law School*, 22 N.Y.S. 663 (1893). However, a Missouri decision indicated that state colleges could not regulate student behavior that occurred off campus after the end of the school day. *State ex rel. Clark v. Osborne*, 32 Mo. App. 536 (1888).

26. Other than *Pratt*, the concept was only mentioned in two American higher education cases prior to 1910: *Clark*, 32 Mo. App. at 541, and *North*, 137 Ill. at 304.

27. Questions about expulsion procedures factored into five out of nine of the reported expulsion cases won by students before 1910. *Commonwealth ex rel. Hill v. McCauley*, 2 Pa. Co. Ct. 459 (1887); *Cecil v. Bellevue College*, 14 N.Y.S. 490 (1891); *Jackson v.*

Majors, 57 Neb. 183 (1898); *Gleason v. University of Minnesota*, 104 Minn. 359 (1908); *Nelson v. Lincoln Medical*, 81 Neb. 533 (1908).

28. *Commonwealth ex rel. Hill v. McCauley*, 2 Pa. Co. Ct. 459 (1887). The case is typically portrayed as an outlier. See, for example, Gerard A. Fowler, "The Legal Relationship between the American College Student and the College: An Historical Perspective and the Renewal of a Proposal," *Journal of Law and Education* 13 (1984): 402–4.

29. Strains in the student-faculty relationship dated back to 1873, when students refused to participate in the classes of Professor William Trickett. Students maintained their protest for two weeks before Trickett agreed to modify his instruction. Elizabeth A. Low, "I Was a Coed" (1891), unpublished manuscript, Dickinson College Archives and Special Collections, 24; James Henry Morgan, *Dickinson College: The History of One Hundred and Fifty Years, 1783–1933* (Carlisle, PA: Dickinson College, 1933), 353–54; Charles Coleman Sellers, *Dickinson College: A History* (Middletown, CT: Wesleyan University Press, 1973), 273–74.

30. Low, "I Was a Coed," 23; *Dickinsonian*, February 1887, 8, and December 1886, 4, 7–8, 14.

31. Minutes of November 8, 1886, Dickinson College Faculty Meeting Records (hereafter Dickinson minutes), Dickinson College Special Collections; *Dickinsonian*, November 1886, 6, December 1886, 13–14, and March 1887, 11. Hill was one of four students expelled after the incident, but he was the only student who was not eventually reenrolled. Whereas the other students and their fathers asked President McCauley to reconsider, Hill adamantly protested his expulsion and claimed that the college was too biased to provide him with a fair trial. Minutes of November 16, November 22, and November 23, 1886, Dickinson minutes. Several of the students who were suspended for the original hazing incident were also readmitted after they apologized, shook the hands of their victims, and signed a pledge of good conduct. Minutes of November 10, 1886, Dickinson minutes.

32. According to a local newspaper, the college was subjected to "a constant stream of unkind and malicious" criticism in publications across the country. Someone sent a stack of these clippings to one of Dickinson's most important feeder schools. *American Volunteer*, February 23, 1887, 2; *President's Report to the Board of Trustees of Dickinson College* (1887), Courtesy of Dickinson College Special Collections.

33. *Dickinsonian*, December 1886, 12–13.

34. *Hill*, 2 Pa. Co. Ct. at 461–62. Also see Note, "Common Law Rights for Private University Students: Beyond the State Action Principle," *Yale Law Journal* 84 (1974): 120–50.

35. Amy Dru Stanley, *From Bondage to Contract: Wage Labor, Marriage, and the Market in the Age of Slave Emancipation* (New York: Cambridge University Press, 1998); John V. Orth, "Contract and the Common Law," in Harry N. Scheiber, ed., *The State and Freedom of Contract* (Palo Alto, CA: Stanford University Press, 1998), 62–64.

36. Colleges often enrolled students as young as fourteen during much of the eighteenth and nineteenth centuries. Brian Jackson, "The Lingering Legacy of In Loco Parentis: An Historical Survey and Proposal for Reform," *Vanderbilt Law Review* 44 (1991): 1152–53; Gregory E. Michael, "The Unitary Theory: A Proposal for a Stable Student-School Legal Relationship," *Journal of Law and Education* 1 (1972): 417–22; Comment, "Private Government on the Campus," 1377–79; Gajda, *The Trials of Academe*, 209.

37. Van Alstyne, "The Tentative Emergence of Student Power in the United States," 403–17; Rabban, "Judicial Review of the University-Student Relationship," 97n15.

38. This interpretation was shaped in part by the increasing power of corporations, which unsettled traditional assumptions about the voluntary nature of contracts. Friedrich Kessler, "Contracts of Adhesion—Some Thoughts about Freedom of Contract," *Columbia Law Review* 43 (1943): 629–42; Morton J. Horwitz, *The Transformation of American Law, 1870–1960: The Crisis of Legal Orthodoxy* (New York: Oxford University Press, 1992), 50; Lawrence M. Friedman, *American Law in the Twentieth Century* (New Haven, CT: Yale University Press, 2002), 382.

39. This assertion runs counter to most previous studies, which have suggested that early courts resolved almost all contractual disputes in favor of colleges. Bickel and Lake, *The Rights and Responsibilities of the Modern University*, 43–44; Laura Krugman Ray, "Toward Contractual Rights for College Students," *Journal of Law and Education* 10 (1981): 163–89; Victoria J. Dodd, "The Non-contractual Nature of the Student-University Contractual Relationship," *University of Kansas Law Review* 33 (1985): 701–31.

40. *People ex rel. Cecil v. Bellevue Hospital Medical College*, 14 N.Y.S. 490 (1891); "An Autocratic Faculty," *Druggist Circular and Chemical Gazette* 35 (1891): 1. Regarding the status of this case as the first to recognize student contractual protections, see Robert L. Cherry Jr. and John P. Geary, "The College Catalog as a Contract," *Journal of Law and Education* 21 (1992), 1–32.

41. *University of Baltimore v. Colton*, 98 Md. 630, 631 (1904).

42. *Burg v. Milwaukee Medical College*, 128 Wis. 7 (1906).

43. *Booker v. Grand Rapids Medical College*, 156 Mich. 100 (1909).

44. *Koblitz v. Western Reserve*, 21 Ohio Cir. Ct. 153, 157 (1901).

45. *Goldstein v. New York University*, 78 N.Y.S. 741 (1902).

46. William A. Kaplin and Barbara A. Lee, *The Law of Higher Education: A Comprehensive Guide to Legal Implications of Administrative Decision Making*, 4th ed., vol. 1 (San Francisco: Jossey-Bass, 2006), 132; Rabban, "Judicial Review of the University-Student Relationship," 113.

47. *People v. New York Homeopathic Medical College*, 20 N.Y.S. 379 (1892). Also see *Niles v. Orange Training School for Nurses*, 63 N.J.L. 528 (1899).

48. *Addy v. Western Pennsylvania Medical College*, 11 Pa. D. 687 (1902).

49. Robert M. Hendrickson, Jason E. Lane, James T. Harris, and Richard H. Dorman, *Academic Leadership and Governance of Higher Education: A Guide for Trustees, Leaders, and Aspiring Leaders of Two- and Four-Year Institutions* (Sterling, VA: Stylus, 2013), 146.

50. *Nelson v. Lincoln Medical School*, 81 Neb. 536, 538–40 (1908).

51. The only academic expulsion case that was decided against a student hinged on technical grounds: the court ruled that the student should have sued the faculty rather than the trustees. *Steinhauer v. Arkins*, 18 Colo. App. 49 (1902).

52. *Brown v. Board of Education*, 8 Ohio Dec. 383 (1899).

53. A letter to the student's father stated that his expulsion was ordered "without reference to his guilt or innocence in matters with which his name has been connected." *Jackson v. State ex rel. Majors*, 57 Neb. 187 (1898).

54. *Miller v. Dailey*, 136 Cal. 219 (1902). Also see *San Francisco Call*, April 4, 1901, 1.

55. *Gleason v. University of Minnesota*, 104 Minn. 359 (1908).

56. Student's undated typescript titled "A History of Gymnastics Competition at the University of Minnesota," Willie Kerr Foster Papers, 1898–1950, University of Minnesota Archives, collection no. 721, box 1, folder 2; *Minneapolis Journal*, November 28, 1906, 6; *Duluth News Tribune*, May 30, 1908, 10; Alternative Writ of Mandamus, *Gleason v. University of Minnesota* (1908) (hereafter *Gleason* case files), Minnesota Supreme Court records and briefs, Minnesota State Law Library. Regarding the national campaign to reform college football, see Ronald A. Smith, *Pay for Play: A History of Big-Time College Athletic Reform* (Champaign: University of Illinois Press, 2011); Leslie, *Gentlemen and Scholars*, 191; John R. Thelin, *Games Colleges Play: Scandal and Reform in Intercollegiate Athletics* (Baltimore: Johns Hopkins University Press, 1994).

57. Leonard later supported the American Civil Liberties Union and served on the governing board of the University of Minnesota. "Biography of George B. Leonard," George B. Leonard Papers, Minnesota Historical Society.

58. Relator's Brief, *Gleason* case files; *Gleason v. University of Minnesota*, 104 Minn. 359 (1908).

59. Brief of Appellants, *Gleason* case files.

60. Alternative Writ of Mandamus, *Gleason* case files; *Gleason*, 104 Minn. at 364.

61. James D. Hurley, "Colleges: Nature of Relation to Student: Right of Dismissal," *Cornell Law Quarterly* 13 (1927): 85; Note, "Expulsion of Students from Private Educational Institutions," *Columbia Law Review* 35 (1935): 898–905.

62. Fifteen out of twenty-one of these opinions ordered reinstatements or mentioned that the court would consider taking this action in certain circumstances. This tally includes nine cases ruled in favor of students, and the following six cases, in which judges suggested that colleges were (or might be) obligated to provide some form of due process prior to expulsion: *North v. University of Illinois*, 137 Ill. 296 (1891); *Niles v. Orange*, 63 N.J.L. 528 (1899); *Koblitz v. Western Reserve University*, 21 Ohio Cir. Ct. 144 (1901); *Steinhauer v. Arkins*, 18 Colo. App. 49 (1902); *Goldstein v. New York University*, 78 N.Y.S. 739 (1902); *Burg v. Milwaukee Medical College*, 128 Wis. 7 (1906).

63. Oliver A. Harker, "The Use of Mandamus to Compel Educational Institutions to Confer Degrees," *Yale Law Journal* 20 (1911): 352.

64. Lane, "Student and Collegiate Contracts," 84.

65. See appendix A. The most categorically deferential decisions continued to come out of eastern courts. *Barker v. Bryn Mawr*, 278 Pa. 121 (1923); *Anthony v. Syracuse*, 231 N.Y.S. 435 (1928).

66. However, the court also suggested that it might invalidate academic standards that were not "easily met by the average student." *West v. Board of Trustees*, 41 Ohio App. 382 (1931). After 1910, courts uniformly refused to evaluate the decisions of private colleges that denied diplomas to students who earned low grades. *Tate v. North Pacific College*, 70 Or. 160 (1914); *Pacella v. Bennett*, 205 Ill. App. 324 (1917).

67. *Foley v. Benedict*, 122 Tex. 193 (1932). The court qualified this statement by suggesting that a reasonable standard should be within reach of an "average student."

68. On the increasing scale and complexity of higher education during the interwar period, see David O. Levine, *The American College and the Culture of Aspiration, 1915–1940* (Ithaca, NY: Cornell University Press, 1986), 165–66.

69. *Statutes of California: 1952 and 1953*, vol. 2 (n.p., 1953), 3332.

70. On the development of California's Master Plan, see John A. Douglass, *The California Idea and American Higher Education: 1850 to the 1960 Master Plan* (Palo Alto, CA: Stanford University Press, 2000).

71. *Gott v. Berea College*, 156 Ky. 376 (1913). A textbook published in 1961 referred to *Gott* as the prime example of the in loco parentis doctrine. Thomas E. Blackwell, *College Law: A Guide for Administrators* (Washington, DC: American Council on Education, 1961), 104. A more recent textbook continues to list *Gott* as the first case in its section on due process for expelled students. Bickel and Lake, *The Rights and Responsibilities of the Modern University*, 22.

72. *Gott*, 156 Ky. at 378–79; Fowler, "The Legal Relationship between the American College Student and the College," 408.

73. For example, the Supreme Court of Florida ruled that contractual language in the Stetson University catalog entitled the institution to expel a student for hazing classmates and ringing a cowbell after curfew in a dormitory. *Stetson University v. Hunt*, 88 Fla. 510 (1925).

74. *Ownbey v. Morgan*, 256 U.S. 94 (1921); Alexander M. Bickel and Benno C. Schmidt Jr., *The Judiciary and Responsible Government, 1910–1921*, part I (New York: Macmillan, 1984), 633–35.

75. Note, "Common Law Rights for Private University Students," 120–50; William W. Van Alstyne, "Procedural Due Process and State University Students," *UCLA Law Review* 10 (1963): 373; Alexander Brody, *The American State and Higher Education: The Legal, Political, and Constitutional Relationship* (Washington, DC: American Council on Education, 1935), 139; Rabban, "Judicial Review of the University-Student Relationship," 113.

76. Comment, "Private Government on the Campus," 1394; Bickel and Lake, *The Rights and Responsibilities of the Modern University*, 29.

77. Reuben, *The Making of the Modern University*, 255–62; Christopher P. Loss, *Between Citizens and the State: The Politics of American Higher Education in the Twentieth Century* (Princeton, NJ: Princeton University Press, 2012), 38–48; Horowitz, *Campus Life*, 119; Horowitz, *Alma Mater*, 149; Paula S. Fass, *The Damned and the Beautiful: American Youth in the 1920's* (New York: Oxford University Press, 1977), 97, 137, 207–9, 467; Rudolph, *The American College and University*, 460.

78. Fass, *The Damned and the Beautiful*, 133, 182, 195–96.

79. Comment, "Private Government on the Campus," 1374.

80. *Barker v. Bryn Mawr*, 278 Pa. 121 (1923).

81. "A Memorandum to the President and Directors of Bryn Mawr College," undated, Hamill & Barker, Inc., Collection (hereafter Barker Papers), box 7, folder 2, Charles Deering McCormick Library of Special Collections, Northwestern University Library; Margery C. Barker to Helen Taft, undated, box 7, folder 2, Barker Papers.

82. "Thomas Interview" (Margery C. Barker's handwritten notes), April 22, 1921, box 7, folder 2, Barker Papers; "A Memorandum to the President and Directors of Bryn Mawr College," Barker Papers; M. Carey Thomas to Marjory C. Barker, April 2, 1921, box 7, folder 8, Barker Papers; *New York Times*, December 18, 1921, and April 2, 1922.

83. Horowitz, *Alma Mater*, 282–93.

84. "A Memorandum to the President and Directors of Bryn Mawr College," Barker Papers; James C. McMath to H. B. Rust, August 10, 1921, box 7, folder 7, Barker Papers.

85. Margery Barker to Margery C. Barker, undated, box 7, folder 1, Barker Papers; Elizabeth Rust to Margery Barker, May 25, 1921, box 7, folder 6, Barker Papers.

86. *New York Times* clipping dated February 22, 1922, box 7, folder 7, Barker Papers; *New York Times*, April 2, 1922.

87. The court suggested that Margery could sue for damages if her reputation had been tarnished without justification. *Barker*, 278 Pa. at 122.

88. The *Gott* opinion indicated that expulsions from public colleges could be scrutinized "somewhat more critically." Gott, 156 Ky. at 380. In 1941, an Ohio court rejected the invocation of *Gott* by a public university, though this decision was also informed by evidence that the administration banned students from a restaurant because of a personal conflict with the property owner rather than to protect the wellbeing of students. *McGinnis v. Walker*, 35 Ohio L. Abs. 245 (1941).

89. *Woods v. Simpson*, 146 Md. 547 (1924).

90. Adele H. Stamp to Burney Piper, January 14, 1924, Adele Stamp to "Pinckney," November 22, 1923, Simpson vs. U of Md. folder, Adele H. Stamp Papers (hereafter Stamp Papers), Collection 72-15, Archives and Manuscripts Department, University of Maryland, series 1, box 4; Transcript of Record from the Baltimore City Court (hereafter *Woods* transcript), *Woods v. Simpson*, case no. 48 (October Term 1924), Maryland Court of Appeals records and briefs, Maryland State Archives, T 2088, 1/65/5/15, 40–41.

91. *Woods* transcript, 118, 122–23, 130; George H. Callcott, *A History of the University of Maryland* (Baltimore: Maryland Historical Society, 1966), 295–98.

92. Untitled typescript by Anna S. Hoerr, Office of the President, University of Maryland records, Collection 72-116, series 6, Albert F. Woods Papers (hereafter Woods Papers), Archives and Manuscripts Department, University of Maryland, box 8, folder 8; untitled typescript by Nadia Wright, Frances D. Lemen, Lillian O. Earnest, and Olive Wallace, Woods Papers, box 8, folder 8; "Charged Girl Wore Kimono at Wrong Hour at University," undated clipping, Simpson vs. U of Md. folder, Stamp Papers, series 1, box 4; *Woods* transcript, 145, 164, 199.

93. "Phyllis Morgan" and "Esther Williams" (undated notes), Virginia Flanagan case folder, Stamp Papers, series 1, box 1.

94. Statement of Adele H. Stamp (undated), and A. F. Woods to Virginia Flanagan, March 21, 1923, Virginia Flanagan case folder, Stamp Papers, series 1, box 1. Deans of women were especially concerned about campus housing because women's dormitories were a relatively recent achievement and colleges assumed that parents expected their daughters to be subject to close supervision. Jana Nidiffer, *Pioneering Deans of Women: More Than Wise and Pious Matrons* (New York: Teachers College Press, 2000), 65–67, 148.

95. Clipping from *Washington Post*, April 29, 1923, Virginia Flanagan case folder, Stamp Papers, series 1, box 1. Regarding the impact of the article, see A. H. Stamp to Burney Piper, January 14, 1924, and Adele H. Stamp to "Pinckney," November 22, 1923, Simpson vs. U of Md. folder, Stamp Papers, series 1, box 4.

96. Appellants' Brief, *Woods v. Simpson*, case no. 48 (October Term 1924), Maryland Court of Appeals records and briefs, Maryland State Archives, T 2088, 1/65/5/15, 24–25.

97. Appellee's Brief, *Woods v. Simpson*, case no. 48 (October Term 1924), Maryland Court of Appeals records and briefs, Maryland State Archives, T 2088, 1/65/5/15, 8–10.

98. Virginia Flanagan to A. F. Woods, March 23, 1923, Woods Papers, box 8, folder 8.

99. Unreported oral opinion from Baltimore City Court, filed May 19, 1924, *Woods* transcript, 291.

100. *Simpson*, 146 Md. at 552.

101. *Anthony v. Syracuse*, 231 N.Y.S. 435 (1928). The case received national publicity. Horowitz, *Campus Life*, 153.

102. *Anthony v. Syracuse*, 223 N.Y.S. 796 (1927).

103. The court ruled that catalogs were binding even if a student never read the relevant section. *Anthony*, 231 N.Y.S. at 439.

104. Between 1910 and 1960, fifteen out of twenty-six reported expulsion cases involved a woman student or some form of political or religious dissent.

105. *Barker v. Bryn Mawr*, 278 Pa. 121 (1923); *Tanton v. McKenney*, 226 Mich. 245 (1924); *Woods v. Simpson*, 146 Md. 547 (1924); *Stetson University v. Hunt*, 88 Fla. 510 (1925); *Ingersoll v. Clapp*, 81 Mont. 200 (1927); *Anthony v. Syracuse*, 231 N.Y.S. 435 (1928); *West v. Board of Trustees*, 41 Ohio App. 367 (1931); *White v. Portia Law School*, 274 Mass. 162 (1931). Regarding women's enrollment, see Barbara Solomon, *In the Company of Educated Women: A History of Women and Higher Education in America* (New Haven, CT: Yale University Press, 1985), 142.

106. Solomon, *In the Company of Educated Women*, 157–59. Also see Amy Thompson McCandless, *The Past in the Present: Women's Higher Education in the Twentieth-Century American South* (Tuscaloosa: University of Alabama Press, 1999), 125, 151.

107. *Tanton v. McKenney*, 226 Mich. 245 (1924).

108. In 1925, Bryn Mawr made waves by legalizing smoking. Solomon, *In the Company of Educated Women*, 160–61; Fass, *The Damned and the Beautiful*, 196, 293–95; Horowitz, *Alma Mater*, 289.

109. *Tanton*, 226 Mich. at 247, 253.

110. *Anthony*, 231 N.Y.S. at 437.

111. Nicholas L. Syrett, *The Company He Keeps: A History of White College Fraternities* (Chapel Hill: University of North Carolina Press, 2009); Solomon, *In the Company of Educated Women*, 164.

112. "General House Regulations, 1921–22," and A. F. Woods to A. Stamp, March 19, 1923, Virginia Flanagan case folder, Stamp Papers, series 1, box 1.

113. *Woods* transcript, 53, 68, 164; "Charged Girl Wore Kimono at Wrong Hour at University," undated clipping, Simpson vs. U of Md. folder, Stamp Papers, series 1, box 4; Callcott, *A History of the University of Maryland*, 292–98.

114. Simpson was an honors student with many extracurricular commitments. *Woods* transcript, 4, 24, 34.

115. Clipping from *Washington Herald*, April 11, 1924, Simpson vs. U of Md. folder, Stamp Papers, series 1, box 4.

116. *Woods* transcript, 152; handwritten note by Ruth Alderman, March 21, 1924, and clipping from *Diamondback*, April 1, 1924, Virginia Flanagan case folder, Stamp Papers, series 1, box 1; "To all whom it may concern" (undated), Simpson vs. U of Md. folder, Stamp Papers, series 1, box 4.

117. *Woods* transcript, 187; "Anna Dorsey" (undated), Virginia Flanagan case folder, Stamp Papers, series 1, box 1.

118. "Amos v. Flanagan" (undated), Virginia Flanagan case folder, Stamp Papers, series 1, box 1.

119. Statements of Ella Hadaway and Phyllis Morgan (undated), Virginia Flanagan case folder, Stamp Papers, series 1, box 1.

120. Clipping from *Washington Post*, April 29, 1923, Virginia Flanagan case folder, Stamp Papers, series 1, box 1.

121. *Woods*, 146 Md. at 551. Vivian Simpson went on to earn a law degree from George Washington University and became the first woman to serve as Maryland's secretary of state. *Washington Post*, December 5, 1949; *Baltimore Sun*, March 24, 2001. Also see Vivian V. Simpson Papers (1903–1987), Maryland State Archives MSA SC 3520-13450.

122. Kaplin and Lee, *The Law of Higher Education*, vol. 1, 738; William W. Van Alstyne, "Student Academic Freedom and the Rule-Making Powers of Public Universities: Some Constitutional Considerations," *Law in Transition Quarterly* 2 (1965): 15.

123. *Samson v. Columbia*, 167 N.Y.S. 202, 205–6 (1917).

124. Carol S. Gruber, *Mars and Minerva: World War I and the Uses of Higher Learning in America* (Baton Rouge: Louisiana State University Press, 1975); David M. Kennedy, *Over Here: The First World War and American Society* (New York: Oxford University Press, 1980), 83–86.

125. *New York Tribune*, March 9, 1917, 6. Regarding student antiwar protests during World War I, see Philip G. Altbach, *Student Politics in America: A Historical Analysis* (New York: McGraw-Hill, 1974), 26–27; Max Horn, *The Intercollegiate Socialist Society, 1905–1921: Origins of the Modern American Student Movement* (Boulder, CO: Westview, 1979), 129–64.

126. *New York Times*, June 12, 1917.

127. *Samson*, 167 N.Y.S. at 204.

128. *Goldenkoff v. Albany*, 191 N.Y.S. 349 (1921).

129. Fass, *The Damned and the Beautiful*, 334, 339–41; Horowitz, *Campus Life*, 152, 467.

130. *University of Maryland v. Coale*, 165 Md. 224 (1933). Also see *Hanauer v. Elkins*, 217 Md. 213 (1958).

131. *Hamilton v. Regents of the University of California*, 293 U.S. 245 (1934).

132. The tide began to turn toward increased protection of student speech after *West Virginia State Board of Education v. Barnette*, 319 U.S. 624 (1943).

133. *Zarichny v. State Board of Agriculture* (1949) (unreported) *cert. denied*, 338 U.S. 816 (1949). James Zarichny, the student, also attempted to organize an auto factory. United States Congress, Committee on Un-American Activities, *Investigation of Communist activities in the State of Michigan* (Washington, DC: United States Government Printing Office, 1954), 5489, 5496.

134. *New York Times*, May 11, 1951, 29. Regarding the vulnerability of dissenting faculty during this era, see Marjorie Heins, *Priests of Our Democracy: The Supreme Court, Academic Freedom, and the Anti-Communist Purge* (New York: New York University Press, 2013); Ellen Schrecker, *No Ivory Tower: McCarthyism and the Universities* (New York: Oxford University Press, 1986).

135. *Robinson v. University of Miami*, 100 So. 2d 442 (1958).

136. Zechariah Chafee Jr., "The Internal Affairs of Associations Not for Profit," *Harvard Law Review* 43 (1930): 1026–27.

137. Chafee, "The Internal Affairs of Associations Not for Profit," 1026–27.

138. Comment, "Private Government on the Campus," 1374. As early as 1931, it seemed clear that students were entitled to respond to specific charges at a hearing. John E.

Kirkpatrick, *Academic Organization and Control* (Yellow Springs, OH: Antioch, 1931), 182–88.

139. A lower court had ruled that the student was entitled to a hearing. One state supreme court judge dissented for a similar reason, noting that the expulsion had been based on "prejudices resulting from rumors." *Ingersoll v. Clapp*, 81 Mont. 200 (1927).

140. *White v. Portia Law School*, 274 Mass. 162 (1931). The student had been dismissed for "misusing" her legal training by suing a local police chief for slander and ordering groceries on credit with the intention of charging her ex-husband. Also see J. Clay Smith Jr., *Emancipation: The Making of the Black Lawyer, 1844–1944* (Philadelphia: University of Pennsylvania Press, 1993), 69n74.

141. *State ex el. Sherman v. Hyman*, 180 Tenn. 99, 111 (1942). Regarding the frequent misinterpretation of this case, see Van Alstyne, "Procedural Due Process and State University Students," 373n23.

142. "Constitution of the United States National Student Association" (1947), in Eugene G. Schwartz, ed., *American Students Organize: Founding the National Student Association after World War II* (Washington, DC: American Council on Education, 2006), 1111; Angus Johnston, "The United States National Student Association: Democracy, Activism, and the Idea of the Student, 1947–1978" (PhD diss., City University of New York, 2009), 144–48.

143. *The Statutes of California: 1947* (Sacramento: California State Printing Office, 1947), 2994; *Acts of the Legislature of the State of Louisiana* (Baton Rouge: Thomas J. Moran's Sons, 1950), 477–81.

144. *Joint Anti-Fascist Refugee Committee v. McGrath*, 341 U.S. 123 (1951).

145. *Dehaan v. Brandeis*, 150 F. Supp. 626 (1957); Comment, "A Student's Right to Hearing on Dismissal from a University," *Stanford Law Review* 10 (1958): 746–47, 748n22. Also see William W. Van Alstyne and Kenneth L. Karst, "State Action," *Stanford Law Review* 14 (1961): 3–58.

146. *Bluett v. University of Illinois*, 10 Ill. App. 2d 207 (1956); Warren A. Seavey, "Dismissal of Students: 'Due Process,'" *Harvard Law Review* 70 (1957): 1407–10. Also see Van Alstyne, "Procedural Due Process and State University Students," 373n27.

147. *Steier v. New York State Education Commission*, 271 F.2d 13 (1959).

148. Philip Lee, "The Case of *Dixon v. Alabama*: From Civil Rights to Students' Rights and Back Again," *Teachers College Record* 116 (2014): 1–18.

149. The *Dixon* ruling cited both of these cases. *Dixon*, 294 F.2d at 158.

150. Van Alstyne, "Procedural Due Process and State University Students," 386–69.

151. Lee, "The Case of *Dixon v. Alabama*"; Bickel and Lake, *The Rights and Responsibilities of the Modern University*, 38n7.

152. Comment, "Private Government on the Campus," 1380.

153. *Knight v. State Board of Education*, 200 F. Supp. 174 (1961).

Chapter 5. Tuition

1. J. J. Lane, *History of the University of Texas: Based on Facts and Records* (Austin: State Printer, 1891), 26–28. For similar remarks from other university leaders, see James B. Angell, "The State Universities of the West," in Johns Hopkins University, *State Aid to Higher Education: A Series of Addresses Delivered at the Johns Hopkins University*

(Baltimore: Johns Hopkins Press, 1898), 37; Charles R. Van Hise, "Inaugural Address," in Hugh Hawkins ed., *The Emerging University and Industrial America* (Malabar, FL: Krieger, 1985), 27.

2. Richard Henry Jesse, "The Function of the State University," *Journal of Proceedings and Addresses of the National Educational Association* (1891), 606–7; Jana Nidiffer and Jeffrey P. Bouman, "The Chasm between Rhetoric and Reality: The Fate of the 'Democratic Ideal' When a Public University Becomes Elite," *Educational Policy* 15 (2001): 437; G. F. Mellen, *Popular Errors Concerning Higher Education in the United States and the Remedy* (Leipsic: Gressner and Schramm, 1890), 46–47; John Aubrey Douglass, *The Conditions for Admission: Access, Equity, and the Social Contract of Public Universities* (Palo Alto, CA: Stanford University Press, 2007), 18–19; C. H. Thurber, "Fiscal Support of State Universities and State Colleges," *Bulletin of the American Association of University Professors* 11 (1925): 265–70.

3. See appendix A. See also the introduction for a cautionary discussion about assigning "winners" and "losers" to cases. Since this book focuses on access, the tally of tuition cases omits suits that simply demanded refunds. In these cases, courts typically allowed colleges to retain tuition and fees unless students were expelled without cause, were not informed of rules and their consequences, or were too ill to continue. William T. O'Hara and John G. Hill, *The Student, the College, the Law* (New York: Teachers College Press, 1972), 23.

4. See appendix A.

5. M. M. Chambers, "Constitutional Provisions Regarding State Universities," *Educational Law and Administration* 2 (1933): 38; Edward C. Eliot and M. M. Chambers, *Charters and Basic Laws of Selected American Universities and Colleges* (New York: Carnegie Foundation for the Advancement of Teaching, 1934), 338; *Laws and Resolutions of the State of North Carolina Passed by the General Assembly at Its Session of 1887* (Raleigh: State Printer, 1887), 469.

6. *Laws of the State of New York passed at the 88th Session of the Legislature* (Albany: William Gould, 1865), 1192. The Florida legislature used almost identical language. *General Acts and Resolutions Adopted by the Legislature of Florida at its 10th Regular Session* (Tallahassee: State Printer, 1905), 54.

7. There were no tuition cases involving private colleges reported between 1928 and 1968. Robert L. Cherry Jr. and John P. Geary, "The College Catalog as a Contract," *Journal of Law and Education* 21 (1992): 24.

8. The distinction becomes larger when room, board, and other costs are considered. Roger L. Geiger, *To Advance Knowledge: The Growth of America's Research Universities, 1900–1940* (New York: Oxford University Press, 1986), 41; James Hulme Canfield, *The College Student and His Problems* (New York: Macmillan, 1902), 196–97.

9. *The Statutes of California and Amendments to the Codes Passed at the 34th Session of the Legislature* (San Francisco: Bancroft-Whitney, 1901), 4–5; *Acts of the General Assembly of Alabama Passed by the Session of 1898–99* (Jacksonville, FL: Vance, 1899), 1622. Stanford was authorized to charge tuition in 1921. *Statutes of California: General Laws, Amendments to Codes, Resolutions, Constitutional Amendments Passed at the Regular Session of the 44th Legislature* (Sacramento: State Printer, 1921), 541.

10. *Illinois Female College v. Cooper*, 25 Ill. 133 (1861). These sorts of scholarships entitled the purchaser to educate a child at some point in the future.

11. The court did allow the university to charge laboratory fees to these students because participation in the courses that required them was voluntary. *New Orleans v. Tulane*, 123 La. 550 (1909).

12. *Niedermeyer v. University of Missouri*, 61 Mo. App. 654, 660–61 (1895).

13. A. W. Lawrence et al. to Board of Curators, April 11, 1895, Turner, Hinton, and Turner to J. G. Babb, April 16, 1895, and William E. Eads to J. G. Babb, May 22, 1895, University of Missouri Board of Curators Executive Board Files (1888–97) (hereafter MU Papers), record group 1/1/2, box 3, folder 17, University of Missouri–Columbia Archives.

14. Report on Fees at State Universities, September 5, 1900, Papers of the Board of Regents (hereafter NU Regents), University of Nebraska (1869–1910), record group 01-01-01, box 14, folder 117, Archives and Special Collections, University of Nebraska–Lincoln Libraries; Canfield, *The College Student and His Problems*, 196–97; Mellen, *Popular Errors Concerning Higher Education in the United States and the Remedy*, 46–47; Nidiffer and Bouman, "The Chasm between Rhetoric and Reality," 442; John A. Douglass, *The California Idea and American Higher Education: 1850 to the 1960 Master Plan* (Palo Alto, CA: Stanford University Press, 2000), 109.

15. *State ex rel. Priest v. Regents of the University of Wisconsin*, 54 Wis. 159 (1882). This level of discretion was unusual for a state agency in that era. Kern Alexander and Klinton A. Alexander, *Higher Education Law: Policy and Perspectives* (New York: Routledge, 2011), 104.

16. Merle Curti and Vernon Carstensen, *University of Wisconsin: A History, 1848–1925*, vol. 1 (Madison: University of Wisconsin Press, 1949), 54–55, 305, 310–16, 366–68; *University Press*, September 30, 1881; Minutes of the University of Wisconsin Board of Regents, June 22, 1881, vol. c, 366, record group 1, University of Wisconsin–Madison Archives; *University of Wisconsin Class Album* (1882), 82, accessed August 9, 2012, http://digital.library.wisc.edu/1711.dl/UW.ClassAlbum1882.

17. Relator's Brief, August 1881, *State ex rel. Priest v. Regents of the University of Wisconsin*, Wisconsin Supreme Court records and briefs, Wisconsin State Law Library, 7, 14–15, 21–23. Also see Brief of S. U. Pinney, filed December 19, 1881, *State ex rel. Priest v. Regents of the University of Wisconsin*, Wisconsin Supreme Court records and briefs, Wisconsin Historical Society.

18. Brief for Respondents, filed December 19, 1881, *State ex rel. Priest v. Regents of the University of Wisconsin*, Wisconsin Supreme Court records and briefs, Wisconsin Historical Society.

19. *Priest*, 54 Wis. at 166–68. For disappointed reaction from a student newspaper, see *Badger*, January 12, 1882, 4–5. In 1903, a bill that would have outlawed the collection of "fees" passed the state senate but lost in the assembly. Curti and Carstensen, *University of Wisconsin*, 581.

20. Previously, corporations were expected to deliver relatively direct public benefits in order to receive their legislative charters. Morton J. Horwitz, *The Transformation of American Law, 1870–1960: The Crisis of Legal Orthodoxy* (New York: Oxford University Press, 1992), 72–78.

21. *State ex rel. Little v. Regents of University of Kansas*, 55 Kan. 389 (1895).

22. *The Laws of the State of Kansas Passed at the 4th Session of Legislature* (Lawrence: State Printer, 1864), 197.

23. Clifford S. Griffin, *The University of Kansas* (Lawrence: University of Kansas Press, 1974), 30, 104–5.

24. Francis H. Snow to C. F. Scott, November 3, 1894, Chancellor's Office Papers, General Correspondence (hereafter Snow correspondence), Series 2/6/1, Spencer Research Library, University of Kansas; Francis H. Snow to L. A. Thrasher, November 6, 1894, Snow correspondence; *Jeffersonian*, November 8, 1894, 4.

25. Francis H. Snow to C. S. Gleed, September 30, 1893, Chancellor's Office Papers, Regents et al. Correspondence (June 1892–April 1899), series 2/6/3, Spencer Research Library, University of Kansas; University of Kansas Board of Regents Minutes (hereafter KU Minutes), December 5, 1893, Board of Regents Papers, series 1/2, Spencer Research Library, University of Kansas.

26. *Jeffersonian*, November 29, 1894, 2. On Little's affiliation with populism, see Ed Blair, *History of Johnson County, Kansas* (Lawrence, KS: Standard, 1915), 248. Ironically, Chancellor Snow would later reflect that the end of tuition and fees was one of the biggest accomplishments of his tenure. Francis H. Snow, "Address," *Graduate Magazine of the University of Kansas* (1902), 46–47. In 1895, the legislature affirmed its expectation that the university should refrain from charging tuition. *Laws of the State of Kansas: Session Laws of 1895* (Topeka: State Printer, 1895), 373.

27. Edwin A. Austin, "The Supreme Court of the State of Kansas," *Collections of the Kansas State Historical Society* 13 (1915), 101.

28. Peter Karsten, *Heart versus Head: Judge-Made Law in Nineteenth-Century America* (Chapel Hill: University of North Carolina Press, 1997), 228. Also see Scott M. Gelber, *University and the People: Envisioning American Higher Education in an Era of Populist Protest* (Madison: University of Wisconsin Press, 2011).

29. KU Minutes, September 13, 1894; untitled and undated typescript, William Henry Sears Papers, box 1, letterbook, 239–42, Kansas State Historical Society; *Jeffersonian*, January 28, 1897, 2.

30. *Lawrence Journal*, January 30, 1897, 9. Also see Griffin, *The University of Kansas*, 233.

31. *Little*, 55 Kan. at 400.

32. *Little*, 55 Kan. at 400–401. Although he supported the conventional view of contract law, Judge Allen advocated for the progressive income tax and government ownership of railroads. He dissented when the court upheld the removal of a Populist regent of KU in 1894. James L. Hunt, "Populism, Law, and the Corporation: The 1897 Kansas Supreme Court," *Agricultural History* 66 (1992): 28–54; Brian J. Moline, "The Populist Court: Frank J. Doster and Stephen H. Allen," *Journal of the Kansas Bar Association* 58 (1989): 23–29; Michael Brodhead, "Populism and the Law: Some Notes on Stephen H. Allen," *Kansas Quarterly* 1 (1969): 76–84.

33. *Little*, 55 Kan. at 393, 398–99.

34. *Connell v. Gray*, 33 Okla. 591 (1912).

35. Philip R. Rulon, *Oklahoma State University since 1890* (Stillwater: Oklahoma State University Press, 1975), 127–28, 132.

36. Brief of the Defendant in Error, filed September 17, 1912, *Connell v. Gray*, case no. 4342, Oklahoma Supreme Court records and briefs, Oklahoma Department of Libraries. Regarding Miller's biography, see Joseph Bradfield Thoburn, *A Standard History of Oklahoma*, vol. 5 (New York: American Historical Society, 1916), 2079–81.

37. Brief for the Plaintiff in Error, filed September 17, 1912, *Connell v. Gray*, case no. 4342, Oklahoma Supreme Court records and briefs, Oklahoma Department of Libraries.

38. *Connell*, 33 Okla. at 600; *Tulsa Daily World*, September 8, 1912, 6. For Williams's biography, see Edward Everett Dale and James D. Morrison, *Pioneer Judge: The Life of Robert Lee Williams* (Cedar Rapids, IA: Torch, 1958).

39. According to a LexisNexis search, *Priest* has been cited fifty-five times, whereas *Little* has been cited thirty-three times, though many of these citations pertained to Wisconsin or Kansas cases that did not involve higher education (search performed on July 26, 2013).

40. R. Pound to J. S. Dales, December 3, 1903, NU Regents, box 16, folder 132.

41. See appendix A. The two tuition cases that universities lost in this period were related to nonresident charges rather than tuition or fees in general.

42. *Litchman v. Shannon*, 90 Wash. 186 (1916).

43. *3rd Biennial Report of the Regents of the University of Washington* (Olympia: State Printer, 1894).

44. Charles M. Gates, *The First Century at the University of Washington, 1861–1961* (Seattle: University of Washington Press, 1961), 126, 141.

45. It is important to note that this suit differs from the others discussed in this chapter because it sought to invalidate a statute rather than an administrative policy. "Resolution" (n.d.), Mark M. Litchman Papers (hereafter Litchman Papers), collection no. 165, box 3, folder 9, Special Collections, University of Washington Libraries. At least one newspaper criticized the tuition law and pointed out that many students supported themselves without parental assistance. *Tacoma Times*, March 4, 1915.

46. Litchman called himself a "soldier in the revolution." A few years after arguing this case, he helped to found the Seattle Labor College and served as its first president. Mark M. Litchman to Leon Rubenstein, April 16, 1934, Litchman Papers, box 2, folder 16; Albert F. Gunns, *Civil Liberties in Crisis: The Pacific Northwest, 1917–1940* (New York: Garland, 1983), 99–101.

47. Gates, *The First Century at the University of Washington*, 114–15, 133–35.

48. *Morning Oregonian*, March 9, 1915, 7.

49. Brief of Appellants, *Litchman v. Shannon*, Washington Supreme Court case no. 13209, Litchman Papers, box 3, folder 9. Emphasis in the original.

50. *Litchman*, 90 Wash. at 193. Before serving as a judge, Holcomb was appointed by a populistic governor to be state commissioner of arid lands. Charles H. Sheldon, *The Washington High Bench: A Biographical History of the State Supreme Court, 1889–1991* (Pullman: Washington State University Press, 1992), 210–12. Litchman petitioned in vain for a rehearing by arguing that the state constitution mentioned a "system of public schools" that should include the university. Appellants' Petition for Re-Hearing En Banc, *Litchman v. Shannon*, Supreme Court Case no. 13209, Litchman Papers, box 3, folder 9.

51. *Olympia Daily Recorder*, March 8, 1916, 2.

52. Lloyd Morey, "Student Fees in State Universities and Colleges," *School and Society* 28 (1928): 185–92; Christopher P. Loss, *Between Citizens and the State: The Politics of American Higher Education in the Twentieth Century* (Princeton, NJ: Princeton University Press, 2012), 30.

53. M. Lyle Spencer to *University of Washington Daily*, April 29, 1929, R. H. Hartley to M. L. Spencer, May 6, 1929, and David Thomson to Governor Roland H. Hartley, May 10, 1929, University of Washington, Office of the President, collection no. 71-034, box 136, folder 139, Special Collections, University of Washington Libraries.

54. The regents estimated that these charges prevented one hundred to two hundred students from attending in 1902. *Biennial Report of the University of Kansas Board of Regents* (1903–4), 2; Griffin, *The University of Kansas*, 422.

55. *Acts and Joint Resolutions of the General Assembly of the State of Virginia* (Richmond: State Printer, 1924), 212; *Acts and Joint Resolutions of the General Assembly of the State of Virginia* (Richmond: State Printer, 1926), 155.

56. *General and Special Laws of the State of Texas Passed by the 40th Legislature at the Regular Session* (n.p., 1927), 351–53; *General Laws of the State of Texas, Passed by the 43rd Legislature at the Regular Session* (n.p., 1933), 596–97.

57. *New York Times*, October 5, 1930, cited in David O. Levine, *The American College and the Culture of Aspiration, 1915–1940* (Ithaca, NY: Cornell University Press, 1986), 215.

58. *State Teachers College v. Morris*, 165 Miss. 758, 778 (1932).

59. *Lynch v. Commissioner of Education*, 317 Mass. 73, 75, 79 (1944).

60. *Rheam v. Board of Regents of University of Oklahoma*, 161 Okla. 268 (1933).

61. Whereas the students' attorney invoked *Little* and cited a statute requiring free tuition, the court concluded that the ability to charge the fee was an implied power associated with the governing board's statutory authority over buildings and grounds. *State ex rel. Veeder v. State Board of Education*, 97 Mont. 121 (1934).

62. *State v. Regents of the University of Georgia*, 179 Ga. 210, 226 (1934).

63. *Rainey v. Malone*, 141 S.W.2d 713, 717 (1940).

64. Revenue from tuition and fees amounted to only 12 percent of state university income during the 1920s, and fees alone represented just 16 percent of total revenue as late as 1950. Morey, "Student Fees in State Universities and Colleges," 185–92; John D. Millett, *Conflict in Higher Education: State Government versus Institutional Independence* (Washington, DC: Jossey-Bass, 1984), 13–14.

65. Malcolm Moos and Francis Rourke, *The Campus and the State* (Baltimore: Johns Hopkins Press, 1959), 1, 11, 72, 269.

66. Many states also exempted students from residency requirements if they served the institution (as employees) or the state/nation (as military personnel). Michael A. Olivas, "Administering Intentions: Law, Theory, and Practice of Postsecondary Residency Requirements," *Journal of Higher Education* 59 (1988): 270–71.

67. *Priest*, 54 Wis. 159; Morey, "Student Fees," 185–92; Olivas, "Administering Intentions," 263–64.

68. *Bryan v. Regents of the University of California*, 188 Cal. 559, 562 (1922).

69. *State ex rel. Kaplan v. Kuhn*, 11 Ohio Dec. 321 (1901); *Halaby v. Board of Directors*, 162 Ohio St. 290 (1954).

70. *Newman v. Graham*, 82 Idaho 90 (1960).

71. Carlton E. Spencer, "The Legal Aspects of the Nonresident Tuition Fee," *Oregon Law Review* 6 (1927): 333; Thomas E. Blackwell, *College Law: A Guide for Administrators* (Washington, DC: American Council on Education, 1961), 266. Also see Olivas, "Administering Intentions," 273.

72. *Laws of the State of New York Passed at the 88th Session of the Legislature* (Albany: William Gould, 1865), 1192–93; *Acts and Joint Resolutions of the General Assembly of the State of Virginia Passed at the Session of 1871–72* (Richmond: State Printer, 1872), 312; *Acts and Resolves Passed by the General Court of Massachusetts in the Year 1883* (Boston: State Printer, 1883), 616. In general, see Thomas J. Giddens, "Origins of State Scholarship Programs: 1647–1913," *College and University* 46 (1970): 37–45.

73. Thomas M. Cooley, *A Treatise on the Constitutional Limitations Which Rest upon the Legislative Power of the States of the American Union* (Boston: Little, Brown, 1868); Horwitz, *The Transformation of American Law*, 21–32; Clyde E. Jacobs, *Law Writers and the Courts: The Influence of Thomas M. Cooley, Christopher G. Tiedeman, and John F. Dillon upon American Constitutional Law* (Berkeley: University of California Press, 1954), 122–24.

74. *Loan Association v. City of Topeka*, 87 U.S. 655, 664 (1874).

75. Howard Gillman, *The Constitution Besieged: The Rise and Demise of the Lochner Era Police Powers Jurisprudence* (Durham, NC: Duke University Press, 1993), 68–73, 93, 203.

76. The public purpose doctrine was not derived from constitutional language but was more or less written into law by judges seeking to limit economic interventions and regulations. Jacobs, *Law Writers and the Courts*, 107, 118; Horwitz, *The Transformation of American Law*, 26.

77. B. J. Burrell and R. H. Eckelberry, "The High-School Question before the Courts in the Post-Civil-War Period," *School Review* 42 (1934): 255–65; Douglass, *The California Idea and American Higher Education*, 131.

78. Alexander Brody, *The American State and Higher Education: The Legal, Political, and Constitutional Relationship* (Washington, DC: American Council on Education, 1935), 49–57, 74–78; Mabel Hardy Pollitt, *A Biography of James Kennedy Patterson* (Louisville, KY: Westerfield-Bonte, 1925), 261.

79. E. Benjamin Andrews, "Eastern Universities and Western," *Independent* 57 (1904): 676. Perhaps out of concern for the competitive disadvantage of his institution, Harvard president Charles Eliot also opposed free tuition at state universities. Hugh Hawkins, *Between Harvard and America: The Educational Leadership of Charles W. Eliot* (New York: Oxford University Press, 1972), 152–56.

80. *Journal of Proceedings and Addresses of the National Educational Association* (1880), 159–61. Also see Thomas Dyer, *The University of Georgia: A Bicentennial History, 1785–1985* (Athens: University of Georgia Press, 1985), 124–25. Regarding the influence of this sort of social Darwinism in general, see Mike Hawkins, *Social Darwinism in European and American Thought, 1860–1945: Nature as Model and Nature as Threat* (New York: Cambridge University Press, 1997).

81. G. Stephens to unnamed professor, July 29, 1899, University of North Carolina Papers, collection no. 40005, box 20, folder 678, Wilson Library, University of North

Carolina Archives; James R. Montgomery, *The Volunteer State Forges Its University: The University of Tennessee, 1887–1919* (Knoxville: University of Tennessee Record, 1966), 4, 28; Gelber, *The University and the People*, 92.

82. *Acts of the General Assembly of the Commonwealth of Kentucky* (Louisville: Globe, 1908), 7–9.

83. *Laws and Resolutions of the State of North Carolina Passed by the General Assembly at Its Session of 1887* (Raleigh: State Printer, 1887), 469; *Biennial Report of the Superintendent of Public Instruction of North Carolina* (1888), 117.

84. John Milton Cooper, *Walter Hines Page: The Southerner as American, 1855–1918* (Chapel Hill: University of North Carolina Press, 1977), 24. Also see David F. Allmendinger Jr., *Paupers and Scholars: The Transformation of Student Life in Nineteenth-Century New England* (New York: St. Martin's, 1975).

85. *Acts of the General Assembly of the State of Virginia Passed at the Session of 1863–64* (Richmond: State Printer, 1864), 29–30. Also see *Acts of the General Assembly of the State of Georgia Passed in Milledgeville at an Annual Session in 1866* (Macon: State Printer, 1867), 143–44.

86. *Public Laws of the State of Illinois Passed by the 25th General Assembly* (Springfield: Baker, Bailhach, 1868), 126; *Laws of the State of New York Passed at the 117th Session of the Legislature*, vol. 2 (Albany: James B. Lyon, 1894), 1275.

87. *Laws of the State of Illinois Enacted by the 51st General Assembly* (Springfield: State Printer, 1919), 923; *Public Acts Passed by the General Assembly of the State of Connecticut in the Year 1929* (Hartford: State Printer, 1929), 4657.

88. *State ex rel. Atwood v. Johnson*, 170 Wisc. 251 (1919); *Veterans Welfare Board v. Riley*, 189 Cal. 159 (1922).

89. Keith W. Olson, *The G.I. Bill, The Veterans, and the Colleges* (Lexington: University Press of Kentucky, 1974); Kathleen J. Frydl, *The GI Bill* (New York: Cambridge University Press, 2009).

90. Isaac P. Roberts, *Autobiography of a Farm Boy* (Ithaca, NY: Cornell University Press, 1946), 37.

91. *Acts of the General Assembly of Alabama Passed by the Session of 1892–93* (Montgomery: State Printer, 1893), 1042; *Acts and Joint Resolutions of the General Assembly of the State of Virginia Passed at the Session of 1887–88* (Richmond: State Printer, 1888), 513; *General Laws of the State of Texas, Passed at the Regular Session of the 27th Legislature* (Austin: State Printer, 1901), 10.

92. *Laws and Resolutions of the State of North Carolina Passed by the General Assembly at Its Session of 1881* (Raleigh: State Printer, 1881), 291–93. Also see *The Statutes of the State of Missouri, to Which Are Prefixed the Constitutions of the United States and the State of Missouri*, vol. 2 (St. Louis: W. J. Gilbert, 1870), 1295–96.

93. *Territory of Alaska: Session Laws, Resolutions, and Memorials Passed by the 22nd Regular Session of the Territorial Legislature* (Juneau: Juneau Independent, 1955), 279. Also see *Laws, Resolutions, and Memorials of the State of Montana Passed by the 32nd Legislative Assembly in Regular Session* (Helena: State Printer, 1951), 185. Especially since the 1990s, scholarships dedicated to students of color have faced opposition from opponents to affirmative action. Michael A. Olivas, "Federal Law and Scholarship Policy: An Essay on

the Office of Civil Rights, Title VI, and Racial Restrictions," *Journal of College and University Law* 18 (1991): 21–28.

94. *Acts and Resolves Passed by the 71st Legislature of the State of Maine, 1903* (Augusta: Kennebec Journal, 1903), 169; *General Acts and Resolutions Adopted by the Legislature of Florida at its 15th Regular Session*, vol. 1 (Tallahassee: State Printer, 1915), 75.

95. The Morrill Act of 1862, *United States Statutes at Large*, vol. 12, 503–5; Coy F. Cross II, *Justin Smith Morrill: Father of the Land Grant Colleges* (East Lansing: Michigan State University Press, 1999); Roger L. Williams, *The Origins of Federal Support for Higher Education: George Atherton and the Land Grant Movement* (University Park: Pennsylvania State University Press, 1991).

96. *General Laws of the State of Texas, Passed at the Regular Session of the 17th Legislature* (Galveston: State Printer, 1881), 91. Also see William L. Carpenter, *Knowledge Is Power: A History of the School of Agriculture and Life Sciences at North Carolina State University, 1877–1984* (Raleigh: North Carolina State University, 1987), 130.

97. *Acts and Resolves Passed by the General Court of Massachusetts in the Year 1911* (Boston: State Printer, 1911), 1186.

98. *McDonald v. Hagins*, 7 Indiana (Blackford) 525 (1845).

99. *The State of Ohio: General and Local Acts Passed and Joint Resolutions Adopted by the 77th General Assembly* (Springfield: State Printer, 1906), 311; *Laws of Missouri Passed at the Session of the 45th General Assembly* (Jefferson City: Hugh Stephens, 1909), 889–90; *Compiled Statutes of the State of Nebraska, 1922, Comprising All the Statutory Law of a General Character in Force July 1, 1922* (Columbia, MO: E. W. Stephens, 1922), 2114; *Acts of the General Assembly of the Commonwealth of Kentucky* (Frankfort: State Printer, 1865), 47–48; *Laws of the State of New York passed at the 136th Session of the Legislature*, vol. 1 (Albany: James B. Lyon, 1913), 530.

100. *Acts of the 136th Legislature of the State of New Jersey* (Trenton: State Printer, 1912), 585–87. The seven other states were Missouri, California, Ohio, Minnesota, Wisconsin, and Pennsylvania. *The Statutes of California and Amendments to the Codes Passed at the 40th Session of the Legislature* (San Francisco: Bancroft-Whitney, 1913), 806; *Laws of Missouri Passed at the Session of the 51st General Assembly* (n.p., 1921), 648; Charles Ben Minner, "The Question of Higher Education for the Blind," *Pedagogical Seminary and Journal of Genetic Psychology* 31 (1924): 384–85; Douglas C. Baynton, *Forbidden Signs: American Culture and the Campaign against Sign Language* (Chicago: University of Chicago Press, 1996); Sarah F. Rose, "No Right to Be Idle: The Invention of Disability, 1850–1930" (PhD diss., University of Illinois at Chicago, 2008); Joseph W. Madaus, "Services for College and University Students with Disabilities: A Historical Perspective," *Journal of Postsecondary Education and Disability* 14 (2000), 4–21.

101. *People ex rel. Wright v. Genung*, 2 How. Prac. 324 (1886); *State ex rel. Taylor v. Blease*, 90 S.C. 412 (1912).

102. William J. Novak, *The People's Welfare: Law and Regulation in Nineteenth-Century America* (Chapel Hill: University of North Carolina Press, 1996), 6.

103. Charles Dorn, "From 'Liberal Professions' to 'Lucrative Professions': Bowdoin College, Stanford University, and the Civic Functions of Higher Education," *Teachers College Record* 133 (2011): 1566–96.

104. Morey, "Student Fees," 185–92.

105. *State ex rel. Garth v. Switzler*, 143 Mo. 287 (1898).

106. Frank F. Stephens, *A History of the University of Missouri* (Columbia: University of Missouri Press, 1962), 241; Jonas Viles, *The University of Missouri: A Centennial History* (Columbia: University of Missouri Press, 1939), 213.

107. *Laws of Missouri Passed at the Adjourned Session of the 26th General Assembly* (Jefferson City: State Printer, 1872), 168–69; *Laws of Missouri Passed at the Session of the 38th General Assembly* (Jefferson City: State Printer, 1895), 278–81; *Biennial Report of the Board of Curators of the University of Missouri to the General Assembly for the Two Years Ending December 31, 1896* (Jefferson City: State Printer, 1897), 16.

108. Charles E. Yeater to R. H. Jesse, September 8, 1895, MU Papers, box 4, folder 3.

109. H. A. Whiteside to R. H. Jesse, August 28, 1895, and C. M. Woodward to R. H. Jesse, September 11, 1895, MU Papers, box 4, folder 3.

110. Brief for Relator (hereafter *Garth* relator's brief), filed November 30, 1897, *State ex rel. Wilfley v. Rassieur*, Missouri Supreme Court records and briefs, Missouri State Archives, 12, 23. The Wilfley suit was eventually consolidated into *Garth*.

111. *Garth* relator's brief, 13–16, 34–35; *State ex rel. Griffith v. Osawkee Township*, 14 Kan. 418 (1875).

112. *Garth* relator's brief, 32.

113. *Garth* relator's brief, 38.

114. *Garth* relator's brief, 39, 43.

115. David Thelen, *Paths of Resistance: Tradition and Dignity in Industrializing Missouri* (New York: Oxford University Press, 1986), 212; Ruth Warner Towne, "The Public Career of William Joel Stone" (PhD diss., University of Missouri, 1953); R. H. Jesse to C. E. Yeater, May 10, 1897, MU Papers, box 5, folder 5.

116. Brief for Respondent (hereafter *Garth* respondent's brief), filed December 10, 1897, *State ex rel. Wilfley v. Rassiey* and *State ex rel. Garth v. Switzler* (combined), Missouri Supreme Court records and briefs, Missouri State Archives, 8–12.

117. *Garth* respondent's brief, 16.

118. *Garth* respondent's brief, 20–21.

119. *Biennial Report of the Board of Curators of the University of Missouri to the General Assembly for the Two Years Ending December 31, 1892* (Jefferson City: State Printer, 1893), 22.

120. *Garth*, 143 Mo. at 319, 324. In a different context, the Supreme Court of Kansas was also required to parse the public and private benefits of higher education. When a father sued to force the University of Kansas to comply with a law that established a state mining college, the court had to determine whether he had sufficient personal interest in the matter. The court ruled in favor of the father because the college would confer "direct" private advantages in addition to "remote" public benefits. *Young v. Regents of University of Kansas*, 87 Kan. 239, 246 (1912).

121. *Garth*, 143 Mo. at 322–23, 325. For more on the relationship between these rulings and Cooley's writings, see Jacobs, *Law Writers and the Courts*, 141–42. *Garth* echoed the perspective of MU law professor Christopher Tiedeman, who had argued for judicial checks on legislative interference in economic matters (including taxation) based on property rights and the freedom of contract. Christopher G. Tiedeman, *A Treatise on the*

Limitations of Police Power in the United States (St. Louis: Thomas Law Book, 1886); Barbara H. Fried, *The Progressive Assault on Laissez Faire: Robert Hale and the First Law and Economics Movement* (Cambridge, MA: Harvard University Press, 1998).

122. *Kansas City Journal*, March 16, 1898, 6.

123. Stephens, *A History of the University of Missouri*, 367–68.

124. *General Acts and Resolutions Adopted by the Legislature of Florida at Its 10th Regular Session* (Tallahassee: State Printer, 1905), 54; *Laws of Illinois Enacted by the 44th General Assembly* (Springfield: State Printer, 1906), 380.

125. *Barker v. Crum*, 177 Ky. 637 (1917).

126. Originally, the law provided for two general scholarships per district, plus a third scholarship for teacher trainees. *Acts of the General Assembly of the Commonwealth of Kentucky*, vol. 1 (Frankfort: State Printers, 1880), 41–42.

127. Charles Talbert, *The University of Kentucky: The Maturing Years* (Lexington: University of Kentucky Press, 1965), 38–46; *Bulletin of the University of Kentucky* 9 (1917): 34–35.

128. *Lexington Herald*, March 7, 1917, 6.

129. Transcript of Record (hereafter *Barker* transcript), *Barker v. Crum*, case no. 46049, Kentucky Court of Appeals records and briefs, Kentucky Department for Libraries and Archives, Public Records Division, 3.

130. *Barker* transcript, 11–17.

131. Brief for Appellants, *Barker v. Crum*, case no. 46049, Kentucky Court of Appeals records and briefs, Kentucky Department for Libraries and Archives, Public Records Division, 8–9. In 1892, the legislature reduced the number of general scholarships per district from two to one, while increasing the number reserved for teachers or teacher trainees from one to four. *Acts of the General Assembly of the Commonwealth of Kentucky* (Frankfort: State Printer, 1893), 906–8.

132. Petition by Appellees for Rehearing Division (hereafter *Barker* appellees' petition), filed February 7, 1918, *Barker v. Crum*, case no. 46049, Kentucky Court of Appeals, Kentucky Department for Libraries and Archives, v, 46; *Report of the Proceedings and Debates in the Convention Assembled at Frankfort, on the Eighth Day of September, 1890, to Adapt, Amend, or Change the Constitution of the State of Kentucky* (Frankfort: E. Polk Johnson, 1890), 4517, 4541, 4499–503, 4529.

133. The legislature had specified that the scholarships should be awarded to applicants with the highest examination scores. If two students had the same score, the counties were supposed to favor public school graduates of modest means. *Barker* appellees' petition, 33, 52.

134. *Barker* appellees' petition, iii, 54.

135. *Barker*, 177 Ky. at 638, 643.

136. *University of Kentucky v. Hickman County*, 185 Ky. 630, 641 (1919).

137. Jacobs, *Law Writers and the Courts*, 157.

138. Arthur J. Klein, "Survey of Land-Grant Colleges and Universities," *United States Office of Education Bulletin*, vol. 2 (Washington, DC: Government Printing Office, 1930), 485; *Nichols Company v. City of Kansas City*, 639 S.W.2d 886 (1982); Comment, "Missouri's Changing Public Purpose Doctrine," *St. Louis University Law Journal* 16 (1972): 658–74.

Chapter 6. Child Support

1. Child support in Michigan typically ended when children turned eighteen. Record on Appeal, January 18, 1957, *Johnson v. Johnson*, case no. 4829, Michigan Supreme Court records and briefs, Michigan State Law Library, 27–28.

2. This stance was inherited from British common law. William Blackstone, *Commentaries on the Laws of England*, vol. 1 (New York: Duyckinck, Long, Collins and Hannay, 1827), 359. Also see *American Law Reports*, vol. 133 (Rochester, NY: Lawyers Co-operative, 1941), 903.

3. Monica Hof Wallace, "A Federal Referendum: Extending Child Support for Higher Education," *University of Kansas Law Review* 58 (2010): 665.

4. In general, divorce proceedings prompt courts to make explicit statements about societal expectations that often remain unspoken otherwise. Mary Ann Mason, *From Father's Property to Children's Rights: The History of Child Custody in the United States* (New York: Columbia University Press, 1994), xi.

5. See appendix C. This chapter examines ninety reported cases. After 1971, these cases focused more on issues related to the lower age of majority rather than the necessity of college. *American Law Reports*, vol. 99 (Rochester, NY: Lawyers Co-operative, 1980), 334–40.

6. It should also be noted that most of these cases preceded the era of no-fault divorce and often involved some compensation for past harm. For example, a father's abandonment of a frail wife and disabled daughter encouraged a judge to order payments for a son's college tuition. *Tribe v. Tribe*, 59 Utah 112 (1921). Also see *Cohen v. Cohen*, 82 N.Y.S.2d 513 (1948).

7. In general, child support cases invited "unbridled judicial discretion" during the twentieth century. Joanna L. Grossman and Lawrence M. Friedman, *Inside the Castle: Law and Family in 20th Century America* (Princeton, NJ: Princeton University Press, 2011), 225.

8. *Middlebury College v. Chandler*, 16 Vt. 683 (1844).

9. The practice of preventing minors from making binding contracts was intended to protect them from unscrupulous lenders. *Middlebury*, 16 Vt. at 684, 686, 686 (1844). Authorities in Massachusetts and Connecticut agreed that college students were not experienced enough to enter into loan or credit agreements with merchants. Edward Elliot and M. M. Chambers, *The Colleges and the Courts: Judicial Decisions Regarding Institutions of Higher Education in the United States* (New York: Carnegie Foundation for the Advancement of Teaching, 1936), 22–23.

10. For example, see *Turner v. Gaither*, 83 N.C. 357 (1880).

11. *Streitwolf v. Streitwolf*, 58 N.J. Eq. 570, 576 (1899).

12. *Core v. Cook*, 24 R.I. 421, 424 (1902).

13. *Nielson v. International Textbook Co.*, 106 Me. 104, 105 (1909). The brief submitted on behalf of the correspondence school had asserted this point, while also arguing more ambitiously that courts should take a permissive stance because "everyone has the right to aspire to fill a higher and better position." David C. Harrington, *Education of Minors, What Are "Necessaries"?* (Scranton, PA: n.p., n.d.), 1, 10.

14. *Ruling Case Law*, vol. 14 (Rochester, NY: Lawyers Co-operative, 1916), 256–58.

15. *Esteb v. Esteb*, 138 Wash. 174 (1926).

16. This trend was influenced by the increasing autonomy of women working outside of the home, as well as by an increasing emphasis on personal satisfaction (rather than self-sacrifice) within marriage. Elaine Tyler May, *Great Expectations: Marriage and Divorce in Post-Victorian America* (Chicago: University of Chicago Press, 1980), 2, 49–59; J. Herbie DiFonzo, *Beneath the Fault Line: The Popular and Legal Culture of Divorce in Twentieth-Century America* (Charlottesville: University Press of Virginia, 1997), 10, 50–51, 89; Glenda Riley, *Divorce: An American Tradition* (New York: Oxford University Press, 1991), 133, 159.

17. Mason, *From Father's Property to Children's Rights*, 114–15; Nancy F. Cott, *Public Vows: A History of Marriage and the Nation* (Cambridge, MA: Harvard University Press, 2000), 168.

18. Thomas B. Shrewsbury, "What's Your Verdict?," *Personnel and Guidance Journal* 34 (1955): 48. Mothers were almost always the custodial parents and plaintiffs in these cases. For an exception, see *Beasley v. Beasley*, 159 N.W.2d 449 (1968).

19. Mason, *From Father's Property to Children's Rights*, 86–87; DiFonzo, *Beneath the Fault Line*, 14; Tracy L. Steffes, *School, Society, and State: A New Education to Govern Modern America, 1890–1940* (Chicago: University of Chicago Press, 2012), 122; Grossman and Friedman, *Inside the Castle*, 223.

20. *Commonwealth v. Gilmore*, 97 Pa. Super. 303, 311 (1929).

21. *Esteb*, 138 Wash. 174. Two appellate court decisions had previously ruled that college was a necessary expense but lacked the expansive dicta about the status of higher education that made *Esteb* so influential. *Dunham v. Dunham*, 189 Iowa 802 (1920); *Tribe*, 59 Utah 112.

22. Henry H. Foster Jr., "Family Law," *New York University Law Review* 36 (1961): 634–35; R. Douglas Wrightsel, "College Education as a Legal Necessity," *Vanderbilt Law Review* 18 (1965): 1402–3.

23. Superior Court Statement of Facts, June 12, 1925, *Esteb v. Esteb*, case no. 19490 (hereafter *Esteb* case files), Washington Supreme Court Record Group, State Cases, 1889–1989, Washington State Archives, 36, 83–84.

24. Respondent's Brief, filed September 2, 1925, *Esteb* case files, 14–16, 24–25.

25. Horace Esteb denied that he used this language. Superior Court Statement of Facts, June 12, 1925, *Esteb* case files, 86–87, 106.

26. Appeal from the Judgment of the Superior Court for Pierce County, August 20, 1925, *Esteb* case files, 4–7, 17–22. Income in 2010 dollars calculated with the Bureau of Labor Statistics inflation calculator, accessed August 20, 2010, http://data.bls.gov/cgibin/cpicalc.pl.

27. Superior Court Statement of Facts, June 12, 1925, *Esteb* case files, 36.

28. Appeal from the Judgment of the Superior Court for Pierce County, August 20, 1925, *Esteb* case files, 28–29.

29. Superior Court Statement of Facts, June 12, 1925, *Esteb* case files, 36, 88–90, 131.

30. O. Edgar Reynolds, *The Social and Economic Status of College Students* (New York: Teachers College Bureau of Publications, 1927), 14, 18. Regarding the underrepresentation of working-class college students during that era, also see David O. Levine, *The American College and the Culture of Aspiration, 1915–1940* (Ithaca, NY: Cornell University Press, 1986), 19–20, 114, 126–33.

31. *Los Angeles Times*, January 3, 1920, I3. Askren worked as bellhop and in a pawnshop before becoming a lawyer—he never earned a law degree. Charles H. Sheldon, *The Washington High Bench: A Biographical History of the State Supreme Court, 1889–1991* (Pullman: Washington State University Press, 1992), 77–78.

32. Regarding legal realism, see William W. Fisher, Morton J. Horwitz, and Thomas A. Reed, eds., *American Legal Realism* (New York: Oxford University Press, 1993); Laura Kalman, *Legal Realism at Yale, 1927–1960* (Chapel Hill: University of North Carolina Press, 1986).

33. *Esteb*, 138 Wash. at 188 (1926). The public policy considerations in the opinion reflect the language of progressive reformers who had argued that a father's duty was not just to his wife and children but also to the state. Cott, *Public Vows*, 170. The import of the decision at that time is suggested by the fact that the president of the University of Washington retained a copy in his files. University of Washington, Office of the President records, Accession 71–34, box 127, folder 1, University of Washington Special Collections.

34. Petition for Rehearing, April 19, 1926, *Esteb* case files, 6, 8.

35. Answer to Petition for Rehearing, April 28, 1926, *Esteb* case files, 4, 2.

36. *Underwood v. Underwood*, 162 Wash. 204 (1931). Also see *Feek v. Feek*, 187 Wash. 573 (1936).

37. Bloedorn v. Bloedorn, 67 App. D.C. 214 (1937).

38. *Howton v. Howton*, 51 Cal. App. 2d 323 (1942).

39. White middle-class men also began to view college as a means to preserve their status in a shifting corporate-dominated economy. Daniel A. Clark, *Creating the College Man: American Mass Magazines and Middle-Class Manhood, 1890–1915* (Madison: University of Wisconsin Press, 2010); Levine, *The American College and the Culture of Aspiration*, 60–62.

40. Howard M. Bell, *Youth Tell Their Story: A Study of the Conditions and Attitudes of Young People in Maryland between the Ages of 16 and 24* (Washington, DC: American Council on Education, 1938), 128.

41. Rita S. Halle, *Which College?* (New York: Macmillan, 1928), cited in Clark, *Creating the College Man*, 183; Margaret A. Nash and Lisa Romero, "'Citizenship for the College Girl': Challenges and Opportunities in Higher Education for Women in the 1930s," *Teachers College Record* 114 (2012): 1–35.

42. "Why Send Your Son to College?," *Scribner's Magazine* 103 (1938): 103–4.

43. One year after *Esteb*, an observer of education law made the inaccurate prediction that courts were on the verge of agreeing that college should be considered necessary for most high school graduates. Harry Raymond Trusler, *Essentials of School Law* (Milwaukee: Bruce, 1927).

44. Floyd D. Hamilton, "Parent and Child—Necessaries—College Education," *Oregon Law Review* 20 (1941): 377–87; John R. Thelin, *A History of American Higher Education* (Baltimore: Johns Hopkins University Press, 2004), 254.

45. *Morris v. Morris*, 92 Ind. App. 65 (1930). A New York court reached a similar decision in 1930. *Halsted v. Halsted*, 239 N.Y.S. 422 (1930).

46. *Boens v. Bennett*, 20 Cal. App. 2d 477, 482 (1937). Also see Trial Court Record, *Binney v. Binney*, case no. 209 (October Term 1941), Superior Court of Pennsylvania records

and briefs, State Library of Pennsylvania, 49a–50a; *Binney v. Binney*, 146 Pa. Super. 374 (1941).

47. *Worthington v. Worthington*, 207 Ark. 185, 186 (1944).

48. *Wynn v. Wynn*, 6 Ohio L. Abs. 450 (1928); *Werner v. Werner*, 7 N.J. Super. 229 (1950). Children with disabilities were more often perceived to be entitled to higher education because they were less likely to become self-supporting by performing manual labor. See, for example, *Strom v. Strom*, 13 Ill. App. 2d 354 (1957).

49. *Payette v. Payette*, 85 N.H. 297 (1931).

50. Chancery Court Transcript, April 1959, *Pass v. Pass*, case no. 41407 (hereafter *Pass* case files), Mississippi Supreme Court records and briefs, Mississippi Department of Archives and History, 33; *Pass v. Pass*, 238 Miss. 449 (1960).

51. Transcript of Record (hereafter *Brown* transcript), October 1966, *Commonwealth ex rel. Brown v. Weidner*, case no. 78, Superior Court of Pennsylvania records and briefs, State Library of Pennsylvania, 20a; *Commonwealth ex rel. Brown v. Weidner*, 208 Pa. Super. 114, 120 (1966).

52. See appendix C. For example, a Pennsylvania father was ordered to support one son in college but not another because the appellate court only saw evidence in the trial court records of his prior intent to educate the younger sibling. *Commonwealth ex rel. Stomel v. Stomel*, 180 Pa. Super. 573 (1956).

53. See appendix C. In cases where there was evidence of prior intent, judges approved college support 71 percent (17/24) of the time. Out of the seven cases that rejected support, only *Wynn* (1928) and *Binney* (1941) took clear stands on principle. The other cases were decided either because of the parent's wealth or because of the student's age or academic record.

54. *Howton*, 51 Cal. App. 2d at 325.

55. See appendix C.

56. *Commonwealth ex rel. Ulmer v. Sommerville*, 200 Pa. Super. 640 (1963); *Nebel v. Nebel*, 99 N.J. Super. 256 (1968); *Dorman v. Dorman*, 251 Ind. 272 (1968).

57. *Titus v. Titus*, 311 Mich. 434 (1945); Straub v. Straub, 213 Cal. App. 2d. 792 (1963). Courts were not unanimous on this point, which continues to be unsettled to this day.

58. After World War II, divorce courts increasingly adhered to the model of juvenile courts, which tended to intervene more aggressively and with less concern for precedent. DiFonzo, *Beneath the Fault Line*, 112–21.

59. *Cohen*, 6 N.J. Super. at 30. Also see *Herbert v. Herbert*, 98 N.Y.S.2d 846 (1950).

60. Transcript of Record, February 23, 1960, *Mitchell v. Mitchell*, case no. 36117, Supreme Court of Ohio records and briefs, Office of the Clerk of the Supreme Court of Ohio, 10, 33.

61. *Adamowski v. The Curtiss-Wright Flying Service, Inc.*, 300 Mass. 281, 283 (1938).

62. Circuit Court Bill of Exceptions (hereafter *Atchley* Bill of Exceptions), March 13, 1945, *Atchley v. Atchley*, case no. 644, Tennessee Court of Appeals records and briefs, Tennessee State Library and Archives, 98; *Atchley v. Atchley*, 29 Tenn. App. 124, 127 (1945).

63. *Sportsman v. Sportsman*, 409 S.W.2d 787 (1966).

64. States did not have to establish clear guidelines for calculating child support until the passage of the Family Support Act of 1988. Deborah H. Bell, "Child Support Orders: The Federal-State Partnership," *Mississippi Law Journal* 69 (1999): 597–640.

65. *Ulmer*, 200 Pa. Super. 640; *Commonwealth ex rel. Schearer v. Schearer*, 208 Pa. Super. 196 (1966); *Commonwealth ex rel. Rice v. Rice*, 206 Pa. Super. 393 (1965); *Brown*, 208 Pa. Super. 114; *Commonwealth ex rel. Yannacone v. Yannacone*, 214 Pa. Super. 244 (1968). Income in 2010 dollars calculated with the Bureau of Labor Statistics inflation calculator, accessed August 20, 2010, http://data.bls.gov/cgi-bin/cpicalc.pl. Recall that Horace Esteb earned $37,000 a year in 2010 dollars.

66. *Ulmer*, 200 Pa. Super. at 644.

67. Not only do the cases examined in this chapter suggest that the overall odds of winning college support increased over time, but after 1949 only one case outside of Pennsylvania excused a parent because of inability to pay. *Peck v. Peck*, 272 Wis. 466 (1956).

68. Unreported Chancery Court Opinion (1959), *Pass* case files, 89. Also see *Hoover v. Voigtman*, 103 N.J. Super. 535 (1968). The case that overturned decades of precedent in Indiana concerned two honor students. Appeal from Clark Superior Court, filed October 18, 1968, *Dorman v. Dorman*, case no. 768S108, Supreme Court of Indiana records and briefs, Clerk of the Indiana Supreme Court, 12. A New York family court explained its denial of further support to a less-than-stellar student by observing that "not all of us can be scholars. Some of us have to do the utilitarian work." *Green v. Green*, 111 N.Y.S.2d 72, 75 (1952).

69. Appellant's Opening Brief (hereafter *Jackman* brief), filed February 29, 1940, *Jackman v. Short*, case no. 14407, Oregon Supreme Court records and briefs, drawer no. 9008, Oregon State Archives, 8, 19–22.

70. *Jackman v. Short*, 165 Ore. 626, 656 (1941).

71. *Titus*, 311 Mich. 434. Also see *Mapes v. Mapes*, 336 Mich. 137 (1953); *Gerk v. Gerk*, 259 Iowa 293 (1966); *Davis v. Davis*, 8 Mich. App. 104 (1967).

72. *Atchley* Bill of Exceptions, 76.

73. *Ogle v. Ogle*, 275 Ala. 483 (1963).

74. *Rhoderick v. Rhoderick*, 257 Md. 354 (1970).

75. Notice of Motion, filed October 20, 1967, *Nebel v. Nebel*, case no. M-2995-66, Superior Court of New Jersey records and briefs, Office of the Superior Court Clerk; *Nebel*, 99 N.J. Super. 256; *Limpert v. Limpert*, 119 N.J. Super 438, 441 (1972). However, some courts still maintained limits. A New York judge denied college support to a "peripatetic student" who had dropped out of several institutions. *Bates v. Bates*, 310 N.Y.S.2d 26, 33 (1970).

76. This expansive attitude about who should attend college became increasingly prevalent during the "golden age" of higher education that followed World War II. Linda Eisenmann, *Higher Education for Women in Postwar America, 1945–1965* (Baltimore: Johns Hopkins University Press, 2006); Richard M. Freeland, *Academia's Golden Age: Universities in Massachusetts, 1945–1970* (New York: Oxford University Press, 1992); Martin Trow, "Reflections on the Transition for Mass to Universal Higher Education," *Daedalus* 99 (1970): 1–42.

77. *Higher Education for American Democracy: A Report of the President's Commission on Higher Education* (Washington, DC: United States Government Printing Office, 1947–1948).

78. Ultimately, the GI Bill would not require any aptitude testing. Glenn Altschuler and Stuart Blumin, *The GI Bill: The New Deal for Veterans* (New York: Oxford University Press, 2009), 67.

79. Earl J. McGrath, preface to McGrath, ed., *Universal Higher Education* (New York: McGraw-Hill, 1966), x; Daniel Patrick Moynihan, "Manpower Development and Employment of Youth," in McGrath, *Universal Higher Education*, 68–70.

80. Angus Campbell and W. C. Ackerman, "What People Think about College," *American Education* 1 (1965): 30–32.

81. *Commonwealth v. Wingert*, 173 Pa. Super. 613, 617 (1953).

82. *Brown* transcript, 26a. Even some of the rulings that endorsed daughters' college education still reflected stereotypical views. In one extreme case, a judge granted custody of a minor to college administrators because her mother was poor and her father could not provide "those niceties and refinements which are so essentially a part of ideal womanhood." *Horton v. Horton*, 287 Ky. 586, 587 (1941). The Oklahoma legislature even authorized courts to order child support for the benefit of unmarried women students but not for men. *Irby v. Martin*, 500 P.2d 278 (1972).

83. See appendix C. This sample included cases where only one gender was involved, the child had not exceeded the age when child support typically terminated, and the decision was not based on the parents' inability to afford tuition. Appendix C lists sixty-six cases that fulfill these criteria. Thirteen of these cases were excluded from the sample because their outcomes were affected by agreements to pay tuition that occurred prior to the litigation. The judges who presided over these cases never explicitly mentioned gender as a factor—perhaps because child support laws used gender-neutral language.

84. See appendix C. The cases that denied support to daughters after 1953 cited either the age of the child or the parent's inability to pay.

85. Nine cases involved both sons and daughters or did not indicate gender.

86. Daughters of divorced parents sometimes reported that their mothers encouraged them to aspire toward college in order to avoid following them down the path of economic dependence and limited career options. "Jodi Vandenberg-Daves, "'There's Got to Be More Out There': White Working-Class Women, College, and the 'Better Life,' 1950–1985," *International Labor and Working-Class History* 62 (2002): 102, 110.

87. Eisenmann, *Higher Education for Women in Postwar America*, 26–29, 44, 98. Cold War competition encouraged educators to focus on the training of women as well as men. Indeed, women tended to earn higher grades than men. Vandenberg-Daves, "'There's Got to Be More Out There,'" 104.

88. It is also possible that judges looked favorably on some cases involving daughters because they assumed that girls were more dependent and therefore more deserving of extended child support. For a discussion of how notions of dependence shaped family during this era, see Mason, *From Father's Property to Children's Rights*, 124.

89. Appeal from Order, November 29, 1929, *Halsted v. Halsted*, New York State Supreme Court Law Library, 4th Department, 12.

90. *Rice*, 206 Pa. Super. at 397.

91. For other cases involving teacher education see, Petition, filed October 28, 1958, *Maitzen v. Maitzen*, case no. 43S7466, Superior Court of Cook County records and briefs, Clerk of the Circuit Court of Cook County, Illinois; *Atchley* Bill of Exceptions, 79.

92. *Herbert*, 98 N.Y.S.2d at 848.

93. Chancery Court Transcript, *Pass* case files, 49; *Pass*, 238 Miss. at 459.

94. For evidence of this notion in the periodicals of the 1930s, see Nash and Romero, "'Citizenship for the College Girl.'"

95. Walter M. Lifton, "Will College Be Wasted on Your Child?," *Saturday Evening Post*, June 2, 1962, 6.

96. Charles Dorn, "From 'Liberal Professions' to 'Lucrative Professions': Bowdoin College, Stanford University, and the Civic Functions of Higher Education," *Teachers College Record* 113 (2011): 1566–96. In general, American schools placed increasing emphasis on vocational preparation over the course of the twentieth century. Herbert M. Kliebard, *Schooled to Work: Vocationalism and the American Curriculum, 1876–1946* (New York: Teachers College Press, 1999).

97. *Morris*, 92 Ind. App. at 67.

98. *Commonwealth v. Wingert*, 173 Pa. Super. 613, 615 (1953).

99. The attorney for the father had tried to counter by arguing that many college graduates were unemployed because there was "very little opening in any field of endeavor for the so-called 'white collar worker.'" Brief of Appellant, filed November 30, 1935, *Refer v. Refer*, case no. 7512, Montana Supreme Court records and briefs, Montana Historical Society, 6–8; Brief of Respondent, filed December 17, 1935, *Refer v. Refer*, case no. 7512, Montana Supreme Court records and briefs, Montana Historical Society, 8–9; *Refer v. Refer*, 102 Mont. 121 (1936).

100. *Nebel*, 99 N.J. Super. at 268.

101. For example, Judge Arthur P. Rugg of Massachusetts graduated from Amherst College and collected clippings about curricular debates in higher education. Addresses and Articles Concerning Colleges and Education folder, box 35, Arthur P. Rugg Papers, Massachusetts Historical Society. Rugg wrote the opinion for *Moskow v. Marshall*, a case concerning the "necessity" of dorm rent for a Harvard student. The opinion upheld *Middlebury* based on the facts presented at trial but invited its overturn by noting that it was "very likely" that he could be persuaded otherwise. *Moskow v. Marshall*, 271 Mass. 302, 305 (1930).

102. *Jackman* brief, 2–3, 14–15.

103. *Jackman*, 165 Ore. at 638, 639.

104. David M. Rabban, "Judicial Review of the University-Student Relationship: Expulsion and Governance," *Stanford Law Review* 26 (1973): 115–16.

105. M. M. Chambers, *The Colleges and the Courts, 1946–50: Judicial Decisions Regarding Institutions of Higher Education in the United States* (New York: Columbia University Press, 1952), 13–14.

106. The Cold War also encouraged college training for those who could fill top industrial, scientific, and diplomatic positions. *The National Defense and Education Act of 1958: A Summary and Analysis of the Act* (Washington, DC: United States Government Printing Office, 1958); James Bryant Conant, *The Child, The Parent, and the State* (Cambridge, MA: Harvard University Press, 1959).

107. Christopher P. Loss, *Between Citizens and the State: The Politics of American Higher Education in the Twentieth Century* (Princeton, NJ: Princeton University Press, 2012), 122.

108. *Herbert*, 98 N.Y.S.2d at 848.

109. *Calogeras v. Calogeras*, 10 Ohio Op. 2d 441, 462, 463 (1959).

110. *Pass*, 238 Miss. at 458.

111. *Dorman v. Dorman*, 251 Ind. 272, 277 (1968).

112. *Universal Opportunity for Education beyond the High School* (Washington, DC: National Education Association, 1964).

113. John R. Thelin, "Higher Education's Student Financial Aid Enterprise in Historical Perspective," in Frederick M. Hess, ed., *Footing the Tuition Bill: The New Student Loan Sector* (Washington, DC: American Enterprise Institute, 2007), 25; Malcolm Moos and Francis Rourke, *The Campus and the State* (Baltimore: Johns Hopkins Press, 1959), 1, 11, 72.

114. *Hale v. Hale*, 55 Cal. App. 2d 879 (1942); *Maitzen v. Maitzen*, 24 Ill. App. 2d 32 (1959); Weber v. Weber, 274 N.Y.S.2d 791 (1966); *Calogeras*, 10 Ohio Op. 2d 441. One New York court, in contrast, wanted to see more explicit legislative support for mass higher education before altering its stance on child support. *Green*, 111 N.Y.S.2d 72.

115. *Dixon v. Alabama State Board of Education*, 294 F.2d 150 (1961).

116. Wrightsel, "College Education as a Legal Necessity," 1424–26. This view was also endorsed in the 1990s. Charles F. Wilson, "But Daddy, Why Can't I Go to College? The Frightening De-Kline of Support for Children's Post-Secondary Education," *Boston College Law Review* 37 (1996): 1099.

117. Through statutes or court decisions, a third of states currently allow postmajority support for higher education. Most other states only allow support when there is evidence that a parent agreed to pay for college during or prior to divorce proceedings. Wallace, "A Federal Referendum," 674; Madeline Marzano-Lesnevich and Scott A. Laterra, "Child Support and College: What Is the Correct Result?," *Journal of the American Academy of Matrimonial Lawyers* 22 (2009): 335–89. Also see Kathleen C. Horan, "Post-Minority Support for College Education—A Legally Enforceable Obligation in Divorce Proceeding?," *New Mexico Law Review* 18 (1988): 153–78.

118. Scholars have written a great deal about the declining civic purposes of higher education. See for example, David L. Kirp, *Shakespeare, Einstein, and the Bottom Line: The Marketing of Higher Education* (Cambridge, MA: Harvard University Press, 2004). The evolution of legal scholarship also exhibits this changing emphasis from civics to vocations. Note the contrast between M. M. Chambers, "Higher Education as a 'Necessary,'" *Journal of Higher Education* 12 (1941): 330–33, and Abraham Kuhl, "Post-Majority Educational Support for Children the Twenty-First Century," *Journal of the American Academic of Matrimonial Lawyers* 21 (2008): 763–81.

119. The typical midcentury college student exhibited little interest in foreign affairs or domestic policy initiatives. Loss, *Between Citizens and the State*, 123; Nash and Romero, "Citizenship for the College Girl," 18.

Conclusion

1. The professor stated that the student swore in class and was generally unprofessional. The student accused the university of breach of contract and sexual discrimination. Riley Yates, "Lehigh University Student Sues over Grade," *Morning Call* (Allentown, PA), February 12, 2013, accessed February 28, 2013, http://articles.mcall.com/2013-02-12/news/mc-lehigh-university-student-sues-over-grade-20130211_1_nicholas-ladany-supplemental-internship-partway-lehigh-lawyer.

2. *Nelson v. Lincoln Medical School*, 81 Neb. 533 (1908).

3. For an example of the tendency to trace academic autonomy back to medieval origins, see Carnegie Foundation for the Advancement of Teaching, *The Control of the Campus: A Report on the Governance of Higher Education* (Washington, DC: Carnegie Foundation for the Advancement of Teaching, 1982), 4–7.

4. *Dixon v. Alabama State Board of Education*, 294 F.2d 150 (1961).

5. J. Peter Byrne, "Academic Freedom: A 'Special Concern of the First Amendment,'" *Yale Law Journal* 99 (1989): 280, 323. Furthermore, some of the post-1960 increase in judicial intervention was prompted by factors (such as evolving views of state action) that did not relate directly to the principle of academic deference. Robert M. O'Neil, "Judicial Deference to Academic Decisions: An Outmoded Concept?," *Journal of College and University Law* 36 (2010): 743–45. Also see Michael A. Olivas, *Suing Alma Mater: Higher Education and the Courts* (Baltimore: Johns Hopkins University Press, 2013); Steven G. Olswang, "Academic Abstention Stronger Than Ever, Despite Vaksman," *Journal of Law and Education* 26 (1997): 91–96; Anthony Finaldi, "The Vaksman Approach to Academic Dismissals: A Different Beat to the Same Drum," *Journal of Law and Education* 24 (1995): 499–503.

6. The National Association of College and University Attorneys was founded in 1960. Its membership grew to nearly three thousand by the beginning of twenty-first century. Robert D. Bickel and Peter F. Lake, *The Rights and Responsibilities of the Modern University: Who Assumes the Risks of College Life?* (Durham, NC: Carolina Academic, 1999), 159.

7. William W. Van Alstyne, "A Suggested Seminar in Student Rights," *Journal of Legal Education* 21 (1969): 547–59.

8. Amy Gajda, *The Trials of Academe: The New Era of Campus Litigation* (Cambridge, MA: Harvard University Press, 2009), 208, 217; James F. Shekleton, "Strangers at the Gate: Academic Autonomy, Civil Rights, Civil Liberties and the Well-Judged University," *Journal of College and University Law* 36 (2010): 875–943.

9. Barbara A. Lee, "Fifty Years of Higher Education Law: Turning the Kaleidoscope," *Journal of College and University Law* 36 (2010): 649–90.

10. Olivas, *Suing Alma Mater*, 69–72, 106–7.

11. William A. Kaplin and Barbara A. Lee, *The Law of Higher Education: A Comprehensive Guide to Legal Implications of Administrative Decision Making*, 5th ed., vol. 1 (San Francisco: Jossey-Bass, 2013), 12, 758–68; Robert M. Hendrickson, Jason E. Lane, James T. Harris, and Richard H. Dorman, *Academic Leadership and Governance of Higher Education: A Guide for Trustees, Leaders, and Aspiring Leaders of Two- and Four-Year Institutions* (Sterling, VA: Stylus, 2013), 141; Michael J. Natali, "Judicial Deference and University Academic Policy Modifications: When Should Courts Intervene on Behalf of Injured Students?," *Indiana Law Review* 37 (2003–2004): 508–9; Hazel Glenn Beh, "Student versus University: The University's Implied Obligations of Good Faith and Fair Dealing," *University of Maryland Law Review* 59 (2000): 183–224; Donald L. Reidhaar, "Assault on the Citadel: Reflections on a Quarter Century of Change in the Relationships between Students and the University," *Journal of College and University Law* 12 (1985): 343–61; Gajda, *The Trials of Academe*, 9, 15–16, 238–37; Bickel and Lake, *The Rights and Responsibilities of the Modern University*, 33. The decline of deference toward universities also coincided with a decline of immunity for other charitable and governmental organizations. Lawrence M.

Friedman, *A History of American Law*, 3rd ed. (New York: Simon and Schuster, 2005), 521. The new federal laws included Title VI of the Civil Rights Act of 1964, Title IX of the Education Amendments of 1972, Section 504 of the Rehabilitation Act of 1973, and the Americans with Disabilities Act of 1990.

12. *Dixon*, for example, did not cite any elementary or secondary school cases.

13. Robert C. Cloud, ed., *Legal Issues in the Community College* (San Francisco: Jossey-Bass, 2004).

14. Richard Arum, *Judging School Discipline: The Crisis of Moral Authority* (Cambridge, MA: Harvard University Press, 2003), 17–26; Stephen R. Goldstein, "Reflections on Developing Trends in the Law of Student Rights," *University of Pennsylvania Law Review* 118 (1970): 615–18; Olivas, *Suing Alma Mater*, 101, 146, 182n24; Gajda, *The Trials of Academe*, 13; Lee, "Fifty Years of Higher Education Law," 653.

15. The parents filed suit after the City University of New York rejected their son because his high school grade point average was seven-tenths of a point below the average required for admission. The parents' attorney argued that the university ought to consider that the applicant had attended a high school honors program and would likely have had higher grades if he had been on a nonhonors track. *Lesser v. Board of Education*, 239 N.Y.S.2d 776 (1963).

16. United States District Court, Western District of Missouri, *General Order on Judicial Standards of Procedure and Substance in Review of Student Discipline in Tax-Supported Institutions of Higher Education* (1968), 10.

17. Kaplin and Lee, *The Law of Higher Education*, vol. 1, 876–77.

18. By the 1980s, statewide coordinating agencies or legislatures formally or informally governed entrance requirements at most public universities. Margaret E. Goertz and Linda M. Johnson, *State Policies for Admission to Higher Education* (New York: College Entrance Examination Board, 1985), 2–3; Carnegie Foundation for the Advancement of Teaching, *The Control of the Campus*, 38–39.

19. Henry T. Edwards, *Higher Education and the Unholy Crusade against Governmental Regulation* (Cambridge, MA: Harvard University Institute for Educational Management, 1980), 10, 21–22.

20. *Mississippi University for Women v. Hogan*, 458 U.S. 718 (1982); *United States v. Virginia*, 518 U.S. 515 (1996). These suits were based on the equal protection clause of the Fourteenth Amendment because schools that were historically single-sex were exempted from Title IX of the Education Amendments of 1972. Kaplin and Lee, *The Law of Higher Education*, vol. 1, 888–90.

21. *Adams v. Richardson*, 480 F.2d 1159 (1973); *Adams v. Califano*, 430 F. Supp. 118 (1977). These cases did not directly raise questions about academic deference because they targeted the Department of Health, Education, and Welfare, rather than academic officials.

22. Kaplin and Lee, *The Law of Higher Education*, vol. 1, 884–85.

23. During the Reagan administration, federal courts began to retreat from rulings that held states accountable for segregation. John B. Williams, *Race Discrimination in Public Higher Education: Interpreting Federal Civil Rights Enforcement, 1964–1996* (Westport, CT: Praeger, 1997), 15–27, 136. Yet in 1992, the United States Supreme Court ruled that Mississippi had reinforced segregated enrollment patterns by manipulating admissions

requirements and resource allocation. *United States v. Fordice*, 505 U.S. 717 (1992). Also see Olivas, *Suing Alma Mater*, 54–59.

24. Annalisa Jabaily, "Color Me Colorblind: Deference, Discretion, and Voice in Higher Education after *Grutter*," *Cornell Journal of Law and Public Policy* 17 (2008): 515–77.

25. Olivas, *Suing Alma Mater*, 74.

26. Affirmative action cases exemplify how discussions about judicial deference can encompass debates about the substantive purpose of university policies. In *Bakke*, for instance, Justice Powell concluded that a medical school could justify an affirmative action policy on the grounds that doctors should be prepared to work with diverse populations. This argument, which emphasized the benefits of affirmative action for the student body and society at large (rather than as a response to historical discrimination), has remained a mainstay of affirmative action jurisprudence. *Regents of the University of California v. Bakke*, 438 U.S. 265, 314 (1978).

27. *DeFunis v. Odegaard*, 416 U.S. 312 (1974).

28. *Bakke*, 438 U.S. at 312.

29. *Bakke*, 438 U.S. at 404; Jerome Karabel, *The Chosen: The Hidden History of Admission and Exclusion at Harvard, Yale, and Princeton* (New York: Houghton Mifflin Harcourt, 2006), 484–90.

30. *Grutter v. Bollinger*, 539 U.S. 306 (2003); *Gratz v. Bollinger*, 539 U.S. 244 (2003); J. Peter Bryne, "Constitutional Academic Freedom After *Grutter*," *Colorado Law Review* 77 (2006): 929–53; Edward N. Stoner and Michael Showalter, "Judicial Deference to Educational Judgment: Justice O'Connor's Opinion in *Grutter* Reapplies Longstanding Principles," *Journal of College and University Law* 30 (2004): 614.

31. *Fisher v. University of Texas*, 133 S. Ct. 2411 (2013). The court's most recent affirmative action decision focused on political processes (whether affirmative action could be banned by a ballot initiative) and did not emphasize academic deference. *Schuette v. Coalition to Defend Affirmative Action*, 134 S. Ct. 1623 (2014).

32. Critics of affirmative action assume that admission to flagship universities should be based primarily on mechanical tallies of grades and test scores, whereas advocates for minority applicants find themselves supporting the tradition of judicial deference that was once invoked in defense of segregation (see chapter 3).

33. *Dixon v. Alabama State Board of Education*, 294 F.2d 150 (1961); Gregory E. Michael, "The Unitary Theory: A Proposal for a Student-School Legal Relationship," *Journal of Law and Education* 1 (1972): 413; Comment, "Private Government on the Campus-Judicial Review of University Expulsions," *Yale Law Journal* 72 (1963): 1387.

34. Brian Jackson, "The Lingering Legacy of In Loco Parentis: A Historical Survey and Proposal for Reform," *Vanderbilt Law Review* 44 (1991): 1135–64; Project, "Procedural Due Process and Campus Disorder: A Comparison of Law and Practice," *Duke Law Journal* 19 (1970): 763–818.

35. Gajda, *The Trials of Academe*, 235–36; Christopher P. Loss, *Between Citizens and the State: The Politics of American Higher Education in the Twentieth Century* (Princeton, NJ: Princeton University Press, 2012), 210–11; William W. Van Alstyne, "Procedural Due Process and State University Students," *UCLA Law Review* 10 (1963): 373; William W. Van Alstyne, "Student Academic Freedom and the Rule-Making Powers of Public Universi-

ties: Some Constitutional Considerations," *Law in Transition Quarterly* 2 (1965): 9; William W. Van Alstyne, "The Tentative Emergence of Student Power in the United States," *American Journal of Comparative Law* 17 (1969): 403–17; Kaplin and Lee, *The Law of Higher Education*, vol. 1, 839, 855.

36. Kaplin and Lee, *The Law of Higher Education*, vol. 2, 1196; Bickel and Lake, *The Rights and Responsibilities of the Modern University*, 36–43; Ed Stevens, "Due Process and Higher Education: A Systematic Approach to Fair Decision Making," *ASHE-ERIC Higher Education Report* 27 (1999): 4; Jerry L. Mashaw, *Due Process in the Administrative State* (New Haven, CT: Yale University Press, 1985), 26–27; Note, "Common Law Rights for Private University Students: Beyond the State Action Principle," *Yale Law Journal* 84 (1974): 120–50; David M. Rabban, "Judicial Review of the University-Student Relationship: Expulsion and Governance," *Stanford Law Review* 1 (1973): 107, 115–16; Charles Alan Wright, "The Constitution on the Campus," *Vanderbilt Law Review* 22 (1969): 1027–88.

37. Jackson, "The Lingering Legacy of In Loco Parentis," 1152–53; Natali, "Judicial Deference and University Academic Policy Modifications," 507, 513; Bickel and Lake, *The Rights and Responsibilities of the Modern University*, 46; Kaplin and Lee, *The Law of Higher Education*, vol. 1, 841–42. The modern basis for the "implied contract" is *Carr v. St. John's University*, 187 N.E.2d 18 (1962).

38. Barbara A. Lee, "Student-Faculty Academic Conflicts: Emerging Legal Theories and Judicial Review," *Mississippi Law Journal* 83 (2014): 837–61; Michael A. Olivas, *The Law and Higher Education: Cases and Materials on Colleges in Court*, 3rd ed. (Durham, NC: Carolina Academic, 2006), 699; Robert Hendrickson and Annette Gibbs, *The College, the Constitution, and the Consumer Student: Implications for Policy and Practice* (Washington, DC: Association for the Study of Higher Education, 1986), 10–11; Stevens, "Due Process and Higher Education," 27–29.

39. *University of Missouri v. Horowitz*, 435 U.S. 78 (1978); *University of Michigan v. Ewing*, 474 U.S. 214, 225 (1985).

40. *Horowitz*, 435 U.S. at 86.

41. Hendrickson et al., *Academic Leadership and Governance of Higher Education*, 144–45.

42. A HeinOnline search conducted March 11, 2014, of *Journal of College and University Law* (published by the National Association of College and University Attorneys) yielded just six articles with "tuition" in the title since 1973.

43. Kaplin and Lee, *The Law of Higher Education*, vol. 1, 936–55.

44. Robert L. Cherry Jr. and John P. Geary, "The College Catalog as a Contract," *Journal of Law and Education* 21 (1992): 25.

45. Suits regarding fees tend to focus on funding for religious and political clubs on campus. Courts have generally upheld these fees as long as they are used to promote education. Maxine G. Schmitz, "Mandatory Student Activity Fees in Public Colleges," *Journal of Law and Education* 25 (1996): 601–45.

46. The dynamic perpetuated itself because higher tuition prompted students to demand more from their institutions. Joan S. Stark, *The Many Faces of Educational Consumerism* (Lexington, MA: Lexington Books, 1977); David Riesman, *On Higher Education:*

The Academic Enterprise in an Era of Rising Student Consumerism (San Francisco: Jossey-Bass, 1980).

47. Comment, "Missouri's Changing Public Purpose Doctrine," *St. Louis University Law Journal* 16 (1972): 658–79. The county scholarship program of Washington State was recently discontinued. *Everett (WA) Daily Herald*, May 30, 2012, accessed July 24, 2013, http://www.heraldnet.com/article/20120530/NEWS01/705309872.

48. Donald E. Heller and Patricia Marin, eds., *Who Should We Help? The Negative Social Consequences of Merit Aid Scholarships* (Cambridge, MA: Civil Rights Project, 2002).

49. *Sharif v. New York State Education Department*, 709 F. Supp. 345 (1989). Also see *White v. Engler*, 188 F. Supp. 2d 730 (2001).

50. Gary Orfield et al., *Charting the Future of College Affirmative Action: Legal Victories, Continuing Attacks, and New Research* (Los Angeles: Civil Rights Project at UCLA, 2007); Michael A. Olivas, "Federal Law and Scholarship Policy: An Essay on the Office for Civil Rights, Title VI, and Racial Restrictions," *Journal of College and University Law* 18 (1991): 21–28.

51. In addition to determining eligibility for in-state tuition, residency status can also determine eligibility for preferential admissions, scholarship, or loan programs. Michael A. Olivas, "Administering Intentions: Law, Theory, and Practice of Postsecondary Residency Requirements," *Journal of Higher Education* 59 (1988): 265–68. Also see William T. O'Hara and John G. Hill, *The Student, the College, the Law* (New York: Teachers College Press, 1972), 19; Barry D. Glazer, "Education at a Discount: Qualifying for Resident Tuition at State Universities," *University of Michigan Journal of Law Reform* 5 (1972): 541–55.

52. *Plyler v. Doe*, 457 U.S. 202 (1982); Michael A. Olivas, *No Undocumented Child Left Behind: Plyler v. Doe and the Education of Undocumented Schoolchildren* (New York: New York University Press, 2012), 65–71; Michael A. Olivas, "Storytelling Out of School: Undocumented College Residency, Race, and Reaction," *Hastings Constitutional Law Quarterly* 22 (1995): 1019–86.

53. For example, see D. Bruce Johnstone and Pamela N. Marcucci, *Financing Higher Education Worldwide: Who Pays? Who Should Pay?* (Baltimore: Johns Hopkins University Press, 2010).

54. E. M. West Jr., "Judicial Opinions Governing Admission and Expulsion of College Students," in E. C. Bolmeier, ed., *Legal Issues in Education: Abridged Doctoral Dissertations* (Charlottesville, VA: Michie, 1970), 215; O'Hara and Hill, *The Student, the College, the Law*, 26.

55. Mark Keierleber, "Student Debt and Federal Loan Policy Take Center Stage at Senate Hearing," *Chronicle of Higher Education*, March 28, 2014, accessed June 17, 2014, http://chronicle.com/article/Student-DebtFederal-Loan/145591/; Paul Fain, "Profit and the Public Good," *Inside Higher Education*, March 12, 2013, accessed March 14, 2014, www.insidehighered.com/news/2013/03/12/accreditors-new-standards-raise-bar-serving-public#ixzz2vxAwYJqi.

56. In light of the long odds against increased state funding, one legal scholar has suggested incentivizing greater private contributions to college students by making parental support tax deductible. Margaret Ryznar, "Incentivizing Parental Support for College Tuition through the Tax Code," *Michigan State Law Review* (2013): 827–51.

57. As might be expected, courts have not granted support to students with married parents. Ben Horowitz, "Judge Rules against NJ Teen Who Sued Parents for Financial Support," *Newark Star-Ledger*, March 4, 2014, accessed March 14, 2014, www.nj.com/morris/index.ssf/2014/03/judge_issues_ruling_in_teens_suit_against_parents.html.

58. Vincent A. Cirillo, "*Curtis v. Kline*: Pennsylvania Supreme Court Declares Act 62 Unconstitutional," *Duquesne University Law Review* 34 (1996): 471–502.

59. Lindsay E. Cohen, "Daddy, Will You Buy Me a College Education? Children of Divorce and the Constitutional Implications of Noncustodial Parents Providing for Higher Education," *Missouri Law Review* 66 (2001): 187–204.

60. Joanna L. Grossman and Lawrence M. Friedman, *Inside the Castle: Law and Family in 20th Century America* (Princeton, NJ: Princeton University Press, 2011), 227; Madeline Marzano-Lesnevich and Scott Adam Laterra, "Child Support and College: What Is the Correct Result?," *Journal of the American Academy of Matrimonial Lawyers* 22 (2009): 335–89; John De Witt Gregory, Peter N. Swisher, and Sheryl L. Wolf, *Understanding Family Law*, 3rd ed. (New York: M. Bender, 2005), 345.

61. Nearly 90 percent of married parents provide consistent financial assistance while their children attend college, compared to less than 30 percent of divorced parents. Furthermore, financial aid offices often consider the income of both parents regardless of their willingness to contribute. In part because of these factors, the children of divorced parents across all income levels are less likely to apply to institutions of higher education. Monica Hof Wallace, "A Federal Referendum: Extending Child Support for Higher Education," *University of Kansas Law Review* 58 (2010): 672, 691; Ruth N. López Turley and Matthew Desmond, "Contributions to College Costs by Married, Divorced, and Remarried Parents," *Journal of Family Issues* 20 (2010): 1–24.

62. Michael W. McCann, "How Does Law Matter for Social Movements?," in Bryant G. Garth and Austin Sarat, eds., *How Does Law Matter?* (Chicago: Northwestern University Press, 1998), 76–108. Also see Michael J. Klarman, *From Jim Crow to Civil Rights: The Supreme Court and the Struggle for Racial Equality* (New York: Oxford University Press, 2004).

63. David Karen, "The Politics of Class, Race, and Gender: Access to Higher Education in the United States, 1960–1986," *American Journal of Education* 99 (1991): 208–37; Frances K. Zemans, "Legal Mobilization: The Neglected Roles of the Law in the Political System," *American Political Science Review* 77 (1983): 690–703.

64. John D. Skrenty, "Law and the American State," *Annual Review of Sociology* 32 (2006): 228; Robert A. Kagan, Bryant Garth, and Austin Sarat, "Facilitating and Domesticating Change: Democracy, Capitalism, and the Law's Double Role in the Twentieth Century," in Austin Sarat, Bryant Garth, and Robert A. Kagan, eds., *Looking Back at Law's Century* (Ithaca, NY: Cornell University Press, 2002), 2.

65. Carnegie Foundation for the Advancement of Teaching, *The Control of the Campus*, 7.

66. Lyman A. Glenny and Thomas K. Dalglish, *Public Universities, State Agencies, and the Law: Constitutional Autonomy in Decline* (Berkeley: University of California Center for Research and Development in Higher Education, 1973), 128. Also see Matthew T. Lambert, *Privatization and the Public Good: Public Universities in the Balance* (Cambridge, MA: Harvard Education Press, 2014).

67. Hendrickson et al., *Academic Leadership and Governance of Higher Education*, 140.

68. See, for example, Charles F. Thwing, "Personal Morals and College Government," *North American Review* 166 (1898): 305.

69. Charles Dorn, "From 'Liberal Professions' to 'Lucrative Professions': Bowdoin College, Stanford University, and the Civic Functions of Higher Education," *Teachers College Record* 113 (2011): 1566–96; Loss, *Between Citizens and the State*, 214–15; Barry Checkoway, "Renewing the Civic Mission of the American Research University," *Journal of Higher Education* 72 (2001): 125–47.

70. Carol Geary Schneider and Debra Humphreys, "Putting Liberal Education on the Radar Screen," *Chronicle Review*, September 23, 2005, B20. Also see National Task Force on Civic Learning and Democratic Engagement, *A Crucible Moment: College Learning and Democracy's Future* (Washington, DC: Association of American Colleges and Universities, 2012), 5–7.

Index